Acknowledgements

This book is the result of a conference, "Exploring the Breadth and Depth of Literacy", held at Memorial University of Newfoundland in St. John's from September 30 to October 2, 1988. The conference was supported by grants from the Social Sciences and Humanities Research Council of Canada, Grant Number 443-88-0083, and from the Canadian Educational Researchers' Association. We are grateful to both organizations.

We also thank the Institute for Educational Research and Development for the use of its facilities in hosting the conference and producing the final manuscript. We especially thank Richard C. Anderson and Jana M. Mason, University of Illinois at Urbana-Champaign, for their advice on and participation in the conference; Judy Blundon for administering the details of the grants, and Pat Wall for her diligence and perseverance in typing and editing the many drafts.

STEPHEN P. NORRIS
LINDA M. PHILLIPS

W0019592

Detselig Enterprises Ltd. appreciates the financial assistance for its 1990 publishing program from Alberta Foundation of the Literary Arts.

Preface

Recently, in Canada, there has been a great deal of concern expressed about literacy by educators, politicians, business people, and the general public. While there seems to be considerable agreement on the importance of literacy, there are many different perceptions of the meaning and significance of literacy and often considerable vagueness about what exactly is being discussed. However, if the notion of literacy is to play a central role in setting ideals and goals for education, then it is imperative that there be a clear and educationally defensible concept of literacy with which to work, and a sense of the range of justifiable implications of lower and higher literacy attainment.

The central purpose of this book is to provide educational policy makers the foundations in knowledge and concepts needed for making justifiable literacy policy decisions. Specifically, the collection of essays explores the bounds of literacy, addressing such questions as how the notion might be circumscribed, how it might be expanded, and what notion of literacy is worth having or worth fighting for as an educational ideal. One overall perspective of the essays is that the concept of literacy has varied tremendously over time, place, and populace, and remains ambiguous. It sometimes refers to a functional ability to read some short, simple passages and to answer questions about them. At other times, being literate means being a learned and educated person with favourable attitudes, dispositions, and outlooks toward knowledge and learning.

Despite this conceptual ambiguity, certain empirical and philosophical research has suggested that any tightly limited notion of literacy, such as functional or cultural literacy, is internally inconsistent. Even the ability to read and understand a simple text or poem, a criterion of functional literacy by some accounts, arguably involves many complex reasoning abilities, dispositions, and frames of mind which are masked by the apparent simplicity of the task. According to such expansive accounts, literacy cannot be tightly constrained to a delimited set of narrow skills. Moreover, the functions and uses of literacy have political, sociological, economic, and educational overtones which expand the notion of literacy beyond simply the ability to read and write.

Educational policy makers should find the treatment of these ideas helpful and intellectually stimulating. The volume should be valuable, however, to more than policy makers. One implication of the volume is that research on issues essential to policy making is needed. Thus, literacy and educational researchers should find herein many researchable questions. In addition, the book can serve as a text or as collateral reading for graduate courses in curriculum and instruction, educational administration, educational foundations, and educational psychology.

Table of Contents

Part III
Social Perspectives

Introduction:
Critical Reflection on the Breadth and Depth of Literacy

Linda M. Phillips and Stephen P. Norris
Memorial University of Newfoundland

The report by the Canadian Business Task Force on Literacy (1988) announced that "the Southam Literacy Survey [had] established beyond reasonable doubt the existence of a literacy problem in Canada that is a blight to our self-image as a modern, progressive nation" (p. 4). These are strong words, but maybe the Southam survey of 1987 warranted this level of response. The survey concluded that 24% of Canadian adults are illiterate, and that an additional 9% are only marginally literate. Illiteracy levels were reported lowest in the west, 17% in British Columbia, and highest in the east, 44% in Newfoundland (Southam Newspaper Group, 1987). The Canadian Business Task Force reasoned that such levels of illiteracy cost Canadian business directly about $4 billion annually and cost Canadian society as a whole probably $10 billion.

As a result of such data and conclusions, policy makers in government and education face considerable pressure to address in some way a perceived problem of illiteracy. Thus, for example, on World Literacy Day in 1987, the Secretary of State established a National Literacy Secretariat to enable the Federal Government to "work with the provinces, the private sector, and voluntary organizations to develop resources to ensure that Canadians have access to the literacy skills that are prerequisites for participation in our advanced economy" (Department of the Secretary of State of Canada, 1987, September 8). The Secretariat has since disbursed funds to provinces for various literacy-related projects. But how valid are the data and conclusions about literacy and illiteracy upon which the Secretariat was established and these disbursements were made? Without careful scrutiny, their validity should not be assumed. Moreover, decisions affecting literacy policy should not be made without a clear and justified conception of literacy, and verification of alleged illiteracy levels and the implications drawn from these allegations.

In order to make literacy policy decisions on valid grounds, policy makers require a perspective that enables them to reflect critically upon the information and demands that they face. Is the data on illiteracy to be trusted? Is the data based upon a sufficiently articulated notion of literacy? Is illiteracy the "blight" that some reports would have us believe? Policy makers need the disposition to ask such questions and the ability to support their answers to them with arguments that reflect the state of literacy research.

This volume represents the views on literacy of Canadian educators from a wide variety of disciplines. The purpose is to provide foundations for the sort of critical reflection that decisions about literacy policy require. The foundational stance is derived from such areas as psychology, curriculum and instruction, as well as from the standard educational foundations of history, philosophy, and sociology. The result is an appropriately broad viewpoint on literacy, literacy being a notion that will not be confined easily to mere reading and writing. Literacy has implications for values as diverse as employment, intellectual fulfillment, personal empowerment, self-respect, national economic well-being, and indeed even survival—especially in the case of developing nations, or developing parts of nations with wide economic and political disparities such as Canada.

The chapters have been grouped into philosophical, historical, and social perspectives. However, each chapter approaches its topic from a variety of perspectives, and the chosen grouping serves to emphasize particular aspects. Other aspects could have been highlighted, and to some readers these may be more salient features.

Part I
Philosophical Perspectives

This section examines several crucial conceptual and normative questions whose answers can inform policy decisions. What is the relationship between cultural literacy, reasoning, politics, and literacy construed more narrowly as reading and writing? How is literacy related to competence in everyday affairs? Do typical indicators of functional literacy estimate accurately competence in real-life problems? Is it realistic to hope that literacy can foster the ideal of personal decision making in a technological society? Do conceptions of literacy influence the selection of curriculum material in such a way that important forms of knowing are omitted? Should literacy be restricted solely to being able to read and write, or should it connote more? This section provides ideas and concepts for examining critically and reflectively these and related questions. The section urges strongly that conceptions of literacy and, by implication, reactions to perceived literacy problems, be reconsidered and, perhaps, reformulated.

David Olson's chapter argues that there are several myths about literacy that have pernicious effects. One myth is that illiteracy is the source of virtually all social problems—poverty, malnutrition, unemployment, and educational failure. Olson argues, in contrast, that this view extends illegitimately the implications of illiteracy—not being able to read and write is simply that, he maintains. Another myth is that literacy is a single commodity and, in particular, that functional literacy is one and only one sort of competence. But literacy requires specific experience before it can be functional, so the literacy required to function in one set of tasks might be entirely different from that required in another. Therefore, assessments of functional literacy must take account of the task that is being envisaged. In addition, assessments of literacy must recognize that there are at least four varieties of literacy: the literacy central to general education, specialized functional literacies, lay literacy or general understandings about reading and writing, and scribal literacy or the simple ability to read and write. Until literacy is conceptualized more accurately, Olson argues, too many social problems will be diagnosed incorrectly as literacy problems and, hence, incorrect approaches will be used to solve them.

The chapter by Suzanne de Castell urges that we explore seriously the possibility of undesirable consequences of literacy. She argues that literacy has shaped our ideas of knowledge and of its mode of development and dissemination. The result is that particular forms of knowing, thinking, and understanding—those she calls "embodied"—have been suppressed and gradually wiped out. The schools are partly responsible for this eradication, because the curriculum contains a literate bias, in that it excludes forms of knowing and expression that do not fit the literate assumption that all ideas can be expressed in writing. Thus, significant voices in our society, especially women's and minorities', are omitted from the schools. In addition, the school's equation of knowledge with the written word has led to the omission or degradation of significant forms of experience, including the aesthetic, perceptual, and moral. De Castell argues that these omissions have served to undermine one of the very purposes of general education—the creation of a more just state.

Focusing on one of the four varieties of literacy identified by Olson, James Heap argues that tests of functional literacy typically are flawed, because they misrepresent the competence required to function in real-world problems. For instance, as presented in a test, a task might require (because of test-situation restrictions) that examinees do some reading or writing. However, in the real-world (which the task is intended to represent, but where the test-situation restrictions do not apply) examinees may be able to perform the task through a variety of routes, including ones that do not require reading or writing. Therefore, the test task does not measure what is required to function in the real-world task. In order to provide a form of discourse with which to analyze and talk about such problems with functional literacy, Heap suggests a distinction between text-based, text-aided, and text-omitted functioning. Only the first of these corresponds to functional literacy as currently conceived. Thus, Heap argues, measures of functional literacy necessarily provide a distorted indication of competence in practical contexts because, from a situated perspective, either text-aided or text-omitted functioning may be more rational than text-based functioning. Heap concludes that tests of functional literacy are actually tests of scholastic literacy and, hence, that the concept of functional literacy should be discarded and replaced by a language that distinguishes among modes of operating with texts.

The chapter by Reg Fleming maintains that literacy with texts that deal with the artifacts of a technological society requires special understandings and sensitivities. The point was anticipated by Olson when he stressed that functional literacy is not a single commodity. Fleming presupposes that the aim of literacy is to empower individuals to read the texts of others but not to be bound to those others' meanings. A technologically literate person, according to Fleming, is empowered to critically examine the underlying assumptions of technology. Furthermore, a technologically literate person has acquired an informed skepticism toward technology, views technology as an artifact resulting from social organization rather than simply as some hardware, and realizes that arguments over technology usually mask underlying differences in value. Thus, literacy as conceived by Fleming requires a particular frame of mind, not merely a set of mental skills, when reading texts about technological issues.

J. Anthony Blair, reminiscent of Olson, first wonders about the justification of the popular trend to stretch the referent of literacy beyond reading and writing to include such things as computer literacy and cultural literacy. Perhaps, he suggests, that what is common to all the literacies is the ability to deal with any context of meaning. However, he cautions that literacy in its root sense, the ability to read and write, might require mental abilities and dispositions quite different from these other literacies, so we should not allow linguistic practice alone to determine our psychology. Second, he explores the relationship between literacy and reasoning by pointing to the role of hypotheses, logical connectives and the logic of deontic terms, and implication, in understanding what text means. Finally, Blair explores the contribution of cultural literacy to reasoning about argumentative structures and the contribution of reasoning to the development of cultural literacy. He argues that the connections are so intimate that to suggest they are two distinct capacities is seriously misleading.

Also struggling with the degree to which the concept of literacy should be extended, Lloyd Brown argues strongly that the politicization of literacy, the casting of literacy as a form of cultural politics, oversteps the limits of acceptable extensions of the concept. First, he challenges the view of some radical school critics that the school is an agent of the middle class bent on repressing the working class. He opines that the middle class is not a homogeneous group representing some particular ideology, much less an ideology founded on working-class repression. In particular, he rejects the views that the schools should speak in the voice of the working class and use the culture of the working class as its experiential capital, because either approach would be too restrictive. One does not become educated, Brown maintains, by being immersed only in one's own culture. Furthermore, politics does not exhaust human experience and so should not be the only focus for education. Therefore, teachers should not serve any particular ideology, because to do so would distort their judgement of what to make available to students for consideration.

Part II
Historical Perspectives

This section provides a sense of how conceptions of literacy have evolved and of where they might lead by describing theories that serve as landmarks in thinking about literacy and by showing how these theories affect today's thought. For example, conceptions of literacy have evolved from the mere recognition of individual words and the writing of one's name to literacy as a route to knowledge embedded in social interaction. This evolution suggests that literacy might be extended beyond reading and writing to making meaning in any context dependent upon print, an idea explored by Blair in Part I. Within this framework, the concepts of mathematical literacy, scientific literacy, and technological literacy, which play central roles in this section, are meaningful extensions to the notion of literacy as reading and writing.

The chapters discuss literacy within the context of traditional school subjects mathematics, reading, writing, and science. The authors show how the evolution of thought about literacy has affected curriculum policy, suggest how concepts of literacy might further evolve, and explore how these envisaged changes may yet affect curriculum policy.

The chapter by Carolyn Kieran begins by noting that the expression "mathematical literacy" is quite new to the mathematics education community. But the adoption of the terminology signals a substantive, not merely semantic, change because, for the first time, there is an attempt to structure mathematics education to meet the needs both of non-mathematicians and the discipline of mathematics itself. Such coalescence has come at the end of a century of conflicting visions of mathematics education, represented by alternating periods in which the views of either the general public or the mathematics community dominated. For instance, in the decades immediately before the turn of the century, the school curriculum was structured around the mathematicians' notion of mathematics: solving linear and quadratic equations, and using ratios, proportions, powers, and roots. By the 1920s, a more practical approach to mathematics had been adopted in England, Canada, and the United States, but was soon suppressed by the Cold War fears of the late 1950s with its emphasis on regaining the lead in the scientific, technological, and mathematical world. However, the new math of that era did not achieve its aims because of the widespread opinion that mathematics has little to do with the real world. Kieran analyzes this separation of mathematics from the real world of individuals, and proposes that such separation is unnecessary. She suggests that the computer is one means of breaking down the barrier because, through its programmability, the computer is able to make clear the relations between everyday quantitative problem solving, for which mathematical literacy is needed, and the pursuits of the community of mathematicians.

In his chapter, Glen Aikenhead also addresses the educational implications of separating a scholarly discipline, science, from the everyday lives of individuals who are not academicians. First, Aikenhead postulates that the historical evolution from small to big science and from small-town Canada to global village increases the need for public criticism and analysis of science and technology. He notes that as the century progressed our society became increasingly conscious of its stewardship over the earth and, as a result, there was an increased desire for scientific/technological literacy. Like Fleming, Aikenhead sees scientific/technological literacy as a critical consciousness that empowers individuals to explore, understand, and sometimes control their own fate in a society increasingly shaped by science and technology. The empowerment depends upon a level of literacy that enables them to use their background knowledge of science and technology to interpret science/technology texts, including the specific policies, practices, and activities of scientists and technologists portrayed in them. To nurture this empowerment, Aikenhead recommends a curriculum that teaches scientific facts and principles and then uses these facts and principles to reason critically about some social problem. For example, a unit of instruction could centre around the use of the breathalyser in the control of drinking and driving. The issues that would arise require examining the science and technology underlying the instrument, and the legal, moral, and public policy questions that arise from its use. Aikenhead argues that scientific/technological literacy requires the ability to deal with all these issues.

Just as mathematics and science have been taught as discrete sets of concepts, facts, and procedures devoid of explicit connections to individuals' everyday lives, reading has been taught as sets of discrete skills devoid of connections to understanding. In Chapter 10, Mona Beebe describes the central themes of reading theories of the past one hundred years. In the nineteenth century, reading instruction began with teaching the names of letters and the spelling and sound of two-letter nonsense syllables, and progressed through three-letter nonsense syllables, one-syllable words, two-syllable words, and so on. In these approaches, there was often considerable emphasis on oral fluency as well, and a lack of emphasis on the overall meaning of texts. The focus on separate skills rather than on comprehension was further entrenched in this century with the almost universal use of basal readers, and with the scientific respectability afforded the skills approach by evidence from factor analytic studies of reading. Beebe argues that the commitment to these expensive basal reading programmes so drains schools' budgets that there is often little money left for purchasing authentic reading materials, such as children's literature. To counteract these tendencies, she proposes that the whole language approach to reading be considered. In this approach, less emphasis is placed on skills, and more emphasis placed upon children's prior knowledge of language and the world. Her proposal is a qualified one, though, in that she cautions that much must be saved from older teaching techniques, such as focusing on individual words and letters to acquire meaning in some contexts.

In the final chapter of this section, Stanley Straw argues that curriculum policy makers and those who set funding priorities for literacy hold views of literacy and functional literacy that are too conservative. He sketches the historical development of conceptualizations of literacy, identifying five periods: Transmission, Translation, Interaction, Transaction, and Social Construction. The periods are distinguished by their assumptions about the locus of meaning in literacy acts, about the nature of knowledge presumed needed for literacy acts, and about the purposes of literacy. Straw argues that governmental and educational policy makers presuppose and espouse either a transmission or translation view of literacy, and that these views are then adopted by the general public. According to the transmission and translation viewpoints, the single or most important purpose of language is communication, the locus of meaning resides with authors, and the kinds of knowledge needed to be literate are knowledge of the intentions of authors and knowledge of the decoding skills of reading. Contrasted with this set of beliefs is the view that communication is only one of a wide variety of purposes of literacy, that readers are the most important players in determining the meaning of text, and that the type of knowledge required for literacy is not simply knowledge of author intentions and reading skills but also knowledge that literacy is a constructive and social act that derives its sense only within the context of social interaction. Straw maintains that policy makers should adopt these more expansive conceptions of literacy and base their policy decisions upon them.

Part III
Social Perspectives

The data and arguments provided in this section support a call for a reevaluation of the assumptions underlying a variety of policy decisions. The data provide a basis for challenging long-standing literacy theories and for constructing new theories that take account of the social aspects of literacy. One main thread of argument in the chapters is that literacy skill is transcended and bolstered by affective and social factors and by yet-to-be-identified cognitive factors common to literacy in several languages. Thus, policy makers must be responsive to the cultural values of learners, the need to experience literacy in meaningful contexts of interaction with others, and the role of the native language literacy of Canada's many minorities in acquiring literacy in the country's official languages.

The chapter by Merrill Swain, Sharon Lapkin, Norman Rowen, and Doug Hart addresses the effect of literacy in one's native language on learning a third language. Evidence already in the literature shows that native language literacy does enhance the learning of a *second* language. But many of Canada's aboriginal peoples and many immigrants to Canada have neither of the two official languages as their native language. Hence, they often first learn one of the official languages in addition to their own, and learn subsequently the second official language. Therefore, there is an interest in knowing the effect of literacy in their native language on learning the second official language (their third language). Existing educational policy often discourages literacy acquisition in the native language, if it is not one of the two official ones, on the grounds that speaking to, reading to, and instructing children in their native language will seriously impede their acquisition of the official languages. The research reported in this chapter challenges this empirical assumption. The data support the conclusion that literacy in one's native language enhances third language learning. Indeed, the data support the hypothesis that there are some language learning proficiencies that generalize across languages and, thus, that the provision of a sound basis in native-language literacy is a wise policy decision.

Gen Ling Chang and Gordon Wells describe a study of third and fifth graders' literate thinking. The study was conducted collaboratively with two teachers, and was premised on the belief that writing reveals best the nature of literacy and the potential of language for empowering thinking. Writing has these effects, they postulate, because both the act of writing and the analysis of written text involves dialectic at a number of levels: between what the writer knows and the demands of the text the writer is creating; between what the writer knows and what the writer needs to come to know; and between the writer and readers of the writer's text. Thus, the written record can be the basis of discussion with oneself and with others and, viewed this way in the classroom, can serve to promote the general process of inquiry. The study supports the claim that treating writing as a reason for and a means of thinking and communicating dialectically in the service of acquiring knowledge enhances both writing ability and subject matter knowledge. That is, treating writing as an activity requiring social interaction in the pursuit of knowledge enhances important educational goals.

Consistent with Straw, Beebe, and Chang and Wells, William Fagan argues that literacy development must be seen as more than the transmission of skills. Literacy, he maintains, is a cultural value that is or is not acquired according to the network of socioaffective relations within which one lives. Students are disadvantaged when the cultural values of their homes clash with those of the school, and when the school then denigrates those children's values because they are different. Fagan relies upon Bateson's theory of socioaffective relations to help understand such differentiation of values within the school. Sometimes the differentiation leads to passive and subservient students who accept the teacher's directives out of fear, rather than belief. Other students fight such differentiation by not accepting the school's diagnosis of them as failures or misfits. Fagan collected data on two groups of low-literate adults and one group of achieving grade nine students in order to explore the process of differentiation in school and its effect on literacy development. The data support the conclusions that the low-literate adults entered school with values that conflicted with the school's, had in almost all cases been differentially treated by being assigned to special groups, and had either passively accepted their lot or had engaged in open conflict with the school. The data on the grade nine achievers stand in direct contrast. Fagan concludes that school should not be a place where literacy is merely taught, leaving it up to students to find some place for it in their lives. If students are to acquire literacy, they must see its meaningfulness from the beginning. This means that teachers must respect and take account of the history and values of the communities of different groups of students.

Rodney Clifton, Trevor Williams, and Jeff Clancy report a study that addresses a question central to education in multi-ethnic countries: whether in these countries success in school is determined by individuals' competence or whether the educational system discriminates against ethnic minority groups. The study examines a specific subset of these questions from the perspective of English, Greek, and Italian students in Australia, and focuses on the effects of English-language usage on the Greek and Italian students' achievement and completion of secondary school. The study provides evidence that the academic achievement of the Greek and Italian students is essentially a function of competition among students of different competence within a meritocratic system. There is discrimination in the sense that English-language proficiency is a major cause of success in Australian schools. However, the same Greek and Italian students who are disadvantaged by their proficiency in English are advantaged because their cultural values strongly support the completion of secondary school—the strongest predictor of income and occupational status. When seen in the context of the chapter by Swain, Lapkin, Rowen, and Hart several implications for Canadian education are apparent. First, while proficiency in the official languages is likely to be a strong determiner of school success, literacy in the native language can foster literacy in the official languages. Second, even though students' ethnicity can be disadvantageous, the schools might try to capitalize upon the cultural values of ethnic groups to try to counteract this effect.

Concluding Remarks

Literacy is important—maybe even important enough to be of national concern. Certainly, conceptions of literacy and of its implications have sufficiently important impact on the lives of Canadians that literacy policy must be made in the context of the best available perspectives on literacy. Neither this volume, nor any other volume, provides all the information that policy makers need. However, it offers current thinking from some of Canada's leading educational theorists.

References

Canadian Business Task Force on Literacy. (1988). *Measuring the costs of illiteracy in Canada.*

Department of the Secretary of State of Canada. (1987, September 8). Statement by the Secretary of State The Honorable David Crombie on the occasion of World Literacy Day. Ottawa: Author.

Southam Newspaper Group. (1987). *Literacy in Canada—A research report.* Ottawa: Author.

Part I
Philosophical Perspectives

2

Mythologizing Literacy

David R. Olson
Ontario Institute for Studies in Education

It is difficult to overstate the significance of literacy to a modern society. But in the attempt to find in literacy an explanation for poverty, unemployment, disease, and hopelessness, both in Third World countries and here at home, politicians, educators, and reporters have succeeded in doing just that.

A recent alarm was sounded by the Southam report on illiteracy (Southam Newspaper Group, 1987) which claimed that the level of functional illiteracy in some sections of Canada was more than 60% and increasing annually. Recent newspaper editorials ("Tackling Illiteracy", 1987) uncritically accept the views that "malnutrition, ill-health and illiteracy form a triple scourge for developing nations"; that the illiterate are doomed to "lives of poverty and hopelessness" because they are "deprived of the fundamental tools to forge a better life", namely, literacy; that "illiteracy is a $2 billion drag on the economy of Canada"; and that "the social costs are enormous". Such claims are not uncommon. Indeed they are so common that they make up part of the mythology of developed countries. But is literacy really at the root of these social problems?

Concern for literacy, even extravagant concern, may appear to be at best an incentive to intensify educational efforts, and at worst harmless rhetoric. But if the claims and assumptions are false, they may in fact set back workable programs to deal with major social ills such as poverty and unemployment. Ironically, they may even have the effect of setting back the advancement of literacy. Hence, it is urgent that we evaluate the claims about literacy levels and their implications before policy and programs are based upon them.

Are claims about the levels of literacy in Canada and the social significance of those levels of literacy valid? To answer such a question requires some understanding of just what literacy is, what it is used for, by whom, and in what ways. The Southam report was based on a measure of functional literacy, competence with the types of written materials one would ordinarily be called upon to use, for business or pleasure, in one's daily life. The unquestioned assumption was that some test could be devised to measure a form of literacy that was functional for everyone. That report "produced" extremely high levels of functional illiteracy in Canada, primarily through the choice of items that made up the test. Subjects were asked to do ten things, including circling the long distance charges on a telephone bill, reading and interpreting the dosage on a cough medicine bottle, and finding a store in the Yellow Pages of a telephone directory, things that some Canadians often do, while others rarely do. If, for example, rather than reading dosages, readers were asked to read things that most people often do, such as labels on bottles, packages, cans, or simple narrative texts, or even the more specialized things relevant to work or play of the particular individuals involved, the best estimates are that less than 5% of Canadian adults are illiterate. Tests can be designed as easily to select the top 10% as to exclude only the bottom 10%, that is to produce whatever levels of functional illiteracy in Canada thought reasonable by some criteria.

The problem is that functional literacy is not a single commodity; what is functional for an automotive-parts person who consults enormous volumes of ghoulish complexity may not be functional for a parent with a medicine bottle or a person with a rejection letter from an employer. No ten items, regardless of how cleverly selected, will indicate whether or not people can read the materials relevant to "one's daily life".

Consider the test items that require one to fill in a formulary such as a deposit slip, a bank cheque, or a customs declaration. The ability to deal with any of these items depends not only on whether or not one can read "Name", but on understanding the nature and use of that document. A bank cheque has a blank space after the words "Pay to the order of". To this day I do not know why I do not pay the money to the person named rather than to his or her "order". These are not problems of literacy but rather problems of, first, knowing how to use these particular documents, and second, of realizing that only the experts, usually lawyers, know just why the wording is the peculiar way that it is. Even sophisticated adults cannot understand all of the information printed on a medicine bottle; part of the text is included to meet statutory requirements not to inform an ordinary user.

An implication is that competence with a document depends upon experience in using that document. Every first-time traveller on returning to Canada from abroad has some difficulty in interpreting and complying with a customs declaration form and, as I notice on my travels, often asks the nearest person what particular expressions mean and what they should list on the document. The form requires that a returning Canadian list the total value of goods purchased abroad. A reader using the form for the first time has no way of knowing what exactly is meant by that expression. Does it include the expensive chocolates purchased as you left Belgium but consumed just before arrival in Toronto? Does it include the shoelaces you had to purchase to replace the ones that wore out while you were abroad? These are matters of judgement about the sorts of things that pertain to a Customs Officer. *No document is self-interpreting,* and it is simply naive to believe that people should be able to use a document the first time they are exposed to it. On the other hand, there are very few people who, after they have used a document several times, let us say, a type of cheque, have difficulty in using the document. Competence depends not only upon key literacy but upon experience through use.

Because the ability to interpret and respond appropriately to documents depends to a significant extent on experience with documents of their type, it is unlikely that performance on document-completion items is highly correlated. Technically, this low correlation means that the Southam scales should have low reliability. The upshot is that there can be no general test for functional literacy. As lives are varied, so literacies are varied.

Incidentally, the Southam report makes a naive error that only literates could make, namely, to believe the representation rather than the reality. It defines, arbitrarily, "functional literacy" as a score of 8 out of 10 items correct. When the test was then given to 1,500 people, even 8% of the university graduates failed to get 8 or more items correct. Instead of recognizing that the measure of functional literacy was invalid, the authors claim that university graduates too are illiterate! This, of course, is simply bizarre. Suppose one made up a test to discriminate mad people from normals and constructed a set of questions you thought, or assumed, to be useful for that purpose. You then gave it to inmates of institutions and to the psychiatrists working there. You found that 50% of the psychiatrists scored below your criterion. Would you then claim that 50% of psychiatrists were mad, or would you think your test may be less than perfect? A naive belief in the authority of the documented word over one's common sense is a peculiarity of some literates.

To give a realistic assessment of the literacy standards and practices in Canada would require that we distinguish at least four kinds of literacy: the literacy central to a general education, the primary concern of public schooling; the specialized functional literacies relevant to particular social, economic and religious groups; "lay literacy", namely the general understandings about reading, writing, texts, documents, law, contracts and the like; and finally "scribal literacy", the simple ability to read and write.

As Wells (1986), Heap (this volume), and others have pointed out, it is worth distinguishing the types of functions that texts serve. Narrative texts call for sustained reading, interpreting, and enjoyment. Educational texts call for reading, interpreting, re-interpreting, summarizing and remembering. Documents, on the other hand, are used rather than remembered. When one looks up a logarithm in a table, one does not try to remember the value; it is simply consulted. In the initial concerns about functional literacy it was assumed that schools required children's use of only the first two types of texts. In fact, schools use an enormous variety of documents. Preliminary observations by Bell (1989, May) suggest that a majority of children's classroom time is organized around consulting, using, and creating documents. Information tends to be looked up and used for some rather specific, and often low level purpose, rather than read, reflected on, related to other sources of knowledge, and organized into meaningful patterns.

It is, therefore, quite possible that the kinds of literate competence that are acquired in schools do provide a reasonable basis for coping with the forms of documents that one will encounter "in one's daily life". That competence, however, must be seen not as the ability to use every document that one encounters, but as a sufficient general education that one understands the functions of those documents and that one *could* learn to use that type of document with a minimum of experience and tutoring. Someone with a reasonable level of education would need to be shown how to use a cheque the first two or three times but would be capable of using that document independently thereafter. That is the kind of literate competence worth pursuing and the kind that schools, in fact, currently appear to be pursuing. Functional literacy, then, is putting literacy skills to use, not a new type of literacy.

It is not only that reports on illiteracy are less than ideal, it is also that they are seriously misleading. Sweeping claims, such as that literacy standards are low and falling or that illiteracy is a "$2-billion drag on the economy", are a consequence of mythologizing literacy. It is always a mistake to attribute social problems simply to personal qualities of the individuals involved—poverty to laziness, epidemics to carelessness, lack of education to low intelligence, and the like. Social ills, such as poverty, unemployment, and inadequate medical care, are never simply reducible to a personal quality or characteristic of the individuals involved; they are social rather than simply psychological problems.

Shirali (1988), an Indian scholar, has argued that the illiterates are not the problem in India; the problem is the fact that the limited resources are exploited by the privileged elites. This injustice is rationalized on the basis of illiteracy. She writes:

> All over the earth, it is the illiterate poor, and it is the women who are the poorest of the poor and the most illiterate from the villages, that are the mainstay of a country's economy, through their cheap labour and their contribution in food production. (p. 90)

She continues:

> It is the rich and elite of the cities . . . who are the beneficiaries of the country's educational system. The top 1% enjoys 40% of the National Income and resources, whereas the lowest 55% gets only 4%. (p. 90)

And finally:

> Education and literacy are said to be the fourth cornerstone of development. Much needs to be reflected upon regarding what, how and for whom. An ethics, a morality of development needs to be understood and implemented. Unless and until the various gaps in society, in living, the dualities between people, the rich and the poor, the urban and the rural, the industrial and the agrarian, the first, second, third and fourth worlds, man and woman, father and child; between I and thou are resolved, development, literacy and education will only breed violence, destruction and degeneration. The poser and arrogance of literacy knows no bounds. (p. 91)

When we misdiagnose the poverty problem as a literacy problem, we may be led to offer inappropriate solutions. Unemployment will not be solved by reading lessons; job training and skills upgrading, which are perceived as relevant to "one's daily life", are part of the solution to unemployment. The fundamental part, of course, is job opportunity. To solve a pressing social problem such as poverty or unemployment, it is important to describe the problem correctly. Historians such as Katz (1976) and Graff (1979, 1986) provided evidence that increased literacy is as likely to be a consequence of economic growth as a cause of it. Despite the complexity of the relations between literacy and social change, the simplicities of the literacy myth persist. Graff cites an unpublished paper by Winchester as saying:

> perhaps the most striking features of UNESCO discussions on literacy since 1965, when a campaign to wipe out world illiteracy got going [UNESCO currently hopes to "eradicate illiteracy by the year 2000], is that it is remarkably little based on either experiment or historical precedents. Rather, in spite of Adam Curle's careful warnings in 1964, action seems as much based on self-evident axioms and hope as on anything else. UNESCO assumes that literacy is a good thing—more latterly, functional literacy. Furthermore, in no clearly defined or understood way poverty, disease, and general backwardness are believed connected with illiteracy; progress, health, and economic well-being are equally self-evidently connected with literacy. UNESCO is committed to what amounts to a modernization theory to the effect that economic progress follows upon a change in man from illiterate to literate, preferably in one generation, and, even better, in the very same man. It is presupposed that such a change will lead, if not immediately then inevitably, to such changes and values in a society that economic progress—and in its train good health, longevity, and perhaps, peace—is possible. (Graff, 1986, pp. 77-78)

Literacy is not the solution to the country's nor the world's social problems. Literacy is a means to a variety of functional ends. Those ends, purposes, uses and goals are what are at stake. As literacy becomes more functional, parents and children alike increasingly value education. And schools, when valued by their clients, become more effective.

A misrepresentation of the literacy problem may actually hold back the advancement of literacy in two ways. Identifying literacy with scribal literacy or functional literacy may lead one to overlook the genuine intellectual benefits that literacy can yield through encounters with science and literature, through the development of critical reading, and through personal expressive writing. Second, to focus explicitly on scribal literacy makes the acquisition of literacy particularly difficult especially for children from less literate homes. On the other hand, by allowing learners to use language for a variety of purposes, both orally and through texts, for writing as well as for reading, for work as well as for play, learners not only develop expressive and communicative competence, they acquire scribal skills in the process. When the so-called basic literacy skills are divorced from these more general goals, the result is often a debased form of instruction and a superficial form of learning.

Our current assumptions about literacy are part of a whole network of superficial prejudices. We talk of the "scourge" of illiteracy, of schools "harboring" illiterates, of "cures" for illiteracy, of "eradicating" or "stamping out" illiteracy. And we talk of illiterates as if they were inferior beings, as if they were flawed, marginal persons. Indeed, the term "illiterate" is often little more than a term of abuse. The term "idiot" at first meant, simply, one who was ignorant of Latin and it accrued its pejorative sense as the technical competence came to be treated as a personal limitation or failing. We should consent to having people referred to as illiterates only if we would be willing to have ourselves referred to as idiots. This is not merely a semantic game. The use of the term in current public discourse emphasizes this pejorative sense so much that we literates have succeeded in conveying our disapproval to the non-literates themselves. Consequently, people who are not able to read and write frequently hide their inability because they are ashamed of it; as if non-literacy were a form of deviancy. Yet, it is also a fact that non-literates are by and large completely indistinguishable from their literate counterparts, their inability to read becoming known only because of their confession (or guilt), or because they inadvertently find themselves in a drastically altered social position or faced with unfamiliar written texts. Inability to read or write is simply what it is, the inability to read and write, nothing more and nothing less.

It is bad enough being non-literate in a literate society without the dominant literate culture then blaming you for all the social ills of that society. Until literacy is seen in a more enlightened way, namely, as a specialized linguistic means of importance to some goals and activities while being irrelevant to others, rather than in the traditional way, namely, as a nostrum for such social problems as poverty, malnutrition, unemployment, and educational failure, then we will lack the understanding necessary to deal with those social problems and the understanding necessary to help children and adults acquire, use, and enjoy the literate resources of our culture.

We who have a commitment to the advancement of literacy have no right to impose literacy on others who are less literate (there are few truly illiterate people in a literate society in any case). We do have a responsibility to provide opportunity so that people who want work can find it, those who seek medical care can afford it, those who desire an education can gain access to it, and those who want to learn to read and write can do so. The provision of opportunity is an enormous social undertaking. But the provision of opportunity is certain to be more productive than programs that are framed on the faulty assumptions regarding the "scourge of illiteracy".

Acknowledgement

Shorter versions of this chapter appeared in *The Globe and Mail,* Toronto, August, 1988, and in *English Quarterly,* Volume 21(2), 1988.

References

Bell, K. (1989, May). *The school as workplace.* Paper presented at the Functional Literacy Workshop, University of Toronto, Toronto, Ontario.

Tackling illiteracy. (1987, October 13 & 14). *Globe and mail,* Editorial.

Graff, H. (1979). *The literacy myth: Literacy and social structure in the nineteenth-century city.* New York: Academic Press.

Graff, H. (1986). The legacies of literacy: Continuities and contradictions in western society and culture. In S. de Castell, A. Luke & K. Egan (Eds.), *Literacy, society and* schooling. Cambridge: Cambridge University.

Heap, J. L. (1988, December). *Reading as rational action: Functioning and literacy* in daily life. Paper presented at the National Reading Conference, Tucson, Arizona.

Katz, M. (1976). The origins of public education: A reassessment. *History of Education Quarterly, 14,* 381-407.

Olson, D. R. (1975). Education and literacy: An essay review of Carroll and Chall's "Toward a literate society". Proceedings of the National Academy of Education, 2, 109-178.

Shirali, K. A. (1989). Ganga Devi: A question of literacy and development. *Canadian Women Studies, 9,* 89-91.

Southam Newspaper Group. (1987). *Literacy in Canada—A research report.* Ottawa: Author.

Wells, G. (1986). Apprenticeship in literacy. *Interchange, 18* (1/2), 109-123.

3

Defining Significant Knowledge:
Some Limits to Literacy

Suzanne de Castell
Simon Fraser University

Raymond Williams (1976) distinguishes two senses of "culture": a backward-looking conception of culture that promotes the preservation of that which has gone before—our "cultural heritage"; and a forward-looking conception of culture, from the semantic root "cultivation"—the cultivation in each new generation of that culture which is to come. In the first view, culture is passed on; in the second view, it is created by the continuously renewing energies of human activity.

Scholars of literacy may, I fear, have devoted disproportionate time and energy on a project whose implications endorse this first, backward-looking, conception of cultural tradition. Thereby, they have neglected the ways in which the selected preservation, storage, and incremental accumulation of knowledge, made possible by writing, may have selected *against*, excluded, suppressed and indeed gradually eradicated forms of thinking and understanding that might safeguard us against a reactionary and finally inert cultural traditionalism.

I should like to argue here an optimistic position, premised upon the necessity to recapture what, in an understandable equation of written texts with the material aspects of text-based cultural knowledge, we appear to have abandoned or negated—embodied knowing. I shall also suggest, perhaps somewhat paradoxically, the necessity for a return to tradition, for an intensification of our culture's historical preoccupation with texts, but this time in the spirit of a re-cultivation of culture, its renewal and regeneration through an ongoing process of internalization and well-informed reinterpretation as the primary basis for invention. On a critical note, I shall suggest that not only has bodily knowing been largely negated, but even traditional textual knowledge has become desiccated and diminished, particularly within that most central vehicle of intergenerational acculturation—the school.

Literacy as the Epistemological Foundation of the School Curriculum

The study of literacy offers us a radical reconceptualization of epistemology. Reaching to the very roots of the theory of knowledge that underlies curriculum theory, policy, and practice, such study may unearth fundamental but dubious presuppositions—Illich (1987), with irony, terms these "certainties"—upon which philosophical notions of what is to count as knowledge have grown up. Such traditional philosophical certainties about the nature of knowledge have flourished, I shall argue, to the detriment of humane individual and cultural development.

The hypothesis that theoretical, and particularly philosophical, discourse is a product of the technology of writing permits us to call into question the hitherto unquestioned assumption that writing is a subset of knowledge, and to propose instead that knowledge may be a subset of writing. I do not mean to imply that prior to the development of literacy human beings lacked knowledge, in the sense that they were ignorant. Indeed, there is evidence that a wealth of intelligent accomplishment existed before literacy. Havelock (1988) details, for example, how a vast store of cultural knowledge was preserved, in both the vernacular linguistic and in what he calls the "anthropological grammars" of preliterate Greece. These grammars were more firmly fixed by a form of managed language beyond the vernacular, in poetically codified "custom-laws" preserved in linguistic formulas memorized and continually re-enacted in formal ritual performances. He goes on to point out, however, something of great significance for this chapter's central argument. He elaborates upon these maxims or sayings that preserve and store the culture's proprieties of personal and communal behaviour as follows:

> These proprieties constitute the *mores* of a society, to use a Latin term; in the Greek, they are conveniently referred to by the words *nomos* and *ethos* ... the custom-laws, the folkways, the habit of a people. It is of interest to note that by etymology both these terms, which when literalized can be rendered as "law" and "ethics", signify in their original usage not prin-

ciples or beliefs but localized human activities, that of distributing or managing land in the case of *nomos* and that of living in a place or a haunt in the case of *ethos*. Their inspiration is behaviouristic, not philosophic, legal, or moralist. (p. 226)

What we literates construe abstractly as law and ethics, in other words, turn out to be more accurately referred to as embodied human activities. It is in embodied behaviours, then, that preliterate cultural tradition is known.

Clearly, then, it would be nonsensical to suggest that the preliterate Greek was not knowledgeable. What I mean by suggesting that knowledge is a subset of writing is, rather, that the very *idea* of knowledge, the concept of knowledge "as such", and hence the idea that human beings could lack, develop, transmit, and possess knowledge, may be entirely a literate construction.

The traditional philosophical conception of knowledge, and that which invariably underlies current educational theory and curricular practice, is the venerable conception of knowledge as justified-true-belief. Decomposing the justified-true-belief conception into its constituent elements illustrates how this central epistemological notion is inextricably tied to and irretrievably dependent upon the invention of a literate prose of ideas. Consider the third term first, the concept of belief. Although we all believe certain things, even if such beliefs may often only be implicit in our actions and attitudes, the standard locution is that we all *have,* that is, we all in some sense "possess", rather strange sorts of things called "beliefs". As Ryle (1949) and others have pointed out, this and cognate locutions often lead to fruitless searches for the location of the beliefs that we have and presumably store somewhere, perhaps in the head, possibly deep inside the brain. And when we share a belief that X is the case with other individuals, will all of our beliefs resemble, or perhaps even be identical with the one generic belief, "X is the case"? Central features of belief, so conceived and named, conform to the characterization of literate conceptual construction: multiple embodied processes occurring in time become atemporally abstracted from concrete subjects and circumstances, unified within a single universally referring expression, and transmogrified from fluid process into fixed result (Havelock, 1962). In this way the concept of belief conforms with the classical philosophical grammar that is said to have stemmed directly from the invention of Greek alphabetic literacy.

This analysis seems to apply equally well to the concepts of truth and justification as it does to the concept of belief. Truth, for example, is a property of propositionalized statements, not attitudes, dispositions, decisions, actions, or performances—nor human beings. People may be truthful, that is, sincere; actions, as well as values, principles, and decisions may be morally right (or wrong); rule-governed performances may be correctly (or incorrectly) carried out; but only propositions can be true (or false). The same point can be made for the concept of justification. It is in this sense, then, that I argue that literacy has shaped, first, the very idea of knowledge, and later, the mode of its development and dissemination. What then, does writing do to knowledge, once it has invented the category? And what has all this to do with schooling?

Literate Schooling and the Erosion of Cultural Tradition

It is widely recognized that the impact of alphabetic literacy revolutionized processes of socialization and acculturation. Indeed, it has even been suggested that formal education was an invention of literacy. Illich and Sanders (1988) contend that "only after it had become possible to fix the flow of speech in phonetic transcription did the idea emerge that knowledge—information—could be held in the mind as in a store". But they go on to remind us:

> Only the alphabet has the power to create 'language' and 'words', for the word does not emerge until it is written down ... In the oral beyond, there is no 'content' ... no 'subject-matter' that can be conceived of, entrusted to teachers and acquired by pupils ... (p. 7)

To the extent that we come to think of all language as (at least potentially) *written* language, and to the extent that we regard texts as equivalent to the word as spoken, then it becomes possible to assume that we can, by a straightforward encoding, translate speech into writing. But in fact this constitutes a *transformation*, since embodied speech is, of course, not merely vocal language—it is also action (Austin, 1962; Searle, 1969).

Illich (1987) employs the phrase "lay literacy" to refer to a transformation of mind in which the book becomes the root metaphor for conceiving of human beings, their activities, and their environments. The production of such a literate world view does not require that individuals themselves read or write, but only that they inhabit a literate culture in

which writing regulates public affairs within culturally significant social, economic, religious, and political contexts. Illich (1987) documents, as illustration, the introduction of literacy into the rituals of the
church from the 12th century onwards, and the uses of literacy for
contracts and deeds, and for oath-taking in the law courts of the state. In
this way, literate culture pervades the lives of illiterates just as it pervades
the lives of those who read and write. The result, lay literacy, which Illich
and Sanders (1988) discuss in terms of an "Alphabetization of the
Popular Mind", is seen as a radical transformation of the oral world view,
an epistemological break with the oral past in which new certainties
(assumptions about the nature of the self, of the social world, of organic
nature and physical reality, and indeed of knowledge itself) gradually
come to appear beyond question, beyond criticism. The lay literate, says
Illich, is certain that speech can be frozen, that memories can be stored ?
and retrieved, and that secrets can be engraved in conscience, and
therefore retrieved and examined, whether in voluntary confession or by
involuntary inquisition (Foucault, 1978). More importantly, the lay
literate assumes that experience can be described and these descriptions
preserved and stored as knowledge.

The downside of the literate mind, as Plato long ago recognized,
should not be overlooked or underestimated. It is often remarked that
with the advent of literacy came the possibility of speaking with forked
tongue, like the devil. Illich and Sanders (1988) trace the way in which
this capacity originates in our own literate tradition, explaining how the
capacity for full-blown lying—saying something quite different from
what one is thinking with the intention to deceive, lying as "contra-
diction"—presupposes a self that thinks before it speaks, and reshapes
what it says to contra-dict the truth.

> Only when I have gotten used to thinking as the silent tracing of words
> on the parchment of my memory, can I detach thought from speech and
> contra-dict it. . . . Only when memory is perceived as a text can thought
> become a material to be shaped, re-shaped, and transformed. Only a self
> which has thought what it does say, can say something it does think. (p.
> 84)

(This view of the relationship between literacy and lying may also
remind us of Rousseau's attack in *Emile* on the premature use of books
in education, and the teaching to children of matters outside their own
"natural" experience as teaching children to tell lies.)

Of course many forms of falsehood existed before literacy. However, as Illich and Sanders (1988) point out, none of these preliterate forms imply the opposition to an abstract truth essential to what we nowadays understand as a lie.

> Neither the Greek *pseudos* (used both for the "liar" *and* the "lie") nor the Latin *mendecium* (referring also to the emendation of a line on a wax tablet) in classical times, comes close to our idea of the untruthful. The preliterate "untruth" is always about *things* that are not so, not of thoughts that are willfully contradicted. (p. 85)

In the oral world, a man and his word are not separable. It appears to be only with continental canon law in the 13th century that the judge becomes a reader of another's conscience, from which the truth can be extracted by torture. From then on, Illich and Sanders conclude:

> truth ceases to be displayed in surface action and is now perceived as the outward expression of inner meanings accessible only to the self. (p. 85)

What is critical here is not the implication that literacy produces lying, but that it produces entirely novel *conceptions,* of which truth and lying feature predominantly, and that what we are seeing in this historical progression is an increasing separation of language from speech and a parallel separation of speech from speaker. Both these consequences continuously and cumulatively feed back into the literate world-view from which they first originated, intensifying the rupture between the self and what the self says, and most important of all, between what the self knows, and what the self does. In our time, this form of alienation produces a conception of literacy as sets of technical skills or abilities, conceives of words as "message units", conversation as "oral communication", and what is conversed about as "information". The metaphor of transmission, has replaced the classical Socratic dialogue as model for the educational process with mechanistic information-processing idioms redefining interpersonal conversation as an exchange between transmitter and receiver.

Literacy, Selection, and Omission

In the translation (itself a literate construct) from embodied speech to written language, much may of course be lost, even as much else is gained. Walter Ong (1982), among others, sees that losses as well as gains may result from the incorporation of knowledge in a system of writing. In a discussion of the "artificiality" of writing as against the "naturalness" of speech, Ong proposes the following:

> Alienation from a natural milieu can be good for us and indeed is in many ways essential for human life. To live and to understand fully, we need not only proximity, but also distance. This writing provides for consciousness as nothing else does. (p. 82)

This *not-only-but-also* argument is less convincing for us as educators when we look at the modern school curriculum, when we ask what kind of knowledge we are emphasizing and privileging, and what kinds of knowers we are thereby producing. For we find there a literate bias that all but excludes those ways of knowing and forms of expression to which Ong would *add* writing, with its attendant virtues of alienation and distance.

What makes up a school curriculum? What gets selected as legitimate educational knowledge? We should begin by noticing that today the apparatus of identification itself, taking the form of core curriculum booklets, ministry of education circulars, research reports, policy statements, lists of authorized and prescribed titles, and a wealth of supporting documentation, is entirely textual. Large, centrally controlled bureaucracies, of which the public school system is one, originated with literacy (Goody, 1986) and continue to depend upon writing—documentation, accounting, extensive and intensive correspondence, and written records—as an element essential to their operation (Smith, 1974).

Centralized control over public education systems entails the imposition of structures of accountability that reconstitute the classroom itself along bureaucratic lines. And this in turn entails that texts must be the currency of classroom exchange. Whatever of significance goes on in the classroom must ultimately be rendered in textual form. This paradoxical textualization of the non-textual has in recent years paradigmatically taken the form of transcribed recordings of oral exchanges.

Little wonder, then, that what gets defined in schools as significant knowledge is almost entirely textual in form. Curriculum decisions, made in writing on the basis of written texts, not surprisingly prescribe *as* curriculum other written texts. The modern textbook is a purpose-built technology for the transmission of accumulated scientific and cultural knowledge that has been accorded the status of significant fact (de Castell, Luke, & Luke, 1988). Although there are some optional (and relatively low-status) school subjects such as shop, physical education, drama and music, that are not entirely text-based, in *no* compulsory matriculation subject is student mastery of any of the core subjects tested by means other than written examinations. In some jurisdictions, it is possible to request oral examinations if students are unable to cope with written examinations. But this option is often little known and rarely requested, and the examinations themselves remain literate ones, even if they are conducted in speech rather than written. If there is one lesson that students cannot help but learn, it is that there is no knowledge or skill designated as culturally significant that cannot be articulated by means of written symbols. I am speaking here about an epistemological lesson that is not informally picked up, but that is imposed throughout all modern nations on a mass scale, made compulsory, institutionally legitimated, and coercively enforced.

Embodied Knowledge

And what is wrong with this, one may ask? What of significance is thereby omitted? Is there any form of thought that does *not* require formal symbolic operations? Is there any mechanism for the preservation and dissemination of contemporary cultural knowledge that is *not* textual, whether originally or ultimately? Treading the well-worn path from literacy to reflection, to the growth of knowledge, which has been so masterfully and so clearly mapped out for us (Goody, 1977, ch. 3), can we see any *other* vehicles of individual and social enlightenment besides the text?

We are frequently told that all processes of thinking or conceptualization *must* involve a linguistic component, and that even though we can view graphics, for instance, as an alternative mode of communication to the linguistic, any elaborate use of visual representation always requires the advanced conceptual system intrinsic to language use (Goody, 1987, p. 10). Of course this by itself doesn't entail the necessity to resort to texts, to *written* language. However, it has been forcefully argued that such codification *is* required for the kinds of incremental accumulative knowledge possible by the preservative function of the written text. (The development of modern science is the usual example given of this.)

But there is another side to the argument that has to do with what is *omitted* when knowledge is textually encoded. At the cultural level (I shall discuss the individual level in the next section), most obviously omitted from the textual canon are minority and women's history and know-how, stemming from dominant cultural views about what was deemed worthy of being recorded, as well as from who was deemed worthy of being given instruction in how to record. Just as texts enable some knowledge to accumulate, then they enable other knowledge to be, as it were, cumulatively lost.

Goody documents a similar process of gain and loss with respect to the survival and status of religions of the book, pointing out that "in our schools, the study of world religion inevitably takes as its models religions having written texts—religions of the book" (1986, p. 3). These are the religions that have survived best, and, unlike in the more persuasive case of modern science, one presumably would not want to argue that the survival of these religions over other local religions has anything to do with the universalizing capacities of literacy. Goody (1986) gives the example of Asante, a territorially based religion in which religion is a part of a particular, spatially bounded group's way of life. "You cannot practice Asante religion unless you are an Asante" (p. 5). "Literate religions", Goody goes on to point out, "at least alphabetically literate ones, are generally religions of conversion, not religions of birth. You can spread them, like jam. And you can persuade or force people to give up one set of beliefs and practices and take up another set" (p. 5). Religions of the book, just like other cultural forms encoded textually, can become relatively autonomous and independent of spatial or territorial boundaries.

Religion is a good example to think about here, because it makes clear that such autonomy and independence as are enabled by writing may not necessarily be a good thing. Without raising the spectre of imperialism, we can question whether the tendency of the written word to over-generalize norms, and to replace contextualized notions of goodness and evil with literate universalized norms is invariably desirable, invariably rational. A current case of legislative irrationality involving a woman on welfare sentenced to prison for non-payment of fines resulting from her stealing a packet of cigarettes is a case in point, as is the case Goody mentions of how a complex constellation of human rights gets reduced to a single line of text in a land title (Goody, 1986, p. 81). The point is that neither the reductionist tendencies of writing, nor the replacement of the particular with the universal, are invariably culturally *progressive* developments. For if they enable action to be taken at a distance, they also enable judgements to be rendered in the absence of relevant knowledge and understanding of both the conditions prevailing and the consequences of that judgement.

Knowledge can be far more readily transmitted, but it is not necessarily understood in local contexts. Vicarious experience can come to be seen as an adequate substitute for lived experience, and knowledge thereby presumed where only the faintest trace of it may in fact be possessed. Perhaps most serious among these negative consequences of writing's ability to preserve knowledge is the illusion of progressive enlightenment that may come with the accumulation of texts, the tendency to equate an accumulation of cultural texts with an accumulation of cultural knowledge. Once knowledge assumes a material form, it can not only be preserved and stored, but censored, owned, bought and sold, and, most importantly, contained "shelved" and disregarded. We are often urged that, because of the vast stores of knowledge our culture has accumulated, it is more important that we teach students to *access* information (the term now being used interchangeably with "knowledge") than that we get them to internalize it personally. And here we cannot help but be reminded of Plato's warnings in the Phaedrus:

> You attribute to letters a fortune that they cannot possess. This facility will make souls forgetful because they will no longer school themselves to meditate. Your instruction will give them only a semblance of truth, not the truth itself. You will train ignorant know-alls, nosey know-nothings. (in Ong, 1982)

"Incremental Knowledge" From Culture to Individual

I should like here to consider some important differences between the impacts of literacy at the cultural level and the impacts of literacy at the level of the individual's own learning. Just as there appears to be some respects in which literacy might impede rather than promote desirable and rational cultural development, so there appear to be ways in which the school's concentrated emphasis on textual knowledge might function to impede rather than promote desirable and rational individual development. Quite possibly the effect is even more profound, in the case of the individual.

As we have seen, it is widely assumed and argued that thinking depends upon language, that any systematic cumulative thought depends upon systematic writing, that language-based thinking is prerequisite to

↓ KEY

challenged

rationality, and that it is our *rationality* that distinguishes us as human beings and sets us off from the so-called "lower" animals. In recent years, however, this near-automatic presumption is increasingly being challenged. Sheets-Johnstone, for example, in a 1981 essay "Thinking in Movement" urges that

> To tie thinking down to language and rationality . . . is to take for granted an inherent and/or necessary interdependence before examining experience itself, and prematurely to declare impossible something which may not be impossible at all, and perhaps, on the contrary, quite common, i.e. thinking in movement. (p. 400)

She goes on to discuss the traditional separation of thought from motor activity as derived from the archaic distinction between body and mind: "to deny the possibility of thinking in movement, may also be to uphold the notion that thinking is something only a mind can do, while doing or movement is something a body can do" (p. 401).

But here one feels compelled to return to "origins". For speaking, too, is something a body does, and the significance of this inescapable embodiment of the voice must not be overlooked. Plato's dialogues, for example, are based upon conversational speech, and it seems to make a great deal of difference to the kinds of arguments, including sophisticated ones, that Plato produces (Gadamer, 1980). And yet it often is overlooked, even by those scholars who fully recognize that it is literacy that first brings into existence a *language* out of our speech, even by those who recognize that it is not literacy, but speaking, that is humankind's most radical and most significant creation. Indeed the assumption that we act with our bodies and think with our minds may itself derive partly from the impact of reading on individual bodies. Reading brings movement to a halt, fixing both perceptual and conceptual attention within tightly restricted spatial limits in which, however, new worlds can be actively imagined and vicariously experienced.

In the oral past, a person's truth was that person's word; a person's knowledge was similarly embodied. In such a situation, one could no more lay claim to knowledge never in fact displayed than one could lay claim to a good reputation in the commission of disreputable acts. But the disengagement of speaker from situation and speech from speaker made possible precisely the kind of separation presupposed in denying the possibility of thinking in movement, or in painting (Cezanne), or in sound. My contention is that so long as we continue to deny all such

Key quote ✗

Key aspect of thesis

possibilities, and, conversely, to affirm the separability of interpersonal conversation from its so called "message content", to substitute what Illich with derision refers to as "oral language use" for embodied dialogue we miseducate—and with dire consequences.

We overlook other processes and forms of thinking—or forms of human intelligence—more generally—that are tied to the immediate situation, and responsive to evolution and change. The form of rationality implicit in this situation-bound and body-bound intelligence can be seen as an embodied reason, in which, Sheets-Johnstone says, "The progress of thought, the process of thinking in movement is tied to the evolving, changing situation itself . . . [hence] reasonableness could not be in terms of each movement being logically connected to the next movement by some formal, linear, or otherwise externally imposed regulative scheme" (p. 404). It appears to me that we need a good deal more of this kind of reasoning, as indeed the literature on rationality crises also indicates (Habermas, 1976).

But all this is by no means to invalidate or undermine the importance of a literate tradition. However, as Steiner (1967) has pointed out of the study of literature, it was once "assumed to carry an almost necessary implication of moral force . . . [that it would] enrich not only taste and style but moral feeling; that it would cultivate human judgement and act against barbarism" (p. 57). But, he goes on to point out

> The simple yet appalling fact is that we have very little solid evidence that literary studies do very much to enrich or stabilize moral perception, that they *humanize.* We have little proof that a tradition of literary studies in fact makes a man more humane. What is worse—a certain body of evidence points the other way. When barbarism came to twentieth century Europe, the arts faculties in more than one university offered very little moral resistance, and this is not a trivial or local accident. In a disturbing number of cases, the literary imagination gave service or ecstatic welcome to political bestiality. That bestiality was at times reinforced and refined by individuals educated in the culture of traditional humanism. Knowledge of Goethe, a delight in the poetry of Rilke, seemed no bar to personal and institutionalized sadism. Literary values and the utmost of hideous humanity could co-exist in the same community, in the same individual sensibility. . . I find myself unable to assert confidently that the humanities humanitze. Indeed I would go further: it is at least conceivable that the focusing of consciousness on a written text, which is the substance of our training and pursuit, diminishes the sharpness and readiness of our actual moral response. Because we are trained to give psychological and moral credence to the imaginary, to the character in a play or a novel, to

misconception

the condition of spirit we gather from a poem, we may find it more difficult to identify with the real world, to take the world of actual experience to heart—"to heart" is a suggestive phrase. (p. 61)

Steiner goes on to quote Kierkegaard, "it is not worthwhile remembering that past which cannot become a present" (p. 67). And he concludes that ⌝ *fantastic quote*

to read great literature as if it did not have upon us an urgent desire, to be able to move unchanged after reading Pound's 1st *Canto,* is to do little more than make entries in a librarian's catalogue. (p. 67)

The mind as a librarian's catalogue—isn't this precisely what we promote in education, when we exclude *presence* from mind, when we permit our students to "know" what they do not believe, and to "believe" what they fail to act upon?

Although Steiner's remarks here are concerned only with *literary* texts and with an ethics of immediacy and a morality of presence, nonetheless the necessary parallels are, I hope, evident It is my contention that the school's increasing disregard of the epistemological significance of affective and bodily knowing, and its correlative equation of knowledge with the written word as detached from speaker and circumstance, has resulted in a reliance on educational texts and technology as commodified pedagogy, and in the omission from, or depreciation in, the modern school curriculum of aesthetic-expressive, perceptual, moral-practical, and physical education. This has thereby diminished, rather than enhanced, the practical political consequences of mass education for social identity and emancipatory social action.

we put so much emphasis on texts. we don't talk about other ways of knowing

References

Austin, J. L. (1962) *How to do things with words.* Cambridge, MA: Harvard University Press.

de Castell, S., Luke, A., & Luke, C. (Eds.). (1988). *Language, authority and criticism: Readings on the school textbook.* London: Falmer Press.

Foucault, M. (1978). *The history of sexuality* (Vol. 1). New York: Random House.

Gadamer, H. G. (1980). *Dialogue and dialectic: Eight hermeneutical studies in Plato.* New Haven, CT: Yale University Press.

Goody, J. (1977). *The domestication of the savage mind.* Cambridge: Cambridge University Press.

Goody, J. (1986). *The logic of writing and the organization of society.* Cambridge: Cambridge University Press.

Goody, J. (1987). *The interface between the written and the oral.* Cambridge: Cambridge University Press.

Habermas, J. (1976). *Legitimation crisis.* London: Heinemann.

Havelock, E. (1962). *Preface to Plato.* Cambridge, MA: Harvard University Press.

Havelock, E. (1988). Instruction of preliterate cultures. In S. de Castell, A. Luke, and C. Luke (eds.) *Language, authority and criticism: Readings on the school textbook.* London: Falmer Press.

Illich, I. (1987). A plea for research on lay literacy. *Interchange, 18*(1,2) 9-22.

Illich, I., & Sanders, B. (1988). *A.B.C.: The alphabetization of the popular mind.* San Francisco: Northpoint Press.

Ong, W. (1982). *Orality and literacy: The technologizing of the word.* London: Methuen.

Ryle, G. (1949). *The concept of mind.* New York: Barnes & Noble.

Searle, J. (1969). *Speech acts.* Cambridge: Cambridge University Press.

Sheets-Johnstone, M. (1981). Thinking in movement. *The Journal of Aesthetics and Art Criticism, 34,* 399-407.

Smith, D. (1974). The social construction of documentary reality. *Social Inquiry 44,* 257-268.

Steiner, G. (1967). *Language and silence.* New York: Atheneum.

Williams, R. (1976). *Keywords: A vocabulary of culture and society.* London: Fontana Paperbacks.

4

Effective Functioning in Daily Life:
A Critique of Concepts and Surveys of Functional Literacy

James L. Heap
Ontario Institute for Studies in Education

Definitions and surveys of functional literacy are unsatisfactory. They do not encompass the metacognitive and practical reasoning practices required for rational, successful functioning in daily life. Even the most recent and sophisticated forms of literacy surveys do not measure people's ability to function in society with printed information. They measure scholastic literacy: the ability to perform school-like tasks requiring reading or writing.

To illustrate my claims I focus on two recent reports on literacy, the National Assessment of Educational Progress (NAEP) report on literacy among young adults (Kirsch & Jungeblut, 1986) and the Creative Research Group Report on Literacy commissioned by a Canadian newspaper chain, Southam News (Southam Newspaper Group, 1987; Calamai, 1987).

In the first section, I offer some conceptual clarifications and distinctions so that there can be a common ground of discussion. The second section analyzes the structure of the tasks on the NAEP and Southam surveys, illustrating the claim that these are school-like tasks, not tasks faced in the world outside of school. Finally, the third section pursues more thoroughly the correspondence problem, namely, the problem of how closely the tasks in functional literacy tests simulate everyday tasks.

Conceptual Foundations

The deep interest in literacy outside academia and professional education is almost always an interest in people's competence, their ability to *lit → competence → func. l*

satisfy personal and collective goals in rational ways. Measures of literacy are of interest because they tell us about levels of competence in society.

From both an economic and social-scientific standpoint, a society or group that cannot produce members capable of satisfying personal and collective goals has little chance of survival. When the means to goal achievement include the use of written information (reading or writing), the interest in competence is manifested as an interest in literacy, but not any or all forms of literacy. The interest is in those forms that are efficacious, if not necessary, for achieving economic stability and growth and for the production and reproduction of social order. Since the middle of this century the interest in competence has become an interest in functional literacy.

defn → Competence, formally understood, consists of whatever collection of skills, subskills, processes, procedures, strategies and knowledge that can be used to achieve personal and collective goals in a typical, uniform, repetitive, cohort-independent fashion. From the perspective of members of a culture, the predictable adequacy of these means for achieving specifiable ends establishes these means as rational. Here I am following Talcott Parsons' (1937) widely used notion of rationality, but modified in line with the criticisms of Schutz (1964) and Garfinkel (1967).

Southam News was interested specifically in functional literacy. The research they commissioned adopted the NAEP definition of literacy, along with the NAEP methodology. The NAEP study defined literacy as follows: *↓ defn of l.*

> Using printed and written information to function in society, to achieve one's goals, and to develop one's knowledge and potential. (Kirsch and Jungeblut, 1986, p.3)

However, the linkage between reading and writing and functioning in our information-dependent society is problematic. It is often taken as a necessary connection. What kind of necessity, however, is involved in the linkage between literacy and functioning?

First of all, the necessity is not analytic in Kant's sense—it is not a necessity at a logical or conceptual level. Put differently, the necessity of being able to read and write in order to function in society is not like the necessity of bachelors being unmarried men. The idea of functioning does not entail the notion of literacy, nor vice versa.

Second, the necessity is not empirical. Any empirical relation, say between functioning effectively on some task and the exercise of literacy skills, is a contingent relation, not a necessary one. Put differently, neither having literacy skills nor employing them is a guarantee of effective functioning. Further, not every case of goal achievement where written language *can* be used to function is a case where written language *is* used. And, not every case where written language *is* used is a case where written language *has* to be used. Anecdotes abound (e.g., Berger, 1988) about people who cope with printed information without themselves being able to read.

Third, putting aside the discipline of logic, the use of necessity in definitions of functional literacy trades on a fact and a presupposed belief. The fact is an empirical regularity: in instances of effective functioning on tasks where written language *can* be employed, as when there is some form to read or fill-in as a means to some end such as receiving unemployment benefits, in most cases written language *is* employed. The presupposed belief used to explain this fact is: employing written language is the most effective means to achieving the intended goal—receiving unemployment benefits. There are rational grounds for this belief, but those grounds do not establish that this belief is necessarily true in all cases where texts are encountered.

I have established that literacy logically is not necessary for functioning in situations where printed information can be used as a resource. Literacy, rather, is a *rational means*. From an objectivist perspective (Heap, 1988), at the aggregate level of all instances of functioning where written language can be used, I will not oppose the argument that literacy is the most rational means for functioning. From a situated perspective, however, where the concern is with particular cases as encountered from the position of participants (Heap, 1988), it is an open empirical question as to whether literate means will be the most rational ones available to participants.

Say, for example, you are in a library and wish to use a photocopier, but do not see how to lay your newspaper clipping on the machine's glass plate. You have at least three choices, which reflect three modes of functioning in the presence of texts. If you find directions on the photocopier for laying out the clipping, you can work in a *text*-based mode. If you look, but do not find unambiguous information, you can act upon your best interpretation of the instructions. You can lay out the clipping, make the copy, see whether you were right, and if necessary try again. This second way of functioning can be said to be a *text*-aided mode. If a library worker comes by, you can ask her or him how to use the photocopier. If the worker shows you, or makes the copy for you, you have succeeded in operating in a text-omitted mode.

The problem with definitions of functional literacy is that they assume reading and writing are the most rational means in *any* circumstance where written language can be used for effective functioning. Defined in this way, functional literacy consists solely of text-based functioning. Functional literacy so defined does not include the practical reasoning (Garfinkel, 1967) involved in deciding if and when reading should be done when print is present.

Text-aided functioning requires such practical reasoning. Functioning effectively in a text-aided mode involves moving back and forth between reading a document and what Schutz (1962, p.212) calls "working acts", where we bodily gear into the world of our surroundings. Such movement depends on repeated practical reasoning, involving what cognitive psychologists call metacognitive acts: "the deliberate conscious control of one's own cognitive acts" (Brown, 1980, p.453). In text-aided functioning you must monitor continually the progress made using each means. You must decide when to terminate reading and turn to the surrounding world, and when to stop manipulating an object and return to reading.

Text-omitted functioning also requires practical reasoning. If you omit attention to a text, other means of sense-making and problem solving must be found and used. Of course, their use must be monitored, and discarded if not productive.

Here we are at the heart of the problem. If the criterion of functional literacy is success, that is effective functioning in daily life, the most rational means to success cannot be foreordained. Success in the open-ended, varied circumstances of daily life cannot be achieved in ways insensitive to the developing resources and constraints of those circumstances. Competence in daily life, including workplace competence, necessarily involves practical reasoning. A definition of a subset of competency skills, for example a definition of "functional literacy", is unacceptable if it does not encompass the practical reasoning processes, practices and strategies upon which people depend when employing that subset of skills.

Analysis of Literacy Surveys

I will now compare the structures of survey tasks with the structures of daily tasks which test tasks are designed to simulate. I will focus on one test task from the NAEP survey and its Canadian version, the Southam News survey. However, all items on these surveys have the structure of test tasks. The results of my effort will provide a basis for the claim that so-called functional literacy surveys are actually tests of scholastic literacy: the ability to perform school-like tasks. If our interest is in competency, then surveys of functional literacy are even less useful than the definitions they purport to operationalize.

The Rationalist Analytic Tradition

The methodology that shapes literacy surveys issues from the rationalist analytic tradition. Rationalist analysis begins by converting phenomena of daily life into tokens of abstract, explicit classes. Idealized phenomena and the conditions of their occurrence are fully represented as a closed system with discrete elements. Via reflection and experiments, these elements are analyzed in order to discover their logically possible and empirically actual relations. These relations are believed to hold within what can be called a "closed system"—a phrase denoting a set of elements and conditions, each member of which is taken to have some relevant relation to at least one other element or condition in the set. Each member of such a system has a determinate content or identity. The system is closed in the sense that the characterization of a problem and the proposed solution/explanation depend only upon the content of the elements and conditions interior to the system. The epitome of closed system rationalist analysis is to be found in programs in artificial intelligence, where closed systems are spoken of as "microworlds" (Papert, 1980; Minsky, 1985).

In an open system, there can be no presumption that the content of each element and condition will remain stable across all interactions with that system. Elements of the system may not be explicitly represented or brought to full attention by people who encounter and operate such systems. Further, in an open system there is the possibility that phenomena not represented are, or will turn out to be, relevant to characterizing or solving a problem at hand. The attempt to use closed systems to represent open ones is the root of the correspondence problem, which will be taken up when we compare literacy tests with the daily tasks which they "simulate".

NAEP and Southam News Literacy Surveys

The NAEP and Southam News surveys are closely related, since the Southam News Survey was based on a selection of tasks from the NAEP Survey. I want to outline the ways in which the survey tasks differ systematically from the everyday tasks they were designed to simulate.

First, the request to the Southam News panel of experts that they "determine what level of literacy is necessary to get by in today's society" (Southam Newspaper Group, 1987, fourth appendix) presupposes that the test tasks drawn from the NAEP survey indeed simulate tasks encountered by ordinary people in daily life. Of their tasks the authors of the NAEP study state:

> The simulation tasks represent a variety of purposes people have for using printed material and the variety of the materials associated with these purposes. (Kirsch & Jungeblut, 1986, p.7)

The test tasks are designed to simulate daily tasks, but do they succeed? Collectively and individually, as representations, do they correspond to the tasks and circumstances of everyday life which they are intended to represent? I find ten aspects of difference when comparing NAEP survey tasks to the activities in daily life. All ten bear upon the problem of correspondence in the rationalist analytic tradition.

In order to illustrate the ten aspects, I will present one item from the NAEP/Southam News survey. The item is the repair notice task. Of young Americans 21-25 years old, 72% got the right answer on this item (Kirsch & Jungeblut, 1986, p.16). Of Canadians, 64% were able to perform correctly on this item (Southam Newspaper Group, 1987, p.51). For my argument, what is important is not how well any group performed, or how easy they found the task, or any other task on the survey. The salient issue is the difference between the items on the survey and the actual tasks in daily life which they are intended to simulate.

The format of the repair task consists of clusters of text appearing on a single page. Five of these clusters are enclosed within rectangular boxes. The top box is presented as instructions supplied by a company to customers: "When returning appliance for servicing, include a note telling as clearly and as specifically as possible what is wrong with the appliance." Below this box are four boxes with notes that a repair person receives with four appliances. The task is to "Circle the letter next to the note which best follows the instructions supplied by the company." Box A, for example, reads, "The clock does not run correctly on this clock radio. I tried fixing it, but I couldn't" (Kirsch & Jungeblut, 1986, p.12; Southam Newspaper Group, 1987, p.37; Calamai, 1987, p.38).

Contingent Aspects of Difference

In comparing this test task with the everyday task which it simulates, the first set of aspects of difference can be labelled contingent features of testing. These aspects of difference are not necessary to testing per se. They represent features which test designers can control and modify to some extent. As a result of decisions made by the designers of the NAEP survey, four such contingent aspects of difference between test tasks and everyday tasks can be located.

First, there is a difference in *task* lay out and the structure of completion between the repair notice test task and the task as might be faced in everyday life. In our daily lives, we would encounter only the text in the top box. That text would be printed on a card, on a sheet of paper, in a manual, on a carton, etc. If we were actually to return an appliance we would have to *write* a note.

Second, the *sample content* of a test task may or may not be familiar to the respondent. Moreover, in everyday life repair persons do not circle letters or evaluate how specific a note is. Their daily task is to read notes, and to examine and repair appliances.

Third, in test tasks, respondents *experience no consequences of their efforts.* In the repair notice task, the respondent just circles a letter. In daily life, if we write a note and send off an appliance, we expect feedback, and a repaired appliance.

Fourth, in the NAEP/Southam survey the *completion of all tasks is equally important.* While the difficulty of all items is graded by NAEP, the completion of one item is no more important, or less important, than any other. The completion of each item is equally weighted. Completing the repair notice task is as important as the test tasks of balancing a chequebook or entering personal information on a job application. In daily life even the same task can differ in importance, depending on circumstances: compare reading a fire extinguisher label in a store versus reading the label when a fire breaks out.

Necessary Aspects of Difference

The second set of aspects of difference are necessary features of testing. These features are ones that must be built into tests and tasks as a condition of measuring performance. These are the features that give test tasks their closed-system character. The designers of the NAEP study had no choice but to produce tasks that incorporate the following features.

The *fifth* aspect of difference is the *normative order of task performance*. Normative order concerns what persons ought to do under particular conditions (Parsons, 1937). Normative order includes, among other things, rules, conventions, expectations, preferences, practices, and beliefs. The normative order of task performance includes such obvious things as the enforceable expectation that the respondent will act rationally and in good faith—that is, will comply with interviewer requests to complete tasks, in a certain order, with full and equal attention to each task; will select the course of action among those found that best achieves the apparent purpose of each task; and will attempt to succeed on each task. While obvious, these expectations cannot always be taken for granted. McDermott's (1985) well known research on reading groups and student performance reveals that some students aim to *achieve* school failure, presumably in order to maintain respected relations with peers. The behaviour of these students is rational, but not in accord with the enforceable expectations of teachers about which classroom goals are appropriate.

Work done on the repair notice task by respondents, and indeed work on all tasks in the survey, is done in compliance with the normative order of expectations, made salient, sustained, and enforced by the task designers and interviewers. In daily life, the tasks which the NAEP survey simulates are not performed within an encapsulating normative order enforced by a stranger who comes to your door. Reading a warranty and devising a note to send along with an appliance are not done in the presence of someone who is interested solely in the technical adequacy of your performance. That is not one of the demands put on your performance in daily life. Yet respondent compliance with a normative order is a condition for the success of a closed system, a "microworld", as a measurement environment. The closed system is held together through compliance with a normative order.

The *sixth* aspect is the time boundedness of task performance. Part of what establishes the NAEP/Southam survey tasks as operating within closed systems is that performance time was limited to five minutes per item. There were no opportunities, as there might be in daily life, to go back at a later time and reread or rewrite a passage or to change an answer from "B" to "C" in the repair notice task.

The *seventh* aspect is frame predetermination. Whenever we encounter print, or indeed whenever we pay attention to our surroundings, we must determine the *frame* within which events should be interpreted (Bateson, 1972, Goffman, 1974). In any everyday task setting, assuming that the reading materials are in some way relevant to what we want or are compelled, to do, some determination must be made as to what kind of texts are present at hand. In the case of test tasks in the NAEP survey, the texts themselves provide a solution to the frame problem. In the repair notice task, frame predetermination occurs twice. First, the reader is given a frame for understanding the sentence in the top box—that sentence provides "instructions for returning appliances for service". Below the box the second, or inner, frame is furnished: "A repair person for the company receives four appliances with the following notes attached".

The *eighth* aspect concerns the *setting of purposes*. In test tasks, purposes are set for respondents. In the repair notice task the purpose is set immediately following the determination of the inner frame. The purpose of the task is to "Circle the letter next to the note which best follows the instructions supplied by the company." In daily life, when we encounter warranty information we may not bother to read it. Our purpose may be just to save the warranty by filing it with other warranties on household appliances.

Setting the same purpose within a specified frame for each respondent, is a move in the construction of a closed system. Given some document to be interpreted, frame and purpose are anchors for closed systems. They establish an orientation on the part of the respondent that test designers regard as necessary for the comparison of performances across respondents. It is through the predetermination of frame and purpose that a task is made the same for each respondent, and that a single, self-same task is constructed, with one set of materials, for everyone.

The *ninth* aspect concerns the *relevance of the* phenomenal field. Abiding by the normative frame and purpose of the test task, the respondent needs to adopt a specific interpretive relation to what can be seen, the phenomenal field. If the respondent is to be maximally rational (testwise!), he or she should view the phenomenal field of task materials under a principle of preorganized relevance. The principle is that everything which appears in the field: (a) was put there by the test designers, (b) is believed by test designers to be definitely relevant or irrelevant to the completion of the task, such that, (c) some set of the field's features will be all that a competent respondent needs to complete the task. Under this principle, constrained by the normative order of task performance, the respondent has reason to believe that the phenomenal field provides all the information needed to determine the correct answer. If the task has been designed successfully as a closed system, no additional searching for information should be required.

The respondent has the right to expect a coherence within the boundaries of the task's phenomenal field. The use of the phrase "the following instructions" or "the following notes" can be taken to refer to what appears below these phrases, within the physical boundaries of the page that presents the task. Whatever appears below those phrases can, and should, be treated as exactly what is supposed to appear there. This will be true in spite of the fact that, given a moment's reflection, it is obvious that "the following notes" are not the same physical notes which would have been attached to four different appliances.

Obversely, anything which is not represented within the physical bounds of the task can be taken as irrelevant. The fact that pictures or drawings of the "four appliances" are not included establishes grounds for the belief that the brand, type of clock or radio (digital vs. analogical), or any other feature of those appliances is not relevant to completing the task.

In daily life, where tasks are encountered as open systems, we must engage in practical reasoning to determine what is, is not, may be, or may become relevant to the task at hand. In test tasks, relevance of items must be assured, and must be consistent across all offerings of the task. This is done to ensure that correct responses can be produced on the basis of task information, and to ensure that task demands are appropriate to the skills that the test tasks aim to measure, for example, reading comprehension skills.

The *tenth* and final aspect of difference concerns the *availability of resources*. Given a set purpose, within some frame, and a preorganized, relevant phenomenal field, the question arises: what operational means, what resources, are available for achieving the desired ends?

In test tasks the resources are sharply constrained. If properly designed, the test task will allow the use only of the target skills the task was designed to measure. If other resources could be used, ones not entertained by the task designer, there would be no way for evaluators to determine what performance on the task actually measured.

In daily life if we have a defective clock radio there are a number of resources for getting it repaired. Use of these resources may omit any attention to warranty texts, as when we call the manufacture's toll-free number, or call the store where we purchased the item. We may operate in a text-aided mode, reading the warranty but still calling a store, because it would be easier to take the appliance back than ship it somewhere.

Summary

This second section has formulated ten differences between test tasks and the everyday tasks that they simulate. Because the tasks of daily life are encountered as open systems, and measurement tasks are necessarily closed systems, the degree of correspondence between test tasks and everyday tasks will remain problematic. In order to move to the conclusion of this chapter it will be useful to clarify the problem of correspondence as it applies to literacy test tasks.

The Correspondence Problem

Simulation and Correspondence

In what sense can the test tasks of the NAEP survey be said to simulate everyday tasks? Kirsch and Jungeblut assert that their "simulation tasks represent a variety of purposes people have for using printed material and the variety of the materials associated with these purposes" (1986, p.7). They say that this framework was applied to task development because research has shown that performance on tasks centering on written materials depends on what the reader is expected to do with the materials.

The test tasks do present a variety of materials associated with everyday life. But the materials have a different layout in test tasks; they are prefaced by information that frames the way the materials are to be addressed, and they formulate purposes for addressing the materials (aspects 4, 7, 8). The materials, so addressed, present a phenomenal field under a principle of preorganized relevance (aspect 9). The materials thus have an assured relevance in the test situation which otherwise would have to be discovered and judged in daily life. The materials can be said to "mean differently" in such test situations than they would when encountered in daily life.

Given the disparity between the purposes and materials presented in tests, and those that are taken up and encountered in daily life, I cannot agree that the test tasks are adequate simulations of tasks in everyday life. To be taken seriously as simulations, test tasks designed from within the rationalist analytic tradition would have to replicate the properties that define everyday tasks. These properties would have to include aspects of everyday tasks that I have discussed here. It is an empirical question which aspects of everyday tasks will have to be replicated. The question will turn upon what is to be measured.

Correspondence and Open Systems

The attempt to design literacy task simulations for measurement purposes results in misrepresentations of people's ability to function in society. The tests measure the ability to read and write in particular ways, but they do not measure what they purport to measure: functioning in society when printed materials can be used.

The problem is that functioning in everyday life requires and consists of operating effectively in open systems of action. The NAEP survey's tasks are closed, in that the content of the elements and conditions—the frame, purpose, time, phenomenal field, resources, and normative order—are predetermined and fixed across the duration of task involvement.

In contrast, an open system is one where the same elements are present, but the content of each element is not assured over the duration of task effort. Task effort will continue as long as a task-related purpose, or set of purposes, remains operative. But it is an open question whether, and how long, a set of purposes will dominate. As long as a purpose or purposes are in place, they are the anchors for the system. The frame may change as different phenomenal fields are encountered. And changes in frame may alter one's sense of the organization of the current phenomenal field. Each field, under each frame, will introduce new normative elements which must be faced in appropriate ways, as when we shift from reading an appliance warranty to speaking on the telephone to an appliance repair person. Perhaps most importantly, the resources we bring to bear to complete a task are open to change. We do have some freedom: the freedom to act in whatever ways are most rational, at the time.

In open systems of task completion, practical reasoning is required in order to decide whether a purpose is worth pursuing, and for how long, given its importance (aspect 4). Practical reasoning, monitoring and selecting elements of activity organization, is involved in the determination of frames and in the selection of resources for task completion. Practical reasoning is required in order to determine whether the materials at hand are relevant to the chosen task. Practical reasoning is required in order to act in the most rational way to achieve ends, successfully.

With the introduction of practical reasoning as an essential feature of open-system operation, the last link in my argument is in place. By closing the system of relevance, designers of literacy test tasks delete the element that is essential for effective functioning in society, whether or not print is involved. This is practical reasoning, reasoning about what frames, purposes, normative orders, and resources are relevant, here and now.

In overlooking practical reasoning of the metacognitive sort specified, the designers of literacy tests operationalize the shortcomings of definitions of functional literacy. Reading and writing are made into necessary and sufficient means for "functioning in society". In fact, though, they are only necessary and sufficient for functioning on tests that *require* reading and writing, for example, literacy surveys. Without practical reasoning, and without the openness that characterizes daily task efforts, no simulation can measure people's ability to function in society when written language can be used. Literacy test tasks do not correspond to everyday tasks.

Conclusion

we need to stop using this term

Conceptions of functional literacy are unsatisfactory, and cannot be salvaged. We ought to stop using the phrase "functional literacy". If we wish to denote its referent we can speak of text-based functioning.

Text-based functioning is extremely important in modern societies. It is important precisely for the domain of texts and set of purposes to which "literacy", without adjectives, is appropriate. These are reflective texts (Heap, in press). The purposes for reading this type of text are satisfied solely within acts of reading the text. These are the texts and purposes that have been the centre of interest in research and debate about the cognitive and social consequences of literacy (Olson, 1977, 1986; Goody, 1986).

Tests of functioning in society using printed information are not tests of people's ability to function effectively on daily tasks. Test items on, for example, the NAEP survey work as closed systems. People encounter closed-system tasks in daily life typically in school, under sway of scientific reading (and mathematics) curricula. Lessons, workbooks, and tests work as closed systems. So-called tests of literacy—functional, prose, document, or quantitative—are tests of scholastic literacy: the ability to complete successfully school-like tasks.

In everyday life, when written language can be used, functioning effectively requires metacognitive, practical reasoning to handle the elements of open systems of task completion. Functioning effectively requires rational use of apparently available means to achieve desired ends. When reading or writing can be used, it will not always be most rational to base action solely on reading or writing. Effective functioning may consist of text-aided functioning, moving between texts and objects in the task environment. This is evident in studies of workplace literacy (Diehl & Mikulecky, 1980; Mikulecky, 1982; Mikulecky & Ehlinger, 1986; Mikulecky & Winchester, 1983).

Indeed, once we remove the artificial constraints in definitions and tests of functional literacy, which require all task completion to be text-based, we will no doubt find empirically that text-aided functioning is the dominant mode of text use in daily life. Having removed these artificial constraints, we will be able to appreciate that text-aided functioning is usually the most rational mode for functioning in the presence of printed information.

While text-aided functioning may be the most inclusive category for collecting uses of written language, it must be appreciated that the variety of things done with texts will be as extensive as the types of circumstances, objects, documents, and texts involved. Close observation and careful analyses will be required to determine what "text-aided functioning" denotes as types of literacy-related events.

To close the circle: if general social interest in functional literacy is actually an interest in competence, then measures of text-based functioning are not directly useful. Those measures tell us how well some population can perform on school-like tasks, but they do not give us a clear view of people's ability to function effectively in society. An interest in competence when written language can be used should be understood as an interest in text-aided functioning.

Acknowledgements

Versions of this chapter have been presented at the meetings of the National Reading Conference, Tucson, Arizona, December, 1988, and at the Functional Literacy Workshop, McLuhan Program in Culture and Technology, Toronto, Ontario, May, 1989. Preparation of this chapter was supported by the Social Sciences and Humanities Research Council of Canada, Grant Number 410-88-0494, and by the Ontario Institute for Studies in Education Small Scale Research Grant, Number 62-3240. The author wishes to thank Christine Bennett for helpful discussions on central issues of this essay, and David Ross for his editorial assistance.

References

Bateson, G. (1972). *Steps to an ecology of mind.* New York: Ballantine.

Berger, J. (1988, September 6). Price of illiteracy translates into poverty and humiliation. *The New York Times*, pp. 1, 12.

Brown, A. L. (1980). Metacognitive development and reading. In R. J. Spiro, B. C. Bruce & W. F. Brewer (Eds.), *Theoretical issues in reading comprehension: Perspectives from cognitive psychology, linguistics, artificial intelligence, and education* (pp. 453-481). Hillsdale, NJ: Erlbaum.

Calamai, P. (1987). *Broken words: Why five million Canadians are illiterate.* Ottawa: Southam News.

Diehl, W. A., & Mikulecky, L. (1980). The nature of literacy at work. *Journal of Reading, 24*, 221-227.

Garfinkel, H. (1967). *Studies in ethnomethodology.* Toronto: Prentice-Hall.

Goffman, E. (1974). *Frame analysis.* New York: Harper & Row.

Goody, J. (1986). *The logic of writing and the organization of society.* New York: Cambridge University Press.

Heap, J. L. (1988). *A situated perspective on literacy events.* Occasional paper, University of Toronto, Project on the Socio-Cultural Organization of Writing.

Heap, J. L. (in press). Reading as cultural activities: Enabling and reflective texts. *Curriculum Inquiry.*

Kirsch, I. S., & Jungeblut, A. (1986). *Literacy: Profiles of America's young adults.* Princeton, NJ: The National Assessment of Education Progress.

McDermott, R. P. (1985). Achieving school failure. In H. Singer, & R. B. Ruddell, (Eds.), *Theoretical models and processes of reading,* 3rd Ed., (pp. 558-594). Newark, DE: International Reading Association.

Mikulecky, L. (1982). Job literacy: The relationship between school preparation and workplace actuality. *Reading Research Quarterly, 17,* 400-419.

Mikulecky, L., & Ehlinger, J. (1986). The influence of metacognitive aspects of literacy on job performance of electronics technicians. *Journal of Reading Behaviour, 18*(1), 41-62.

Mikulecky, L., & Winchester, D. (1983). Job literacy and job performance among nurses at varying employment levels. *Adult Education Quarterly, 34*(10), 1-15.

Minsky, M. (1985). *The society of mind.* New York: Simon & Schuster.

Olson, D. R. (1977). From utterance to text: The bias of language in speech and writing. *Harvard Educational Review, 47,* 257-281.

Olson, D. R. (1986). The cognitive consequences of literacy. *Canadian Psychology, 27,* 109-121.

Papert, S. (1980). *Mindstorms: Children, computers, and powerful ideas.* New York: Basic Books.

Parsons, T. (1937). *The structure of social action.* New York: McGraw-Hill.

Schutz, A. (1962). *The collected papers I: The problem of social reality.* The Hague: Martinus Nijhoff.

Schutz, A. (1964). *The collected papers II: Studies in social theory.* The Hague: Martinus Nijhoff.

Southam Newspaper Group (1987). *Literacy in Canada: A research report.* Ottawa: Author.

5

The Artifact as Text:
Being Literate in a Technological Society

Reg W. Fleming
University of Saskatchewan

The power and versatility of technology often leads to the optimistic view that technology holds the key to economic prosperity. The manifestation of this optimism is seen in concrete benefits to segments of North American society: improved clothing, housing, health care, communications, and so on. Technology has become the focus of homage by segments of the public.

During the latter part of this century, however, more ambivalence has developed toward technology and its social role. Many of the products of technology are no longer received without question. Vigorous debate has centred on issues as varied as genetic manipulation, nuclear engineering, air pollution, and agribusiness. Such debate places an onus on citizens to attempt to understand complex issues surrounding technology and its uses. Understanding the issues of technology requires that people be technologically literate.

Technological literacy, however, goes far beyond merely understanding the uses of technological artifacts. As Thoreau indicates, in his comments on artifacts:

> Each one yields me a thought. I come nearer to the maker of it than if I found his bones. It is no single inscription on a particular rock, but a footprint, rather a mind print . . . fossil thoughts, forever reminding me of the mind that shaped them . . . I am on the trail of mind. (Torrey, 1968, p. 91)

Quite simply, studying technological artifacts is studying the mind and the culture of the mind that produced the artifact. The artifact is a text, allowing for a critical "reading" of the culture that produced it. This chapter argues that there are several understandings and skills people must have in order to examine technology critically. They include knowing the meaning of both literacy and technology, knowing the nature of technological knowledge, and having decision-making skills.

A Meaning for Literacy

As Emig (1983, pp. 172-173) suggests, a possible yet incomplete description of literacy would be "the ability to comprehend, through reading the texts of others, what is new information". Unfortunately, such a perspective ignores the genesis of the text. Staying inside another's text may force one to accept another's meanings. Such intellectual passivity may well serve any majority or minority position. The active role for reading is the desired role. This active role for reading requires the use of one's knowledge base plus critical thinking when examining the text.

Writing demands that the writer move from the mechanics of writing (handwriting and copying) to the extraordinarily internal (authoring; namely, the translation of inner speech to the written word). This latter act of translation is synthesis and therefore original. In practice, writing is probably all these things. Combining reading with writing should, then, be a *freeing* activity, which removes one from the complete dependence on others' ideas. This occurs when one can cast the ideas gleaned from reading in one's own language while writing. Thus literacy gives one power—one is empowered in one's culture and may be able to move beyond it to create new, more powerful cultural forms. The essential word here is "may". It is not enough that one has the *potential* to act; rather, one must have the *disposition* to act (Norris, 1989). According to Habermas (1972), such empowerment is the concern of the emancipatory cognitive ability; namely, the ability of individuals and groups to take control of their own lives in autonomous and responsible ways.

A Meaning for Technology

"Technology" has become a catchword with a confusion of meanings. Kline (1985) attempts to untangle these meanings by identifying three commonly held positions. The most common usage is technology as *hardware*. By hardware he means all non-natural objects manufactured by humans. He then describes the second most common usage—technology as the *process of manufacturing the hardware*. Kline argues that this descriptor must include *all* elements necessary to manufacture particular hardware: people, machines, resources, as well as the physical, legal, economic, and political environments. He labels this the sociotechnical system of manufacture. The third perspective suggested by Kline is technology as know-how. Know-how is the information, skills, processes, and procedures for accomplishing tasks. These are Kline's interpretations of the three most commonly held views, and I do not wish to imply that they give either a consistent or complete conceptual analysis of technology; but they are helpful.

Kline goes on to argue that these three perspectives are inadequate. He suggests that a fourth is necessary to give purpose to the manufacture of hardware. This fourth perspective is technology as a *sociotechnical system of use*. It contains the hardware and the people necessary to extend human capacities:

> . . . we embody automobiles in a system of roads, gas stations, laws for ownership and operation, rules of the road, etc., and use the combined system (the autos plus all the rest) to extend the human capacity for moving ourselves and our possessions about. (Kline, 1985, p. 216)

Thus, without a sociotechnical system of use, the manufacture of hardware has limited purpose. Kline elaborates by stating that "sociotechnical systems of manufacture and sociotechnical systems of use form the physical bases of all human societies past and present" (p. 217). This pattern of purposeful innovation in sociotechnical systems distinguishes humans from other animals. Kline concludes by saying that "few topics are more basic . . . than an understanding of the nature of sociotechnical systems and the pattern in which we humans use them to create the physical bases for our societies past and present" (p. 18).

Consider another model for technology proposed by Pacey (1983). To expand the model past the merely technical, he alters the term to become technology-practice. The term encompasses the technical knowledge, as well as the organizational and cultural aspects of technology. The technical knowledge appears to be synonymous with Kline's hardware and know-how. The organizational aspect is most crucial to the politically minded. It represents public policy and its resultant administration; the activities of engineers, designers, and technicians; the needs of unions; and the needs of users of technology. This is quite similar to

Kline's sociotechnical system of manufacture, for Kline also discusses the people involved in manufacture in the context of their legal, economic, and political environments.

For those interested in ideological issues, Pacey's model offers the cultural aspect of technology-practice. This aspect focuses on the ideology of progress, habits of thinking in technical activity, values of engineers, and ethical codes. This may reflect many of the ideas in Kline's sociotechnical system of use.

The combination of these ideas results in a definition for technology-practice that will be used throughout this chapter. Technology-practice is "the application of scientific and other knowledge to practical tasks by ordered systems that involve people and organizations, living things and machines" (Pacey, 1983, p. 6). This is often called "sociotechnology", a social process in which the knowledge created by science and the knowledge created by technology are "put at the disposal of people who in general are not themselves competent in these knowledge bases, and who would wield them on behalf of ends reflecting a parochial interpretation of prevailing personal, institutional, and social values" (Goldman, 1984, p. 121). In other words, technology users decide what benefits may accrue from the use of these knowledge bases. It is these decisions that determine what will be the ultimate products of technology, not the scientific and technical knowledge. To understand sociotechnology, then, requires also that one understand the social forces brought to bear on those who make the decisions.

Technological Literacy

If one understands sociotechnology, then one is empowered to imagine alternatives, rather than confined to others' ideas. For example, the mind can construct "possible worlds inhabited by possible others" or imagine "alternative social, economic and sexual structures and arrangements . . ." (Emig, 1983, p. 177). Or, as Grundy summarizes, one is empowered "to engage in autonomous action arising out of authentic, critical insights into the social construction of human society" (1987, p. 19).

A technologically literate person has the power to examine and question the issues of importance in sociotechnology. Some of these could be: (a) the idea of progress through technology; (b) the appropriateness of various technologies; (c) the benefits and costs of technological development; (d) the economic models involving technology; (e) the decisions involved in consuming the products of technology; and (f) the decisions made by the managers of technology as they shape its application.

This list is merely illustrative of the areas in which a technologically literate person would be empowered. This empowerment would enable such a person to be critical about technology, to examine the potential benefits and costs of any technological development, and to perceive the underlying political and social forces driving the development. In addition to having these abilities, people must be disposed to conduct this critical examination. This behavioural disposition is a tendency that is justified and motivated by educational norms (Norris, 1989). The tendency here is to examine critically the social message or text portrayed by the artifact. To do this, one must examine the knowledge and cultural bases of the artifact—the sociotechnical systems of manufacture and use.

The above portrayal of technological literacy raises two crucial issues: (a) the nature of technological knowledge, for it is here that the relationship between science and technology unfolds; and (b) the nature of the decisions that people must make while living in a technological culture. These two issues will be the focus of the remainder of the chapter.

The Nature of Technological Knowledge

Technological knowledge can be perceived as a unique form of cognition. This perception is in direct contrast to the technology-as-applied-science perspective. This latter perception is very popular. In it, science discovers, and technology applies these discoveries to improve the quality of life. It may be possible to trace this perception to the misguided attempts by many scientists to justify the expenditure of public funds on the basis of future benefits in the form of new refrigerators, microwave ovens, and the like. Many politicians were quick to capitalize on this idea, particularly as the benefits of applied science led to economic prosperity and the possibility of re-election.

However, the applied-science perspective presents technology in far too passive a light. In the first instance, the technology-as-applied-science perspective is based on the premise that science represents the objective knowledge from which technology derives its meaning. If, however, one considers science as "a limited style whose methodologi-

cal constraints and particular historical traditions make it helpful for
some cognitive tasks and not others" (Staudenmaier, 1985, p. 102), then
other styles of knowing are equally viable. Given such a perspective, it
is not possible to assert that science is a more primary source of
knowledge than technology. Rather, science can be seen as *one* source,
and technology as a possible other source.

Second, empirical studies suggest the applied-science model is overly
simplistic. As Bijker, Hughes, and Pinch (1987) suggest:

> "Technology/science," "pure/applied," "internal/ external," and "techni-
> cal/social" are some of the dichotomies that were foreign to the integrating
> inventors, engineers, and managers of the system-and-network-building
> era. To have asked problem solving inventors if they were doing science
> or technology probably would have brought an uncomprehending stare.
> Even scientists who thought of themselves as pure would not have set up
> barriers between the internal and the external, if these would have
> prevented the search for solutions wherever the problem-solving thread
> might have led. Entrepreneurs and system builders creating regional
> production complexes incorporated such seemingly foreign actors as
> legislators and financiers in networks, if they could functionally con-
> tribute to the system-building goal. Instead of taking multidivisional
> organizational layouts as airtight categories, integrating managers sew a
> seamless web. (p. 10)

As examples of this web, Pinch and Bijker (1987), using their data
from a case study of the development of the bicycle, conclude that both
science and technology are socially constructed cultures and that the
boundary between them is a matter for social negotiation and represents
no underlying distinction.

Callon (1987), studying the French attempts to market an electric car,
asserts as well that the fabric has no seams. Specifically, drawing on his
case study, he asks why one should categorize differently the elements
in a system or network "when these elements are permanently interact-
ing, being associated, and being tested by the actors who innovate" (p.
11). From the perspective of the general public, on the other hand,
science is perceived as serving a utilitarian purpose; that is, science exists
as an instrument for achieving social goals. This allows for a blurring of
any differences between science and technology, resulting in a combined
enterprise called "technoscience".

A contemporary term for technoscience may be "research and
development" (R&D). To most members of the general public, R&D
implies mission-oriented research whose ultimate goal is the creation of

marketable products. This is the description offered by political parties and entrepreneurs, but it overlooks the necessity for basic and strategic research, whose function is to provide a knowledge base for potential use. Even an utilitarian model of science must allow for these two procedures.

Science and technology, then, are linked by the necessity for pure research as well as the necessity for business success. There is a dialectic between knowledge and production. This dialectic is the essential tension between science and technology.

Despite the uncertainty over the possibility of any demarcation between science and technology, Staudenmaier posits four components of technological knowledge—*scientific concepts*, problematic data, *engineering theory*, and technological skill. Each of these will be explored with respect to its contribution to technological knowledge. One must remember that none of these characteristics stands alone. Again drawing on Staudenmaier, an appropriate guiding principle would be that "all four characteristics derive their unique cognitive qualities from the tension between technical design and its [cultural] ambience, which defines the nature of technology itself" (p. 103). A description of the four components of technological knowledge will elaborate this claim.

Scientific Concepts

Let us assume, as does Staudenmaier, that technological knowledge is structured by the tension between "the demands of functional design and the specific constraints of its [cultural] ambience" (p. 104). What could be the role of scientific concepts in all of this? Unlike the abstract nature of scientific concepts, technological knowledge is hampered by the abstract. The abstract does not deal with the exigencies of time, cost, and personnel. As a result, the abstract of scientific design must be restructured to meet the demands of the specific design project at hand. As Skolimowski (1966) states, "science, that is pure science, is but a servant to technology, a charwoman serving technological progress . . . the basic methodological factors that account for the growth of technology are quite different from the factors that account for the growth of science". Technologically literate citizens understand that science knowledge is radically altered to accommodate the needs of technologists. The resulting knowledge is unique to technology.

Problematic Data

Problematic data are "specific information aimed at the solution of a particular technological problem" (Staudenmaier, 1985, p. 110). The need for problematic data arises when the attempts at solving technical problems encounter areas of ignorance which require new data to resolve the problem. In most cases, these areas of ignorance are those components of some system which have fallen behind or are out of phase with all the other components. Such out-of-phase components are called "reverse salients" (Hughes, 1987). Problematic data, then, are those data needed to deal with reverse salients. Reverse salients, for example, could be found in difficulties with emerging technologies, difficulties encountered during normal use of a technology, or difficulties anticipated by agencies that examine possible effects of technology. As Staudenmaier (1985) asserts:

> The conceptual content of the data being sought necessarily reflects the structural design of the technology. This congruence is due to the fundamental characteristic of all technology, which consists of historically specific tensions between design concepts and the limited material and societal contexts in which they exist. Since technology never exists in an abstract, a historical domain, it necessarily requires knowledge that is problematic in the sense defined here. Unlike scientific data which are congruent with highly abstract theoretical models, technological data are rooted in the specifics of every ambience in which it operates. (p. 107)

Technologically literate citizens must see that technology requires that further data be gathered as the technology unfolds. Simply put, people must understand that no technology is completely understood, and that they must expect questions to be asked and possibly inadequately answered. They must be taught what questions to ask, and be encouraged to harbour a healthy degree of informed skepticism in the face of those who maintain that *all* the answers are known.

Engineering Theory

An engineering theory is "a body of knowledge using experimental methods to construct a formal and mathematically structured intellectual system. The system explains the behavioural characteristics of a particular class of artifacts" (Staudenmaier, 1985, p. 108). In one sense, then, engineering theory seems very "scientific" as it strives to create the artifact (theory). Its abstraction level is much higher than that of problematic data.

On the other hand, it can appear to be very similar to problematic data. Consider Layton's (1976) argument that "engineering theory and experiment came to differ with those of physics because it was concerned with man-made devices rather than directly with nature. Thus, engineering theory often deals with idealizations of machines, beams, heat engines, or similar devices. And the results of engineering science are often statements about such devices rather than statements about nature" (as cited in Staudenmaier, p. 108). In other words, artifacts rather than nature provides engineering science with its focus. As a result, all the procedures of this theoretical perspective are governed by the demands of practice rather than the demands of theoretical knowledge production. The technologically literate person must understand that even when engineers speak about theory, they are discussing the practical world of artifacts. The engineer is not interested in theoretical knowledge for its own sake. Rather, all engineering, including its theories, is focused on practicality. The major function served by engineering theory is to mediate between the idiosyncratic demands that engender the need for problematic data and the demand for general applicability. This is technology's essential tension—the attempt to resolve the demands of a specific case with the more abstract concerns of engineering theory. Engineering theory mediates between the worlds of the practical and the abstract. The world of the practical, however, raises the issue of technical skill, or if one wishes, the distinction between the technical and the trades, or pushing further, the distinction between the designer and the implementor of the design. The tension between skill and theory must be explored further.

Technological Skill

The apprenticeship model for skill development is based on the premise that skills are learned experimentally. As Feibleman (1966) has indicated, these skills are a form of learned intimacy with a particular tool or machine. Another aspect of skill development is that pragmatic judgement takes precedence. Any amateur carpenter who has ever dealt with a journeyman understands intuitively the role differences between theoretical knowledge and pragmatic judgment. The tacit knowledge transmitted during the training program is an essential element of the technical skills received therein. Thus technological skill is a combination of a high level of ability with specific machines and technique plus pragmatic judgements based on tacit knowledge.

Following apprenticeship, and assuming appropriate employment, the technically skilled person is often referred to as "skilled labour". In a technological society skilled labour often finds itself deskilled through the introduction of sophisticated machines. (Deskilling) involves the transition of skills from people to machines, resulting in the need for lower level skills among all workers. The resultant labour-management tensions rarely are the focus of public interest discussion. Rather, the concept of a golden age of employment through high technology is highly touted. It seems obvious that the concept of skilled labour must be tempered by the realization that decisions related to deskilling are usually motivated by non-technical issues such as managerial control of the workplace. It appears that the issue of decisions related to technology plays an important role in deciding the instructional implications of being technologically literate. Hence, decision making in technological society must be carefully examined.

Technology and Social Change

Decision Making by Experts

In a restricted sense, technology can be seen as causing changes only in the physical world: a bridge is created to cross a river, a word processor appears on a desk, a building reaches new heights. In a fuller sense, technology changes the very society in which it operates. A technologically literate person must, then, understand the relationship between technology and social change. In other words, this person must "read" the artifact to find within it the set of societal assumptions that may cause the artifact to effect change in the society. To do this, one must conceptualize technology as a social organization, rather than black-box hardware with external effects (Wynne, 1988).

The process of social change is driven by an elite, a group or organization that commands the economic and political resources necessary to implement a new technology. Because it commands these resources, this group, not the creator of the technology, legitimizes the deployment of the technology. The elite will encourage the testing and large-scale production of a technology only if the technology is seen as useful in maintaining or enhancing its position. A counter-elite may arise in opposition to the position of the elite. If it can muster enough support, it can stop the diffusion of the technology. The movement against the construction of nuclear power plants can be cited as an example of a counter-elite having such an effect.

As well, a counter-elite can seize upon a technique that the elite decides not to employ and use it to enhance its own position to such an extent that it becomes a new elite. The development of barbed wire appears to follow this pattern. As Hayter (1939) states, cattle companies (the elite) were initially opposed to barbed wire and refused to use it. Those who wished to grow crops (the counter-elite) decided to use the new technology. The result, says Hayter, was that

> ... barbed wire fences aided in the downfall of the cattle companies as well as the "cow culture" that had developed on the Western Plains during the seventies and eighties. When trail driving disappeared—largely because of the fences—this cultural pattern began to decline, and in its place came, with the influx of the granges, an economic and social structure that was built, in part at least, on an agricultural system of corn, wheat, and cotton. (p. 95)

Let us assume, however, that an elite has the power to increase the production and dissemination of a technology over the objections of a counter-elite. This is the critical phase, for it is now that the spread of the technology may strain the available resources. If it does not, the technology is compatible with the existing system and we get graceful entry into the society. The ball-point pen is a good example of this. If, however, the technology does strain existing resources, the elite alters the socioeconomic system, redistributing power and resources to support the new technology. In other words, social changes occur. As well, when a new technology causes social strain, it becomes politically and socially interesting. It is this strain which prompts technological assessments and legislation to control the technology.

This attempt to control usually involves the presentation of positions by various experts. Experts interpret the artifact as text to the technologically illiterate. The growth in the use of experts requires the citizen to question the extent to which experts should be given authority, particularly when they advise policy-makers who may use this advice to further political ends. Research with Canadian high school graduates (Fleming, 1987) and undergraduates in a science department (Fleming,

1988) indicates that the majority favour a technocratic model in which scientists and engineers make the important decisions about social issues related to technological involvement. Thus, experts are viewed in a most favourable light.

Habermas (1971) calls a society where experts are on tap but not on top, a decisionistic society. Such a society has a political elite at the top. This elite does not need highly specialized skills. Rather, it needs access to the layer just below it—the experts who pass their expertise up but are expected to restrict the flow of that expertise down to the next layer, the general public. The general public is offered only carefully selected information about technical issues. The resulting ignorance results in a sense of powerlessness and depoliticization. As Barnes (1985) states, the result for the public is that

> their participation in the political process tends to be restricted to the periods before general elections, when on the basis of restricted and distorted information, filtered by the media, degraded, trivialized and biased by advertising agencies and professional communicators, they choose between competing political elites. Not surprisingly, therefore, many among the main body of the population perceive a sharp disjunction between politics and life generally, and become deeply alienated from their political institutions: occasionally there is active hostility to them, more often complete passive indifference. (p. 100)

Thus, opposition to government policies is only possible for those with access to their own experts. In a decisionistic society, then, we have battles between experts acting to legitimate the cases of different sides. Habermas is concerned that during these battles, which are couched almost exclusively in technical language, the expertise offered by those concerned with issues of ethics and human decency is often ignored.

Decision Making by Citizens

It seems that our modern society may be a decisionistic one. If this is so, the public probably will not be consulted over technical questions. An important first step, then, for the technologically literate citizen is to gain a realistic picture of the nature of a decisionistic democracy.

For example, citizens in a technological society confront complex issues involving the use of technology. Examples abound: experimentation with recombinant DNA, control of nuclear weapons, uranium mining, disposal of industrial wastes, limits to industrial development, and the sources and uses of energy—especially nuclear power (Patrick & Remy, 1985). To assume that citizens will have the opportunity to confront these issues when voting misrepresents the practices of contemporary democracies. The promise of effective collective decision making may turn out to be political sop. It is important, however, for citizens to examine possible reasons why the issues do not appear on the ballot. The channels available to these "informed citizens" (Aikenhead, this volume) must be explored further.

Patrick and Remy (1985) suggest that people hold ambivalent beliefs about the social effects of technology. There is, they claim, a "paradoxical blend of dread and anticipation, of fear and hope" (p. 13). Citizens may choose, of course, to emphasize their fears instead of their hopes in science and technology where they participate either as voters in referenda and initiatives, as members of political interest groups, or as public officials. This emphasis seems to be misguided. It seems more appropriate to examine, as a starting point, why fears arise over technological developments.

One major reason for fear seems to be uncertainty about the consequences of various courses of action. In simple terms, citizens worry about risk. Part of this worry is caused by their belief that experts have all the information and hence knowledge of all possible outcomes. This belief exhibits a misunderstanding of the nature of science, the nature of technology, and the nature of expertise.

Wynne (1988) offers insights into the public perception of technological risk. Basing his case on the sociology of scientific knowledge, Wynne argues that "a formal public image of technology as mechanical, rule-following behaviour belies a far less clearly rule-bound and determined world of real technological practices" (p. 148). This fuzziness in the real world of technology is revealed, argues Wynne, in technological accidents.

Lack of public understanding of the concept of risk leads to the demands for risk-free technology in which uncertainty must be removed. Research indicates that most people perform very poorly when attempting to make decisions involving uncertainty (Kahneman, Slovic, & Tversky, 1982; Nisbett & Ross, 1980). At the collective level, risk appears to be central to an appreciation of the perceived necessity to consult experts. Expertise often focuses on the acceptability of risk. Discussions with experts on risk issues must of necessity deal with health, occupational safety, job security, profit, and so on. Different values will emerge—protecting worker health versus protecting production and jobs. The compromises made in an attempt to accommodate these value positions are worthy of study. A first step is to help future citizens assess the value-laden relationship between so-called factual information and the decision-making process. Wynne, however, cautions against the 'white boxing' of technology, which

> claims to give an externally accountable version of the inner workings of technology, yet it denies access to and appreciation of the complex, open-ended and incompletely rule-determined technical-social constitution of technologies. It is a laundered version which is itself part of the discourse of social 'closure' and legitimation of technologies. (p. 160)

Experts, he claims, see themselves as constrained on the one hand by public innocence of real technology and, on the other hand, by fear of the response of the public to a more accurate picture of contemporary technology. It is possible, however, that informed citizens, knowledgeable in the ways of real technology, would expect uncertainty in expert decisions. Possibly, this expectation would increase the legitimacy of experts while decreasing their power.

An electorate has little use for personal decision-making skills about technology if all technical decisions are made by the on-tap experts. A first step in becoming a technologically literate citizen would be to understand who makes the decisions, with a particular emphasis on possible biases. The next step might be to examine the proposed technical bases for these decisions. Technical arguments are presented in a logical, rational form. They are designed to defuse controversy. The literate citizen must understand the value claims implicit in the conflicting positions and realize that a struggle over the acceptability of value claims is an inherent part of science and technology. Fundamentally, this is a struggle over whose interpretation of the artifact as text most closely resembles our lived reality. As with other forms of criticism, such a struggle seems obviously to be an ongoing one.

References

Barnes, B. (1985). *About science*. Oxford: Basil Blackwell.

Bijker, W. E, Hughes, T. P., & Pinch, T. (Eds.). (1987). *The social construction of technological systems*. Cambridge, MA: MIT Press.

Callon, M. (1987). Society in the making: The study of technology as a tool for sociological analysis. In W. E. Bijker, T. P. Hughes, & T. Pinch (Eds.), *The social construction of technological systems*. Cambridge, MA: MIT Press.

Emig, J. (1983). *The web of meaning*. Upper Montclair, NJ: Boynton/Cook.

Feibleman, J. K. (1966). Technology as skills. *Technology and Culture, 7*, 318-328.

Fleming, R. W. (1987). High school graduates' beliefs about science-technology-society. II. The interaction among science, technology, and society. *Science Education, 71*, 163-186.

Fleming, R. W. (1988). Undergraduate science students' views on the relationship between science, technology, and society. *International Journal of Science Education, 10*, 449-463.

Goldman, S. L. (1984). The techne of philosophy and the philosophy of technology. In P. Durbin (Ed.). *Research in philosophy and technology* (Vol. 7). Greenwich: JAI Press.

Grundy, S. (1987). *Curriculum: Product or praxis*. London: Falmer Press.

Habermas, J. (1971). *Toward a rational society*. London: Heinemann.

Habermas, J. (1972). *Knowledge and human interests* (2nd Ed.). London: Heinemann.

Hayter, E. W. (1939). Barbed wire - a prairie invention. *Journal of Agricultural History, 13*, 189-207.

Hughes, T. P. (1987). The evolution of large technological systems. In W. E. Bijker, T. P. Hughes, & T. Pinch (Eds.), *The social construction of technological systems*. Cambridge, MA: MIT Press.

Kahneman, D., Slovic, P., & Tversky, A. (1982). *Judgment under uncertainty: Heuristics and biases*. Cambridge: Cambridge University Press.

Kline, S. J. (1985). What is technology? *The Bulletin of Science, Technology and Society, 5*, 215-218.

Layton, E. T. Jr. (1976). American ideologies of science and engineering. *Technology and Culture, 17*, 688-701.

Nisbett, R., & Ross, L. (1980). *Human inference: Strategies and shortcomings of social judgment*. Englewood Cliffs, NJ: Prentice-Hall.

Norris, S. P. (1989). Can we test validity for critical thinking? *Educational Researcher, 18*(9), 21-26.

Pacey, A. (1983). *The culture of technology.* Cambridge, MA: The MIT Press.

Patrick, J. J., & Remy, R. C. (1985). *Connecting science, technology, and society in the education of citizens.* Boulder, CO: Social Science Education Consortium.

Pinch, T., & Bijker, W. E. (1987). The social construction of facts and artifacts: Or how the sociology of science and the sociology of technology benefit each other. In W. Bijker, T. P. Hughes, & T. Pinch (Eds.), *The social construction of technological systems.* Cambridge, MA: MIT Press.

Skolimowski, H. (1966). The structure of thinking in technology. *Technology and Culture, 7,* 371-383.

Staudenmaier, J. M. (1985). *Technology's storytellers.* Cambridge, MA: MIT Press.

Torrey, B. (Ed.) (1968). *The writings of Henry David Thoreau* (Vol. 12). New York: AMS Press.

Wynne, B. (1988). Unruly technology: Practical rules, impractical discourses and public understanding. *Social Studies of Science, 18*(1), 147-167.

6

Reasoning and Literacy

J. Anthony Blair
University of Windsor

The literary custom of beginning with a definition of one's topic and its terms makes sense. Author and reader can then begin from a common understanding, if not agreement. However, I fear that separate definitions here would be an excessive digression, given the complexity of these two concepts and the limited scope of this chapter. In the remainder of this first section, I speculate about some uses of the term "literacy", but I shall rely on the context to make clear how I am using the term "reasoning".

In the remainder of the chapter, I explore the connections between reasoning and literacy in two respects. First, I consider some ways in which being able to perform certain reasoning operations seem to be connected with being able to read with understanding and to write meaningfully. Second, I consider some ways in which what might be called "cultural literacy" seems to be a prerequisite for certain everyday reasoning operations.

On the Meanings of "Literacy"

Although "literacy" originally meant knowledge of letters, namely being able to read and write, we nowadays talk of things such as math literacy, science literacy, technological literacy, cultural literacy, media literacy, and computer literacy. How did the reference get extended from knowing how to read and write to being able to use a word processor or to understanding the dynamics of television? I would speculate that the extension of the term is due to a generalization from being able to read and write.

It is well known that what is entailed in being able to read and write is enormously complex. The approach to understanding reading and writing that looks toward their *purposes* seems promising, since both are human activities, and human activities are most broadly intelligible when understood in terms of the purposes or functions they serve. Reading and writing can have various purposes, so the ability to read and write will be relative to the particular purpose at hand. One who is able to read and write for one purpose (such as navigating a city's transportation system, or writing a grocery list) may be unable to do so for another (such as reading technical instructions for the operation of machinery, or writing a lab report). So literacy can be regarded, more generally, as the ability to read and write for a particular purpose or set of purposes.

It is but a short step from there to thinking of the ability to function with respect to *any given* context of meaning for a given purpose. And it is understandable, though linguistically inelegant, that the term "literacy" was then stretched beyond its historical reference to the medium of letters, or written texts, and made to refer—with an appropriate modifier—to the ability to function in other contexts of meaning. So, computer literacy refers to the ability to function with computers; cultural literacy refers to the ability to function in the culture in question; and so on.

We should be cautious about these extensions of the term "literacy". For one thing, they encourage us to assume that there is a connection between being able to read and write and, for example, being able to use a computer or being conversant with a culture—a connection that might not exist. It might turn out that the abilities needed to function with computers are not at all similar to those needed to function with written texts. Another caution is that extending the term "literacy" might be taken to imply that we can apply our understanding of functioning with written texts elsewhere, and that is a questionable application. The caution of academics has no appreciable impact on general usage, so I am not trying to revise anybody's terminology. But popular terms can tempt anyone, including academics, to make unjustified assumptions. I suspect that what are called "scientific literacy" or "cultural literacy", for example, are quite different from literacy in its root sense.

The arguments in favour of extending the term to other contexts of meaning—that the carry-over from the original narrow sense of literacy

substitute discourse communities for cultural literacy

is conceptually suggestive, and politically useful—certainly carry weight. Indeed, I find it illuminating, later in the chapter, to make use of a concept of "cultural literacy". Also, it assuredly is worthwhile to investigate what are denoted by "media literacy", "scientific literacy", and so on. I am not arguing against those projects at all.

I suppose I am reduced to the speculation that an exploration of the breadth and depth of literacy might look into rather different things, if "literacy" is used in extended ways. If there is a crisis of literacy in our educational systems, or even just a worry about literacy, there might be more than one crisis or worry, and what some critics bemoan might turn out to be different from what concerns others.

In the following section, I focus first on literacy in its root sense and consider how reasoning is related to reading and writing. Then I speculate about the connections between reasoning and cultural literacy (going against my warnings about extending the term). Hereafter, I will use the unmodified word "literacy" to refer to the ability to read and write (in all its complexities), and will add a modifier if referring to those other literacies.

Reading, Writing, and Reasoning

The discussion in this section depends on the assumption that possessing literacy implies being able to understand or interpret what one reads and being able to write meaningfully at the requisite level. To illustrate: one must not only be able to tell that the letters, "m-e-n-a-t-w-o-r-k" spell the words, "men at work", but one must also be able to tell that those words on a sign beside the roadway mean that some repair or installation is being carried out, even if everyone in sight is leaning on a shovel.

The fact that understanding, interpretation, and meaningfulness are entailed by literacy implies that reasoning is entailed by literacy, because reading with understanding, interpreting what one reads, and writing meaningfully all entail reasoning. Consider some ways this is so.

Reading and Hypothesizing

Phillips (1988) and others have shown how hypothesis formation and testing seem to be used (with varying degrees of success) in reading. One reads the first sentence of a paragraph and on the basis of it (and of broader contextual knowledge, if it applies) one formulates at least one hypothesis about the topic of the paragraph. The second sentence is interpreted in the light of that hypothesis. The initial hypothesis might be revised as a result of reading the second sentence, or it might be reinforced. In addition, the second sentence might give rise to new hypotheses. The reader proceeds through a paragraph by formulating hypotheses and confirming or revising them as he or she goes.

The same process occurs in reading single multiclause sentences, and is illustrated by examples of ambiguity. De Sousa quotes an example he attributes to Paul Ziff: "I saw her duck when they were throwing rotten eggs, and then I saw it swim out into the middle of the lake" (De Sousa, 1987, p. 192). The fact that we are stymied for a microsecond when we read the second half of this sentence shows that, having finished reading only the first half, we already have formulated the hypothesis that the sentence reports the writer observing a female in whose direction rotten eggs were being thrown and who was ducking to avoid them. As we read on, we revise that hypothesis in light of the information incompatible with it provided in the second half—summed up by saying that the word "duck" here refers to an aquatic bird. Further revisions would be needed were the text to continue in a way that is inconsistent with the second hypothesis, for instance if the next sentences were these:

> I was amazed. But there was no doubt about it. The little bundle of synthetic feathers with its plastic beak and rubber legs was actually swimming across the lake, quacking cheerfully to its natural cousins.

Not only would we revise our hypothesis about the referent of the word "duck", but we might revise the contextual hypothesis, that the discourse is actual reportage, and consider the possibility that it is fiction. We revise our interpretation of the context to make it consistent with a reasonable interpretation of the text. In the light of that broader hypothesis, we then interpret subsequent sentences. So there is hypothesis formation, testing, revision, and retesting going on at different levels when someone is reading—at the sentence-meaning level and at the context level.

Another example (Haugeland, 1985, p. 202) shows reasoning to the best explanation at work in resolving ambiguity when reading: "I left my raincoat in the bathtub, because it was still wet". Here there is no puzzle, but according to the rules of grammar the referent of "it" should be the immediately preceding noun—"bathtub". We take the writer to mean that the raincoat, not the bathtub, was still wet, because we can see how a raincoat's being wet makes it reasonable to leave it in a bathtub but we can't readily see how a bathtub's being wet makes it a sensible place to leave a raincoat (Morton, 1988).

Thus, a reader's competence will be partly a function of his or her reasoning ability, even at the level of simple texts. If a reader can formulate only one hypothesis about the immediate context, when two or three equally plausible ones are consistent with what the sentence states and relevant background information, then the reader will not read as well as one who can formulate several hypotheses. The poorer reader does not have the same imagination or the same flexibility with respect to hypothesis formation. An even poorer reader will not treat these implications of a sentence as hypotheses at all, but will fix on one and treat it as a given. Such a reader will have great difficulty making sense of texts that contain subsequent sentences that are incompatible with initial inflexible assumptions.

So one reasoning skill that seems inherent in the reading of even the simplest texts is hypothesis formation, testing and revision, and its special case, reasoning to the best explanation.

Understanding Logical Connectives

Reasoning is also entailed in understanding the meaning or use of the truth-functional connectives of deductive logic: "not", "some", "all", "if . . .,then . . .", "or", and so on.

For example, a reader or writer understands the word "all", only if he or she knows that (1) "All the books on the table are paperbacks" is incompatible with (2) "None of the books on the table is a paperback" and (3) "Some of the books on the table are not paperbacks." I don't mean that the reader must be schooled in class logic in order to understand the words "all", "none", "some", and "not". I mean that a necessary condition of knowing what they mean is being able to understand their logical implications.

Understanding the "Logic" or Implications of Other Words

Further examples come from other logics. The deontic terms, "permitted", "forbidden", and "obligatory" are logically related: if something is forbidden, it is not permitted, and it is obligatory not to do it; if something is permitted, it is neither forbidden nor obligatory. One does not understand the meaning of any one of these terms without understanding the corresponding implications for the applications of the others.

The modal qualifiers—"necessary" and "possible"—are similarly logically related. An event or relation that is necessary cannot possibly not be the case; one that is possible is not necessarily not the case and not necessarily the case. Suppose someone reads the following instructions for an appliance: "It is necessary to align the two red switches, but not necessary to align the three green ones, if damage to the motor is to be avoided." To understand the meaning of "necessary", the person would have to see that the appliance's motor will be damaged if the two red switches are not aligned.

To be sure, understanding such sentences requires understanding more than the meanings of the words discussed. However, understanding those words implies being able to draw correct inferences from their use, and thus entails some skill in the reasoning operation of drawing inferences.

"Reading In" and Reasoning

I take correct interpretation in reading to include such things as understanding what is said, understanding what is implied by what is said, understanding what is implied by the fact that it is said, and being able to tell, operationally, the differences between these. In practice, this means taking someone to mean what he or she has written or implied, and *not* "reading in" statements that the person has not made and not implied. The latter is a common form of misreading.

Take assertive prose as an illustration and distinguish the following four things (Pinto & Blair, 1988):

1. **What is implied by a statement in its context.** By this I mean what a reasonable person can conclude merely from the assumption that the statement is true. The statement, "St. John's is a lovely city," uttered at the conference on literacy held in St. John's at which this chapter was originally presented implies that there is a city named "St. John's", that St. John's population is at least in the tens of thousands rather than in the hundreds, that St. John's has been in existence for more than a month, and so on.

2. What is implied by the fact that a statement is made in its context. By this I mean what a reasonable person can conclude from the fact that the statement was made by its author in the circumstances and context in which it was made. My saying, "St. John's is a lovely city," while at the conference in St. John's might be taken to imply that I think St. John's is a lovely city, or it might be taken to imply that, as a visitor to St. John's, I am being polite to my hosts, and so on.

3. What the writer implies by what he or she writes in a context. By this I mean what the writer intends the reader should conclude from what he or she says, or from the fact that he or she said it. If I write on a postcard, "The fog is so thick you can't see more than ten metres in front of you, it's freezing cold and only the end of September, and the stench of the harbour permeates everywhere—ah, St. John's is a lovely city," then what I imply by that last sentence is exactly the opposite of what the sentence normally means.

4. What the reader is justified in concluding. These are the inferences the reader may draw from a statement, from the fact that it is made, or from what he or she takes the speaker or writer to be implying—together with background beliefs and beliefs about the context of the utterance. The reader who knows that the sentence, "St. John's is a lovely city", appears in a report in the "Travel" section of the newspaper, and who knows that this section is devoted to selling tourism, might legitimately conclude that it is as possible that St. John's is not a lovely city as that it is a lovely city.

To the extent that a reader draws unwarranted inferences, or fails to draw warranted inferences, from a set of statements, the reader has not fully understood them. But drawing warranted inferences requires the reasoning skill of distinguishing between the above types of implication. The reader must be able to recognize when the discourse is, and when it is not, intended to mean what it literally means and implies, and being able to do that entails, among other things, being able to draw inferences based on the context and literal meaning and implications of the discourse.

In general, if understanding a text implies drawing the appropriate inferences from it, then a reader unable to perform the reasoning operations of drawing appropriate inferences will fail to understand texts he or she reads. If literate writing implies conveying what one means to say with precision, then a writer who is unaware of these distinctions will not write in a literate way. Distinguishing between different implications and drawing appropriate inferences are reasoning operations. So here is another respect in which literacy entails reasoning.

Topic Dependency

My discussion has not yet touched on the issue of the topic dependency of reasoning when reading and writing. That issue becomes pertinent when we start to think about some practical implications of the connections between reasoning and literacy. Given the connections discussed, it might seem to be a good idea to teach reasoning alongside the teaching of reading and writing—for example some class logic, or the logic of modal and deontic qualifiers, or the logic of hedging qualifiers (such as "maybe", "probably", and so on). The assumption is that if reasoning is essential to literacy, then improving reasoning would improve literacy. If so, then explicitly teaching reasoning and its application to reading and writing should contribute to an improvement in literacy levels.

A possible problem with this suggestion is that the reasoning employed in reading and writing might be topic-dependent. By this I mean that a skill in such reasoning might turn out to be limited in its deployment to just those topics where one has learned it. One might, as a student of history, become good at distinguishing between (a) the implications of historical claims, (b) what an historian is implying when making an historical claim in a particular context, and (c) what is implied by an historian's making a claim in a particular context—yet not thereby improve one's ability to make these distinctions (with the appropriate substitutions) as they apply to the discourse of philosophy or of farming.

This problem is real enough, but it is easily overstated. Partly, the problem will be greater with some aspects of reasoning than with others. We know that a large factor in understanding the implications of statements in different specialized fields depends on understanding their contexts, and that requires knowledge of the substantive issues in the fields. However, it is hard to imagine how learning the truth-functional connectives, "all", "some", "not", etc., in the context of examples from the newspaper will not also prepare students to use them in literary criticism or chemistry class. The student may have difficulties understanding literary criticism or chemistry, and as a result have difficulties understanding sentences about those topics which use truth-functional connectives, but such problems will not be due in any part to having to learn the logical connectives all over again.

Also, I don't think the problem of transfer is an overwhelming objection to teaching reasoning along with reading and writing. From the fact that one cannot draw reliable implications in technical contexts without specialized background knowledge, for example, it does not follow that exposure to and practice with different sorts of implication in contexts that are generally known will not usefully improve students' reading and writing in non-specialized discourse.

Finally, it seems in principle possible—although admittedly difficult to find the time in practice—to teach for transfer. One could take the time to show how the reasoning principles one has learned in application to one topic apply to other topics and give students practice in applying those principles to various new topics.

Whether, in what sense, or to what degree reasoning is topic-dependent are to some extent empirical questions, and deserve study.

Cultural Literacy and Reasoning

What I mean by "cultural literacy" is the background knowledge and understanding of, and facility in, a culture that permits one correctly to interpret and engage in its specific policies, practices, and activities. I have in mind skills as well as propositional knowledge. We speak of being conversant with a culture when we mean having this sort of familiarity with it. In this section I discuss various ways cultural literacy and reasoning seem connected. The first suggests that, at a certain level, the failure to write in a way that communicates successfully and to read with understanding seem due to a combination of cultural illiteracy and inadequate reasoning. The second connection I discuss is the one between cultural literacy and argument competence.

Miscommunication and Literacy

Recently, I had the task of reading some refused sabbatical applications and suggesting ways they could be improved, that is, made more persuasive. In the general statement of purpose of one of them, the author had presented an apparently rambling discourse on his interests and research, starting from his dissertation and ending with the proposal to write a book or a series of papers on a particular literary figure. To anyone reading the proposal quickly, and used to a brief that argued "Here's what I want to do and here's why I should get a sabbatical to do it," the proposal seemed poorly organized and even ill-considered. I think the proposal *was* wrongly organized for the purpose at hand. However it was far from poorly organized, nor was the project ill-conceived. Why did it fail to convince?

My answer is that its author had written a narrative instead of a brief. Read as a narrative, the proposal built up clearly and persuasively to the project the applicant wanted to pursue; but read as a brief, it was rambling and failed to make a striking case.

There is a kind of sophisticated illiteracy illustrated by this example which I shall try to describe. First, the sabbatical applicant was unfamiliar with the conventions of such application writing. He wrote his application in a way that made it almost certain to be misread or misunderstood. As such, he failed to communicate. Such a failure is different in kind from what occurs when a writer's sentences are so ungrammatical as to be unintelligible, but the practical result was not too different. Second, others who read the application were unfamiliar with the conventions of narrative prose. Consequently, they failed to realize that the proposal was not written as a brief and so should not have been read as a brief. So they failed to understand. Their failure was different in kind from that of a reader whose ignorance of vocabulary, grammar, and punctuation lead to failure to understand some perfectly straightforward prose. But, again, the practical result was not very different.

My interest in this case lies in attributing both failures (at least in part) to poor reasoning. Consider the applicant. He could have thought the application process through, recognized the burden of time on those who assess such applications, and realized that academics from very different fields with very different styles of discourse are applying. From these facts he could have inferred that a presentation along the lines of a brief would be most likely to be understood quickly and accurately.

Consider the reviewers. They could have paused before leaping to the conclusion that the applicant was incompetent, and sought other possible explanations of the strange proposal. They might have considered whether it was following different conventions from the norm, and have tried alternative interpretations of the structure of the application. They might have discovered that in terms of the narrative structure the proposal was very plausible.

Both parties showed poor reasoning. They did badly at such reasoning activities as the following: anticipating probable consequences, drawing inferences from probable situations, formulating alternative means of getting a desired result, reasoning to the best explanation, formulating alternative hypotheses, and testing them. The results were, first, a failure to write comprehensibly, and second, a failure to read with under-standing—both, in some sense, lapses from literacy.

Cultural Literacy and Arguments

If reasoning is an element of literacy at the "micro" level of reading and writing sentences and paragraphs, literacy in a broader sense is a prerequisite of reasoning at the "macro" level of analyzing and formulating arguments and explanations. Let me illustrate this point by discussing the analysis and evaluation of arguments—understanding an argument for this purpose to be a set of reasons put forward as support for a claim.

Literacy and interpreting arguments

Outside of textbooks, arguments often appear unannounced; the writer offers them, and leaves it to the reader to recognize them, without even the guidance of illative particles (such as "because" and "therefore") to mark their presence. Such recognition requires recognizing a pattern of relations between statements, but it can also require recognizing that an argument is appropriate or to be expected in the context.

Recognizing a context of argument requires an understanding of the wider contexts in which the discourse is situated, and knowing how they work. There is, first, the immediate context of the type of discourse in which the passage in question appears and that presupposes some knowledge of discourse types and their functions. (By a discourse type I mean such categories as thank-you letters, letters to the editor of newspapers or magazines, opinion columns, editorials, articles, columns in newspapers and magazines, articles in magazines, articles in scholarly journals, short stories, novels, popular non-fiction, scholarly monographs, legal briefs, employment applications, and so on.) The reader needs to know that arguments are the norm in scholarly articles, but not in short stories, for example.

Knowing the context of a piece of discourse also entails knowing something about the current state of the subject matter and the status of the issue in that field. That smoking is a cause of cancer is not problematic among cancer researchers, but the precise mechanisms whereby tar and nicotine cause carcinomas is problematic. Knowing these facts, one expects arguments about the mechanisms but not about the general causal connection. So deciding no more than that one is in the presence of argument can require a degree of literacy in a broader sense—being familiar with various types of discourse context, and being informed about the state of knowledge and debate in different fields.

The recognition that an argument is present blends into the recognition of the details and logic of the argument, so it is not surprising that the interpretation of the precise content and structure of an argument also presupposes such broader literacy. Unstated assumptions (the recognition of which is necessary for the argument to make sense) presuppose a shared understanding about background facts and beliefs between writer and reader. Spotting that a particular comment is a response to a commonly cited objection can be crucial to fitting a segment of the discourse into the argument. In these and other ways the fine-grained interpretation of arguments requires cultural literacy.

I am not suggesting that the very structure of arguments varies from field to field, although it seems evident that certain types of argument occur more frequently in certain fields, and are perhaps even found paradigmatically in certain fields. For example, arguments using inferences from samples to population are symptoms of a social science question, while case-by-case reasoning suggests a legal question (Govier 1988a). If there are types of argument that are found or that tend to be found only in discourse on certain subjects, then evidently some knowledge of those subjects will be immensely helpful, and perhaps necessary, to interpret arguments in them. But the main point is that even for argument types that are ubiquitous, some understanding of background facts and some degree of cultural literacy are needed just in order to recognize what is going on in the argument.

Literacy and evaluating arguments

If one goes on to evaluate an argument's cogency, literacy in the culture or sub-culture of the argument is also essential. This point holds obviously for the issue of when the evidence presented in an argument is sufficient to settle the question. What counts as sufficient will depend on both the minimum standards in the field, and the standard objections to the question that have to be addressed.

Cultural literacy applies elsewhere in argument evaluation. Arguments found in adversary contexts, for instance, are prone to certain well-known fallacious moves that can be recognized only if one is acquainted with the issues in dispute. In such contexts, there is a good chance that a gain by one entails a loss by the other. Disputants tend to want to defeat their opponent, with some third party such as a judge in a court of law, the electorate, or a union membership—and not the nominal opponent in the dispute—being the real judge of the success of argumentative exchanges. Here, what have been called the fallacies of diversion—straw man, red herring, ad hominem, guilt by association—have their natural home (Johnson & Blair, 1983).

In order to recognize a straw-man argument—an argument in which the critic attacks a distorted version of the opponent's position—one must know what the opponent's position is. In order to recognize a fallacious, abusive *ad hominem* argument—an irrelevant attack on some alleged property of the opponent, levelled in order to discredit the opponent's position—one must be able to judge what characteristics of the opponent might be relevant to the position, and doing that requires a knowledge of the issues under dispute and of the opponent's relation to them. Similarly, for other adversary-context fallacies a knowledge of current events, of the issues in dispute, of the various positions that have been taken, of the arguments that have been proposed—all enhance the chance that the reader not only will understand the statements made, but also will recognize their true functions in the argumentative exchanges and will appreciate the cogency of the arguments.

Cultural literacy is also essential for appreciating good reasoning. Consider arguments from *a priori* analogy, for instance. An *a priori* analogy is one in which imaginary examples suffice, and the key desideratum is that the two cases compared share relevant similarities (Govier 1988b). (Example: "You gave him an A for the same answer I had, so I should get an A too.") Such an argument can work only if its readers know enough about the analogue to see which of its features are being compared and how what is true of them is also true of the case in question.

The Contribution of Reasoning Ability to Cultural Literacy

It seems to me highly likely that, just as the state of one's cultural literacy contributes to the cogency of one's reasoning, so too one's reasoning ability contributes to one's cultural literacy. There is the straightforward fact that the better one's reasoning in general, the better one's reasoning about one's culture. Besides that, a fine-grained understanding of good and bad reasoning should enhance cultural awareness and understanding.

Consider some of the adversary-context fallacies I have just discussed. If one is alert to the possibility of straw-man criticisms in adversary contexts, one will be looking for differences between statements of point of view or policy, and as a result should end up with a better understanding of various positions and issues. If one is looking for red-herring rejoinders, one has to have a good sense for what is relevant to an issue and what is not, and consequently one should end up better appreciating the issue's nuances.

I do not think there would be disagreement that certain reasoning abilities facilitate one's capacity for cultural enrichment. Learning how to write a lab report according to the norms of the American Psychological Association entails learning some scientific reasoning. It is impossible to gain much understanding of philosophy without understanding how demonstrative arguments work. Skill at imagining counterexamples is a key to extending one's understanding of almost any academic field, since it leads to an appreciation of how the field deals with objections. Understanding the structure of scientific argument and the methods of scientific research enhance the general reader's understanding of popularizations of science like those found in *Scientific American*.

Whether improved reasoning ability actually does feed cultural literacy in such ways is an empirical question. While people might be expected to make the connections and applications, they may not. But to whatever extent the connections and applications are automatically made, it seems possible in principle to teach for this sort of application when one is teaching argument analysis and other reasoning skills.

Reasoning Literacy?

It is tempting sometimes to introduce a new literacy to the growing list. How about adding reasoning literacy to computer literacy and scientific literacy? The idea has punch. It could be used to denote the standards of reasoning ability to be expected at any given level and context.

However, the temptation should be resisted, and for reasons that are by now obvious. The connections between reasoning of various sorts and literacy are so intimate that to suggest, by the introduction of a separate label, that there are two distinct capacities would be seriously misleading. One cannot read and write if one cannot reason.

Conversely, I would argue that, far from reasoning literacy being distinct from cultural literacy, the ability to reason moderately well is a component of cultural literacy. One is not able to function in the context of the culture unless one is able to reason about matters that arise in the course of its existence. Put another way, the reasoning about science and politics and art and literature that occurs in a culture is not an extra-cultural phenomenon, but part and parcel of the culture.

References

De Sousa, R. (1987). *The rationality of emotions.* Cambridge, MA: MIT Press.

Govier, T. (1988a). *Problems in argument analysis and evaluation.* Dordrecht, The Netherlands: Foris.

Govier, T. (1988b). *A practical study of argument.* Belmont, CA: Wadsworth.

Haugeland, J. (1985). *Artificial intelligence: The very idea.* Cambridge, MA: MIT Press.

Johnson, R. H. & Blair, J. A. (1983). *Logical self-defense,* (2nd ed.). Toronto: McGraw-Hill Ryerson.

Morton, A. (1988). Making arguments explicit: The theoretical interest of practical difficulties. In Fisher, A. (Ed.) Critical thinking (The Proceedings of the First British Conference on Informal Logic and Critical Thinking). Norwich, UK: The University of East Anglia.

Phillips, L. M. (1988). Young readers' inference strategies in reading comprehension. *Cognition and Instruction, 5,* 193-222.

Pinto, R. C., & Blair, J. A. (1988). *Information, inference, and argument.* Windsor, Ontario: University of Windsor, Department of Philosophy.

7

Literacy as Politics:
A Critique of the Views of Some Radical Critics

Lloyd Brown
Memorial University of Newfoundland

In his book, *Growth Through English*, Dixon (1967) discusses three models of literacy. The first, the skills model, he describes as that which "fitted an era when initial literacy was the prime demand" (p. 1). It concerns itself with teaching the rudiments of reading and writing—vocabulary skills, word identification, spelling, proper usage, and correct mechanics. It is, he says, narrow and ignores the learner. The second, the heritage model, he criticizes because it stresses culture as a given, and ignores "culture as the pupil knows it" (p. 3). It confirms the teacher "in presenting experience (in fictions) to his pupils, rather than drawing from them their experience (of reading and self)" (p. 3). Having dismissed these two models, he advocates the personal growth model. Here pupils use language for their own purposes. It helps them, he says, to realize themselves, and it provides opportunities for personal growth (pp. 4-9). However, in the last paragraph of his book, while acknowledging "the recent emphasis on public exchange of ideas rather than private writing and reading" (p. 111), Dixon expresses some doubt about the durability of the personal growth model, and recognizes the need for a new one:

> Is a new model for education struggling to emerge, just at the point when we have spelt out for ourselves the fuller implications of a model based on personal growth? Very well. The limits of the present model will be reached, that is certain, and thus a new model will be needed. (p. 114)

At the Fourth International Conference on the Teaching of English, held in Ottawa during May of 1986, there were some hints about the nature of this new model. Britton (1986) concluded the abstract of his paper with this vague reference to it: "I shall suggest that the growth model needs . . . amending to take account of the fact that education is an effect of community." Dixon (1986) was more specific and more direct. He stated that the personal growth model is not good enough for the eighties decade with its "grass roots" movements, movements which have taught us "to scrutinize . . . language . . . as a pervading form of institutional pressure, enforcing traditions we must challenge and reshape." To challenge "some of the social and ideological assumptions" of these traditions, he suggested the adoption of a new view of education, "that of education as social formation". There were references to this view in other presentations. Green (1986), for example, concluded that "what should be clear . . . is the need to recognize English teaching emphatically as a significant form of cultural politics."

None of these speakers specified what a program concerned with social formation or cultural politics would look like. The purpose of this chapter is to examine the nature of this view of schooling and literacy and to ask where it might lead us. Specifically, the chapter will discuss the ideas of a select number of radical critics (both teachers of language and theoreticians), some supporting the reproductive nature of the school, and others regarding it as a place of resistance. First, the chapter will examine briefly the general view of schooling and culture held by these critics; then it will discuss their ideas on the teaching of composition.

The School, Code, and Culture

It might be useful first to provide some discussion of the ideological foundation that underlies the view that literacy is a form of cultural politics. While there is no homogeneity of ideas among the proponents of this view, there are similarities in their philosophy of education. They all seem to regard the school as a reflection of the dominant culture, and education as rooted in politics. Bowles and Gintis (1977), for example, see school practices and organization as reproducing the capitalist order. Searle (1973), a teacher, is extreme and specific in his discussion of the political role of the school. He sees the school as a tool of the ruling class, and the teacher as "the functionary of state power" (p. 7). As a functionary, he goes on to say that the teacher is "an agent of repression", one who "is delegated the squalid job of persuading or coercing the child . . . to sit quietly and contentedly at a job which will give him no chance to participate in the government of his own life" (p. 12). Searle proceeds to characterize the classroom as a centre of political conflict, one in which teachers, because they are agents of the ruling class, "the established culture", act on its behalf "to break the working class child's confidence in his own individual and collective identity, and to make him easier to manipulate and manage by his future employers" (p. 13).

The morality of the school, he says, is middle class morality, one that is repressive, denying "democratic advancement". It is a "morality of exploitation", and "represents the standards that benefit and perpetuate the status quo" (p. 8). The invective may be stronger here than in the writings of most radical critics, but the denigration of middle class values is a common theme (Anyon, 1980; Bowles & Gintis, 1977; Ohmann, 1976). What strikes me in reading these writers is the degree to which they homogenize the middle class, treating it as if it were an abstraction, as if it represented a uniformity of behaviour and values. It is difficult to take seriously the notion that the great variety of representatives of the middle class such as priests, businesspeople, union leaders, university professors, politicians, and school teachers, have, as a group, agreed to deny democratic advancement, to exploit and dominate others, and, as Searle says, to turn the school into an "agent of repression" (p. 12). First, experience tells us that the middle class is not a homogeneous group with a single view of society. Second, the call for, and practice of, a vigorous criticism of the dominant culture by some (such as professors and priests) from the middle class give the lie to Searle's claim that it is working together to coerce children and imbue them with state ideology.

Searle (1973) and Bowles and Gintis (1977), in describing the school as an institution which simply reproduces the dominant interests and ideology of society, seem to take a rather dim view of the capacity of people for resistance, treating them as if they were merely passive receivers of the dominant culture. They ignore what both experience and research (Willis, 1977) teach us, which is that both students and teachers have a certain autonomy, that they may, and often do, offer resistance to the dominant culture, that their relationship to society is one marked by resistance. Searle must also believe this, for he urges us to change the schools. If domination were as strong as he says, how could criticism and resistance be started, how could renewal be effected? They could not be, and Searle's call for transformation of the schools would be fatuous and empty.

Many recent critics (Willis, 1977; Apple, 1982; Fitzclarence & Giroux, 1984; Giroux, 1983) who regard schools as "sites of intervention" and places where students may exercise a critical voice, have taken issue with this simplistic theory of reproduction and have largely discredited it. These critics have called for a critical pedagogy, one characterized by openness and critical rigour, one that sees the school as a complex, active institution with a certain amount of autonomy.

Whatever their view of the relationship between the school and the dominant culture, whether they see the school as a place of resistance to this culture or as a place that is dominated by it, all radical critics demand the transformation of the school. What, exactly, are some of the changes they advocate? Bowles and Gintis (1977) say that "the educational process . . . should contribute to the development of a revolutionary, democratic socialist movement" (p. 269). Searle (1973) is more specific. He advocates "throwing out the enemy culture"—the established middle class culture—"and making socialism together" (p. 178). He concludes, "the real direction of our energy is to struggle towards the structures and organized love of socialism" (p. 178). Searle, then, while complaining about one kind of indoctrination, wants to replace it with another kind. The school which he calls for would no longer be a "tool of middle class consciousness" (p. 41); it would instead, it seems, be a tool of working class consciousness.

Aronowitz and Giroux (1985) also believe that the school curriculum should be political. However, according to them, this change in the school curriculum is not achieved by indoctrination, by an uncritical acceptance of another view of schooling. It will, they say, be brought about by the practice of a critical pedagogy, one that calls "into question the production, organization, transmission, stratification, allocation and evaluation of knowledge within schools" (p. 145). It is also one that helps

> students, particularly from the oppressed classes, recognize that the dominant school culture is not neutral and does not generally serve their needs, while at the same time raising the issue of how it is that the dominant culture functions to make them, as students, feel powerless. The answer to this issue lies, in part, in revealing myths, lies, injustices of the dominant school culture. (Giroux 1984, p. 37)

This statement shows that Giroux's critical pedagogy is not nearly as open and generous as we were led to believe. It is a one-sided pedagogy. First, it concerns itself only with what Giroux calls "the oppressed classes". It is not clear what Giroux has in mind for those who are not oppressed, those whose needs are met by the school, and who are not powerless. Second, it is concerned only with the lies, myths, and injustices of the dominant culture that are assumed to be there merely to be revealed. It does not even allow for the possibility that a critical examination of the dominant culture—democratic capitalism—might lead one to conclusions quite different from Giroux's assumptions. He seems to be more concerned with politics than he is with truth. And, as Arendt (1987) has pointed out, "no one has ever doubted that truth and politics are on rather bad terms with each other" (p. 22). Giroux seems to be so committed to the socialist ideology and to its implementation that he is rendered incapable of examining that ideology or of conducting an objective analysis of another, such as democratic capitalism. In fact, it is difficult to see how we can call what Giroux describes here as criticism. It is certainly a long way from Arnold's (1961) claim that "it is the business of the critical power . . . to see an object as in itself it really is" (p. 239). Arnold here seems to assume that whatever one's politics one is able to engage in a disinterested examination of ideas, that "prescriptions of reason" transcend ideology, obeying an instinct that prompts it "to try to know the best that is known and thought in the world" (p. 239). Giroux's critical pedagogy seems to be more a hunt for flaws than criticism; and the teacher more an undercover agent than a critic.

Radical critics emphasize the centrality of the students' culture in learning. Simon (1987) says that in order to empower students, the school must "provide a curricular and instructional agenda that enables students to draw upon their own cultural resources" (p. 374). Giroux (1983) writes that "literacy . . . only becomes relevant if it is grounded in the cultural milieu that informs the context of the learners' everyday lives"; and that "the relationship between teachers and students would have to be mediated by forms of discourse and content rooted in the cultural capital of learners" (p. 228). Such discourse and content "give students the opportunity to speak with their own voices, to authenticate their own experiences". He continues, "once students become aware of the dignity of their own perceptions and histories, they can make a leap to the theoretical and begin to examine the truth values of their meanings" (p. 203). These statements prompt certain questions. Most would agree that students should be encouraged to speak with their own voices, but don't these voices need to be developed, made clearer, more thought-ful, precise, and logical? How is this to be done? What critical tools do students need in order to be able to use their own voices well? What are the areas of study necessary for the development of their own voices? What modes of discourse will they need to know in order to go from a recognition of "the dignity of their own perceptions" to the point where they are able "to examine the truth value of their meanings"? The answers to these questions are not clear, but Giroux seems to suggest that only a study of the students' "cultural capital" is necessary. For example, he denigrates the classics (1983, p. 212) and has little time for tradition, as shown by his acceptance of this statement by Marx: "The tradition of all the dead generations weighs like a nightmare on the brain of the living" (p. 133). He objects to the teaching of that which is removed from the "cultural capital of students" because it "provides the context for a pedagogy that disconfirms the historical and cultural experiences of students" (p. 214).

Searle (1973) also argues that the school should reject the alien, established culture in favour of working class culture and its language. Specifically, he says that the teacher must "stand up and affirm the working class . . . language that his students speak" (p. 136). Here he rejects Bernstein's notion that this language is a limited, restricted code, and maintains that it is an "unbounded code", "a truly educational language", one with

> words which inspire generosity and shared experience, people speaking
> together and solidarising, affirming themselves and their class. (p. 136)

It is not necessary, in order to avoid paternalism with respect to working class culture, to engage in such glorification of it. Those who do so, as Hoggart (1977) points out, "are in danger of themselves falling into a new noble savage myth" (p. 52). Hoggart argues that we should "introduce pupils to a common core of intellectual and imaginative values beyond those of a particular historical consensus" (p. 53). He concludes that it is the responsibility of the teacher to educate students for a "fuller literacy and numeracy" so that they may be "articulate, critical, judging human beings" (p. 59).

Inglis (1975) takes a position similar to Hoggart's. He also emphasizes how important it is for teachers to recognize "the humanity and the experience which their pupils [bring] to school with them" (p. 16). Without this recognition, he says, many "children have suffered the assaults of an alien speech and symbolism as an impersonal violence against which they have closed their shutters and remained in hiding" (p. 16). However, Inglis recognizes that education would be narrow if students were limited to a study of their own culture. He believes, as radical critics such as Simon, Giroux, and Searle do not, that education, before it can be radical and critical, must first be conservative; that one must first receive the cultural heritage before one can think new thoughts about the world. Educators, then, Inglis suggests, have a responsibility to help their students recapture traditional culture. The task, he says, is to create ways of seeing traditional culture "in such a way that it confers its significance on the lives of all men and women" (p. 34).

These positions by Hoggart and Inglis seem to me to be fair and reasonable; and they call attention to the weakness in the thesis of those who maintain that working class culture should form the basis of a literacy program. For if, as Hoggart says, working class culture has limitations, to base a literacy program on it is to limit the experiences of children and to provide a very weak foundation for their education. It may, for example, suffer from limited linguistic resources, lacking, what Broudy (1979, p. 4) calls, an "imagic store", thus restricting severely the generation of meaning. The task of the teacher must surely be to enlarge children's repository of images so that they may refine and expand their understanding. Lawton (1975), who is quite sympathetic to linking children's schooling to their community culture, makes a similar point. He says that we may want to begin with the immediate, working class environment but we should certainly look beyond it (p. 49). He suggests looking beyond it to a common culture, represented by the public forms of knowledge. These he regards as an extension and a refinement of the local culture (p. 71).

What, then, in summary, are the basic tenets of the radical critics as discussed here? First, education is rooted in politics and is at present under the dominance of a repressive, middle-class, capitalist ideology. Second, this state of affairs should be changed so that the school can contribute to the development of a democratic socialist system. Third, teachers have an obligation to undermine the present dominant culture in order to bring about socialism. Fourth, central to radical pedagogy is a curriculum grounded in the students' own culture.

Teaching Composition

Radical critics regard composition as a political phenomenon, and present-day composition teaching as a form of acculturation. Rouse (1979), for example, complains that Shaughnessy (1977), with her emphasis on conventions in composition teaching, is attempting "to socialize . . . young people in a manner politically acceptable" (p. 1). He also argues that, in teaching students sentence analysis and the names of language structures, Shaughnessy is socializing students "to accept society's way of classifying things" (p. 10), and classifying is regarded as evil, a way of denying the students' "subjective reality" (p. 11). Ohmann (1976) maintains that freshmen English is "framed in response to needs of the industrial state and its governing class" (p. 94). He later lists some of the things we have attempted to teach in the service of the industrial state:

> organizing information, drawing conclusions from it, making reports, using standard English (i.e. the language of the bourgeois elites), solving problems, keeping one's audience in mind, seeking objectivity and detachment, conducting persuasive arguments . . . These are all abilities that are clearly useful to the new industrial state, and to the extent that English departments nourish them . . . they are giving value for society's money. (pp. 301-302)

Perhaps Ohmann is here exaggerating in order to make the point that we have overemphasized these qualities in order to satisfy social demands, and that in so doing we have largely ignored "the performance—behind the composing itself—of finding something to say, modifying it, deepening it" (p. 139). Perhaps he wants to remind us that composition teaching that overemphasizes these qualities creates "a kind of composition adrift from social process, and from the social identities of students and teachers" (p. 159). If this is so, his points are well taken, but why the anti-intellectual stance? Why the leftist polemic in order to make them? I would have thought that "organizing information", "drawing conclusions from it", "seeking objectivity", and "keeping one's audience in mind" would be useful skills for anyone, even radical critics. It is difficult to know what to make of anyone who argues that these basic skills are elitist, serving the industrial state merely. How does one think radically without being able to think critically? And how does one think critically without the ability to organize, draw conclusions, and seek objectivity? Bizzell (1982) recognizes the importance of this latter question in her discussion of the college composition of basic writing students, and answers it by stating that such students, generally politically oppressed, need to develop their critical understanding in order to gain "control of their own destinies" (p. 196), and to gain this critical understanding "politically oppressed students need to master academic discourse" (p. 196). This academic discourse, she says, calling as it does for an "abstracting, formalizing power" (p. 206), will help students "gain . . . critical distance on their experience" (p. 197).

If the qualities specified by Ohmann are not central to writing, which ones are? What exactly is Ohmann asking for? He is rather vague in his discussion of what ought to be. He asks, in a general way, for "a very different sort of teaching from what we and our employers are used to", teaching that would encourage students to "develop their writing skills in the process of discovering their political needs and as an aid in achieving those needs". He continues by saying that this "different sort of teaching" would mean

> encouraging students to form alliances with one another based on real life interest, and letting the skills of writing grow through collective work . . . .
> In short it would mean bringing politics—everyone's politics—into composition. (p. 160)

It should be pointed out here that there is nothing, apart from this statement, in Ohmann's book to suggest that he is as tolerant as the parenthetical expression, "everyone's politics", suggests. One feels that if "everyone's politics" were brought into Ohmann's composition class, it would not be, to quote Leavis (1964), to encourage "a play of the free intelligence upon the underlying issues" (p. 2). It would rather be to denigrate bourgeois capitalism and to praise socialism. There is some evidence in his book to support this conclusion. Near the end, for example, he concludes that in order for the universities to be emancipatory, they will "have to act as allies of socialism" (p. 332), and that as university instructors we ought "to teach politically with revolution as our end" (p. 335).

It is not clear what Ohmann means by "collective work", but it seems to be similar to Searle's (1973) "group expression" and "verbal solidarity", which allow students to affirm "themselves and their class" (p. 136). Searle sees this "verbal solidarity" expressed in two ways. One way is co-operative writing in which children write "plays about their world together . . . pooling their ideas to reproduce the drama of the neighborhood" (p. 53). The second way encourages the individual student to write "of his own identity, and his life in his community with his peers", thus allowing him to develop "a collective identity" (p. 53).

Searle's book contains many examples of both kinds of writing— poems and prose of conflicts at home, poverty, trouble at school, and racial conflicts in the community. It is, by and large, honest, clear, detailed writing. However, there is also a monotony about it, due to a sameness of subject and imagery. It is perhaps what we would expect from any attempt to construct "a collective co-operative identity", which can only grow from common experience, and, as Searle himself admits, "from a collective imagery, a foundation of mutual language and symbol, which people need to both share experience and achieve a common level of communication" (p. 105). But to confine our students' expression to the neighbourhood, in the neighbourhood's language, is to limit their vision unduly. There is no hint in Searle's book that his students read or were encouraged to read anything outside of pop songs on which they based some of their own poems. In fact, when the school inspector suggested to Searle that the "function of the teacher . . . was to work towards a situation where the children could 'transcend' their environ- ment" (p. 161), he regarded the statement as middle class bias. Searle goes on to classify anything outside of the students' own struggle as "alien knowledge" (p. 162), and anything that does not deal with "social fact and social injustice" (p. 137) as illusion and escapist fantasy. The all-consuming purpose of the teacher, according to Searle, is to force students to realize "their position in the world and their oppressive life-situation" (p. 137). It is this "oppressive life situation" that members of the working class share, and though they may differ in race, creed, and colour, Searle concludes that they "have to look for points of unity and connection" (p. 104) in themselves. However, this search for points of unity is not a universal one; it is confined to the working class. The middle class is the "enemy that is using us . . . and keeping us divided from each other" (p. 104).

On one occasion, Searle's students, objecting to a decision made by the school governors, go on strike and sing:

> We hate the governors
> Oh yes we do,
> We hate the governors
> Oh yes we do. . . (p. 173).

Searle's comments are that "singing together gave a joy, a belief and a recognition of themselves as people with strength" (p. 173). If this is what "collective work" leads to, if this is what "verbal solidarity" means—the development of hatred for, and bitterness toward, others—there is reason to be critical of, if not alarmed by, such a view of English teaching. Though Searle condemns middle-class, capitalist society as one which "creates and thrives on division" (p. 10), he himself seems to encourage and foster divisions by supporting class hatred.

What strikes me about the political approach to writing espoused by Searle is its narrowness, and its anti-imaginative quality. It is narrow because it confines students to the contemporary, the scenes, situations, and problems which they experience. The danger here is, as Allen (1980) points out, "that the child might become trapped in a schooling which mirrors his world and does not show him other possibilities" (p. 70).

Shayer (1972) also complains about the narrowness of this approach. In his discussion of the textbook *Reflections* by Clements, Dixon, and Stratta, he concludes:

> good though it may be to try and make secondary pupils, and especially disadvantaged pupils, aware of the social realities . . . around them, an approach as obviously circumscribed and prosaic as this . . . is too narrow.
> (p. 154)

In trying to create social awareness, this approach also ignores imaginative experience. Because its emphasis is, as Searle (1973) puts it, on "confronting the facts of social injustice", this approach does not allow for fantasy, for playfulness with language and ideas. One feels that behind the poetry of Searle's students is his too obtrusive personality, giving strong direction, limiting the subjects of their writing, clarifying the social problems for them. The students seem to have been manipulated to produce something of social relevance. The emphasis on social relevance is evident in Ohmann's (1985) glowing description of literacy in Cuba. He attributes its success to its being allied to politics and to the "promise of a better life" (p. 687). The children did not study "See Jane Run", he says, but "key political terms" (p. 687). The result of the study was this student's letter to Castro:

> I write this to let you know that now I know how to read and write thanks
> to our Socialist and Democratic Revolution. . . . I take leave with a firm
> Revolutionary . . . salute. (p. 687)

The study apparently worked its effect. It is difficult to imagine writing
that is less original, less an expression of an individual mind than this.
Both Searle and Ohmann show us here didacticism with a vengeance,
functionalism that is restricting and prosaic. One is reminded of Dickens'
Hard Times (1964) and the stifling world of Mr. Gradgrind. As in his
world, there is to be here "no idle imagination" and no "idle storybook"
(p. 24). "You are not to see anywhere what you don't see in fact" (p. 15),
and "you are never to fancy" (p. 16) seem to be the mottoes which
crystallize Searle's and Ohmann's conception of literacy.

In his discussion of those aspects of English composition which have
been taught in the service of the industrial state, Ohmann lists standard
English. Both Searle and Ohmann regard standard English as a middle-
class language, and the teaching of it as an elitist act. Shallcrass (1984)
characterizes teachers who "impose their own dialect on children" (p.
160) as practicing imperialism. He says that to teach the dominant dialect
(standard English) is "to extend the influence of existing power blocs in
society" (pp. 160-161). To teach standard language, then, is regarded by
radical critics as a form of oppression by the teacher of the child, and is,
therefore, to propagate social injustice. Insofar as this position calls
attention to the importance of the language and culture that a child brings
to school, there are few who would disagree with it. That psychological
harm may be done to children if we condemn their dialect is widely
accepted. However, it is not necessary, in order to correct this error, to
deny children access to their common heritage. For standard language
is not just another dialect. As Postman (1979) writes, it has "a wider
range of expressiveness" than any regional dialect. He continues, it

> contains the fullest living account of the history and psychology of English
> speaking people. By this I mean it has been used, in spoken and written
> form, by people of widely different time, place, social class and ex-
> perience to express every conceivable state of mind . . . Its resources have
> been . . . developed by our most intelligent people and therefore there is
> a . . . richness to it that cannot be approached by any social . . . or ethnic
> dialect. (p. 177)

Hirsch (1977) argues that standard language is "not a dialect at all in
the sense that a purely oral language of a speech community is a dialect.

It is a different kind of language system" (p. 43). He characterizes it as a "grapholect", a "transdialectal instrument for communication between social and regional groups" (p. 45). He also adds that it allows us to communicate

> with the dead and the yet unborn. When a child of ten can read . . .
> *Gulliver's Travels*, a book over two hundred years old, the conservative
> and normative power of the grapholect transcends class, time, and place.
> (p. 45)

Although a grapholect "has the greatest currency among those who have been most intensively trained in its use", Hirsch sees it as an "artificial construct", belonging to "no group or place in particular" (p. 44). He concludes that to teach the grapholect is to teach "an instrument of communicability on a national and even international scale" (p. 45), and that "without a normative grapholect, a classless society could not be plausibly imagined" (p. 46). However, Hirsch does recognize the need to encourage the development of students' "cultural and personal individuality", and argues that this individuality can be nurtured within the grapholect, which tolerates a wide range of variations, much wider than any regional dialect does (p. 47). This position recognizes the students and their language, while at the same time emphasizing the importance of standard language. That is, while it recognizes the right of students to their own language, it also maintains the school's responsibility to broaden the horizons of its students by introducing them to "what it regards as the instrument of civilized discourse" (Postman 1979, p. 178).

This position, it seems to me, is a reasonable, defensible one. It is much more defensible than that of the radical critics like Searle and Ohmann who, while writing their books in standard English, say it is elitist to teach working class students the language they themselves use with facility. They are the true elites, members of the middle class, the privileged, speaking for the underprivileged, telling them what they need, while denying them the privileges which they, the enlightened, have.

Furthermore, the notion that standard language is, as the language of the ruling middle class, an instrument of control and oppression cannot stand up to criticism. First, as Ellul (1985) points out, this position is valid only if one subscribes to a mechanistic view of language; if, that is, one holds that language corresponds exactly to the user's intention, if the words reproduce ideology exactly. This is not the case. Discourse, as Ellul describes it, "is full of empty spaces; there are fractures in the word and gaps in the language" (p. 176). In other words, listeners and readers must interpret what is said and written, and these interpretations vary. There is, then, no "perfect reproduction of the bourgeois mind-set" (p. 176) in standard language.

A second criticism of the position that standard language is an instrument of the state used to maintain the status quo is made by both Ellul (1985) and Hirsch (1988). Hirsch argues cogently that literate culture and the national language (standard language) are the most effective instruments for political and social change. He uses the language of *The Black Panther*, a radical, revolutionary newspaper, to show that radical sentiments are generally expressed in conservative language (pp. 22-23). Historically, standard language has been the instrument of rebels. One thinks of Marx, Lenin, Tom Paine. If this is so; if, that is, standard language has been used to express rebellion, how can we argue that it is merely a tool of the bourgeoisie for producing conformity? Moreover, the radical critics themselves undermine their own argument by writing of revolution in standard language.

Summary

What have we discovered from our brief examination of a select number of critics who hold the view that literacy is a form of cultural politics? The following is a summary of the main points discussed in this chapter, points that seem to be central in the writings of these critics:

1. Education in general, and literacy in particular, are a form of acculturation by the dominant class culture.

2. Working class values, culture, and language should be central in teaching.

3. The skills of writing that we had traditionally regarded as qualities of good writing (organization, clarity, recognition of one's audience) are regarded as skills in the service of the bourgeois elites.

4. Writing is a process of discovering one's political needs and achieving political ends.

5. Writing is not an individual act, but an act of collective identity. Personal expression is regarded as "verbal self-indulgence", and is to be replaced by "verbal solidarity".

6. The topics of writing should grow out of the social environment. Writing is to be concerned with "social fact and social injustice".

7. Standard language is a middle-class, elitist dialect and should not be taught.

Conclusion

I have here examined the views of a select, though, I believe not an unrepresentative, number of writers who regard literacy as a form of cultural politics. Throughout this examination I have registered certain objections to and difficulties with the case they make. I shall conclude the chapter by discussing briefly what I consider to be the main flaws in that case.

First, those who regard literacy and the teaching of it as a form of politics seem to think that politics exhausts our lives, that we are political creatures only. As a result, a rather tiresome earnestness characterizes their writing. They seem to have no time for delight and wonder and celebration; and seem to forget that human nature, as Morse (1972) points out, also "includes a capacity to produce and enjoy beautiful things" (p. 22). They have, to use Arnold (1961) out of context, gone "into drab—the drab of the earnest, prosaic, practical, austerely literal future" (p. 234).

Radical critics also seem to forget that there are basic human needs about which politics does not speak, and does not even have the vocabulary about which to speak. Inglis (1975) sums it up this way:

> We do not have a politics capable of speaking as though men have souls. It cannot speak of love, or generosity, or tenderness. Its most dignified terms are 'rights' and 'justice'—good terms both, but not enough with which to imagine a brave new world. (p. 36)

The point to be emphasized is that there are basic human needs, such as the need for dignity, honour, love, respect, forgiveness, ultimate meaning, that are outside the purview of politics, needs that cannot be subjected to legal or administrative control, but that must be satisfied if we are to be truly human. It is the task of literacy teaching to keep alive language that allows us to name and share with others those basic human needs, thus reminding ourselves that we are more than creatures of the state, that we share a common humanity, one that transcends the command of the government. The vocabulary of politics—"equality", "rights", "justice"—is a necessary vocabulary to clarify what is due us as residents of the state, but inadequate to express the needs of the spirit. If we ignore or distort the vocabulary capable of expressing these latter needs, it will atrophy and we will be left with a language inadequate for expressing and defining an important part of our humanity.

In accepting the notion that truth is political and collective, the radical critics appear to undermine any claim of the individual to truth, and to regard any such claim as a form of self-indulgence. In emphasizing solidarity, they reject the contribution of literacy to personal growth and personal discovery. Their position, for instance, is radically different from Polanyi's (1972) which stresses the centrality of the knower in knowing:

> Nothing that is said, written or printed, can ever mean anything in itself: for it is only a *person* who utters something—or who listens to it or reads it—who can mean something by it. (p. 22)

This suggests that there is no meaning without the personal participation of the knower. However, Polanyi does not overemphasize personal freedom and autonomy in learning. He stresses the limits of personal freedom, and these limits are imposed by the learner's experiences and culture. For example, the learner who listens to and reads messages, understands them by making a tacit contribution of his own; and this tacit contribution comes from the learner's experiences in the culture— both contemporary and traditional. This position, unlike that of the radical critics, establishes a balance between the individual and culture. However, this relationship is dynamic, stressing the continued existence of the culture while at the same time encouraging creativity and renewal.

Abbs (1982) writes that "education . . . is a fearless enquiry into human meaning . . . it is not a pre-selected political struggle" (pp. 22-23). If we accept, as I do, this "fearless enquiry into human meaning" as the goal of literacy, we must conclude that to regard literacy as a form of politics is to restrict it and to make it unimaginative. In stressing that the goal of literacy is to create a particular political system—socialism—the proponents of literacy as politics make the world of politics, as it were, a closed text. They seem to be saying that the truth is known; that there remains only the task of persuading others of this truth and establishing the system that will embody it. This position has two effects. First, in calling for the acceptance of a system already defined, it fails to encourage the development of imagination, that quality which allows us to realize the possibilities of things, to think of new ways of transforming and renewing what is. The purpose of literacy is more visionary, more open than the radical critics define it. It is to help students to understand themselves and their world that they may be free to think new thoughts about, and act for the good of, both. The political system created as the result of this thinking and acting may or may not be socialism.

Second, to accept the goal of literacy as the making of socialism (or any other -ism) is to become the servant of a system. If this happens; if, that is, teachers serve any particular ideology, they limit their judgement. Their criticism is confined only to that which their ideology opposes. If their ideology achieves power, they become silent. For the aim of any particular political movement when it achieves power is to keep it. It will expect its supporters to remain silent in order to do so. For this reason I distrust the political mind. It is the enemy of independent thought, the enemy of what Arnold (1961) calls, the "disinterested love of a free play of the mind on all subjects", as it tries "to know the best that is known and thought in the world, irrespectively of practice, politics, and everything of the kind" (p. 245).

The proponents of the cultural politics model of literacy dismiss the teaching of skills, regarding them as bourgeois conventions (Rouse 1979; Ohmann 1976). Few would disagree that as a model of literacy the skills model is incomplete. But are skills of no consequence? Have they no place in the teaching of composition? Bizzell (1982) argues that students must learn the conventions and skills of the academic discourse community in order to develop critical thinking as practiced by it. That is, students must "indwell", must learn and practice the language and discourse conventions of an academic discourse community to know its particular view of the world and its particular way of reasoning about it.

"Indwell" is Polanyi's term. He regards skills as subsidiaries which, when we have mastered them, become a part of our tacit resources allowing us to practice our craft. They are never thought of in isolation, divorced from performance, but always as a means to an end, some larger purpose. Polanyi, then, assigns skills their proper place—secondary to meaning, serving as tacitly known subsidiaries in the creation of meaning, and necessary for the communication of meaning. If what Bizzell and Polanyi say is true, we could argue, as Graff (1979) does, that if we are to train our students to think critically, the skills that Ohmann dismisses as bourgeois—"organizing information", "drawing conclusions", "seeking objectivity and detachment"—must be emphasized; for surely, these are aspects of critical thinking. As Graff concludes, although such skills of thinking and writing may have been used "to further the interests of the elite and the upwardly mobile", our task "ought to be not to dismantle these techniques but to restore them to the groups from which they have been stolen" (p. 120).

As we have already noted, the radical critics, in emphasizing the teaching of a student's own culture, denigrate the value of cultural heritage, of what Polanyi (1972) describes as the "articulate heritage to which we are apprenticed" (p. 34). This lack of attention by the radical critics to the heritage of Western Civilization is serious. For if we agree with Hirsch (1988) and Blair (this volume) that a fully developed literacy depends on a background of shared knowledge, we must conclude that the school should provide its students with this knowledge. This knowledge takes the forms of the modes or disciplines of knowing, which provide us with a variety of human utterances with which we must be acquainted if we are to be truly literate. It is to these that Steiner (1971) refers when he defines as necessary for literacy, a "minimal gamut of shared recognitions and designative codes without which there can be neither a coherent society nor a continuation . . . of a 'lived culture'" (p. 78). Oakshott (1962) expresses a similar view. He says that we are inheritors of a conversation and that the responsibility of educators is to initiate students

> into the skill and partnership of this conversation in which we learn to recognize the voices, to distinguish the proper occasions of utterance, and in which we acquire the intellectual and moral habits appropriate to conversation. (p. 199)

When I think of the utterances of those who have contributed to this great conversation, I think especially of Thoreau's chapter (1950), "Reading", in *Walden*. Here he advises us that reading is not that which "lulls us as a luxury", but that reading, "in a high sense", is "what we have to stand on tiptoe to read" (p. 137). Thoreau must have followed his own advise, for in *Walden* we have one who speaks in a language permeated with the ideas of great minds, in a language which, with its particularity, its clarity, its responsiveness, its generous reverberations, its sonorous rhythms, is, while personal, not merely personal; it is also "the product of immemorially collaborative creativity" (Leavis 1975, p. 33). To read this chapter on reading in *Walden* is to realize how mistaken are those who seek to confine the conversations of students to their own culture and experiences and language, and how important, how crucial, it is for schools in their development of literacy to provide students with "the best that is known and thought in the world", with the classics, the "bibles of mankind", with, that is, the universal, informing, enduring utterances that permeate our lives.

References

Abbs, P. (1982). *English within the arts*. London: Hodder and Stoughton.

Allen, D. (1980). *English teaching since 1965: How much growth?* London: Heinemann.

Anyon, J. (1980). Social class and the hidden curriculum. *Journal of Education, 162*(1), 67-92..

Apple, M. W. (1982). *Education and power*. London: Routledge & Kegan Paul.

Arendt, H. (1987). *Between past and future*. Middlesex, U.K.: Penguin.

Arnold, M. (1961). The function of criticism at the present time. In A. D. Culler (Ed.), *Poetry and criticism of Matthew Arnold*. Boston: Houghton Mifflin.

Aronowitz, S., & Giroux, H. A. (1985). *Education Under Siege*. South Hadley, MA: Bergin & Harvey.

Bantock, G. H. (1980). *Dilemmas of the curriculum*. New York: Wiley.

Bizzell, P. (1982). College composition: initiation into the academic discourse community. *Curriculum Inquiry, 12*, 191-207.

Bowles, S., & Gintis, H. (1977). Schooling in capitalist America. New York: Basic Books.

Britton, J. N. (1986). Dartmouth: Elegy or eulogy. [Abstract]. *Proceedings of the Fourth International Conference on the Teaching of English.*

Broudy, H. S. (1979). Tacit knowing as a rationale for liberal education. *Teachers College Record, 80*, 446-462.

Dickens, C. (1964). *Hard times*. New York: The New American Library.

Dixon, J. (1967). *Growth through english*. Reading, UK: National Association for the Teaching of English.

Dixon, J. (1986). Is it growth or social inculcation: Dartmouth revisited. [Abstract]. *Proceedings of the Fourth International Conference on the Teaching of English.*

Ellul, J. (1985). *The humiliation of the word.* Grand Rapids, MI: Eerdmans.

Fitzclarence, L., & Giroux, H. A. (1984). The paradox of power in educational theory and practice. *Language Arts, 61,* 462-477.

Giroux, H. A. (1984). Rethinking the language of schooling. *Language Arts, 61,* 33-40.

Giroux, H. A. (1981). *Ideology, culture and the process of schooling.* Philadelphia: Temple University Press.

Giroux, H. A. (1983). *Theory and resistance in education: A pedagogy for opposition.* South Hadley, MA: Bergin & Harvey.

Graff, G. (1979). *Literature against itself.* Chicago: University of Chicago Press.

Green, W. (1986). Literature teaching in question: English teaching as culture politics. [Abstract]. *Proceedings of the Fourth International Conference on the Teaching of English.*

Hirsch, E. D. Jr. (1988). Cultural literacy: What every American needs to know. New York: Vintage.

Hirsch, E. D. (1977). *The Philosophy of composition.* Chicago: The University of Chicago Press.

Hoggart, R. (1977). The language of culture: Gains and losses. In P. Gallivan & R. J. Merrett (Eds.), *Literature, language and culture.* Edmonton: Athabascan Publishing.

Inglis, F. (1975). *Ideology and the imagination.* London: Cambridge University Press.

Lawton, D. (1975). *Class, culture and the curriculum.* London: Routledge and Kegan Paul.

Leavis, F. R. (1984). Manifesto. In E. Bentley (Ed.), *The importance of scrutiny.* New York: New York University Press.

Leavis, F. R. (1975). *The living principle "English" as a discipline of thought.* London: Chatto and Windus.

Mathieson, M. (1975). *The preachers of culture.* New Jersey: Rowman and Littlefield.

Morse, J. M. (1972). *The irrelevant english teacher.* Philadelphia: Temple University Press.

Oakshott, M. (1962). *Rationalism in politics.* New York: Basic Books.

Ohmann, R. (1976). *English in America.* New York: Oxford University Press.

Ohmann, R. (1985). Literacy, technology, and monopoly capital. *College English, 47,* 675-689.

Polanyi, M. (1967). *The tacit dimension.* New York: Anchors Books.

Polanyi, M. (1972). *The study of man.* Chicago: University of Chicago Press.

Postman, N. (1979). *Teaching as a conserving activity.* New York: Delacorte Press.

Rouse, J. (1979). The politics of composition. *College English, 41,* 1-12.

Searle, C. (1973). *This new season.* London: Calder and Boyars.

Shallcrass, J. (1984). The politics of english teaching: A broad view: Have vision and do what is possible. In James Britton (Ed.), *English teaching: An international exchange.* London: Heinemann.

Shaughnessy, M. P. (1977). *Errors and expectations.* New York: Oxford University Press.

Shayer, D. (1972). *The Teaching of english in schools 1900-1970.* London: Routledge and Kegan Paul.

Simon, R. I. (1987). Empowerment as a pedagogy of possibility. *Language Arts, 64,* 370-382.

Steiner, G. (1971). *In Bluebeard's castle: Some notes towards the re-definition of culture.* London: Faber and Faber.

Thoreau, H. D. (1950). *Walden.* New York: Harper and Brothers.

Willis, P. E. (1977). *Learning to labour.* Westmead, England: Saxon House.

Part II
Historical Perspectives

8

Perspectives on Mathematical Literacy

Carolyn Kieran
Université du Québec à Montréal

Mathematical literacy, what is it? Until very recently, this term was rarely heard among members of the mathematics education community or the public at large. That situation has now changed. The National Council of Teachers of Mathematics has just published the long-awaited *Curriculum and Evaluation Standards for School Mathematics* (National Council of Teachers of Mathematics, 1989). In this document, *mathematical literacy* denotes "an individual's ability to explore, to conjecture, and to reason logically, as well as to use a variety of mathematical methods effectively to solve problems" (p. 6).

However, the *Standards* is more than a statement on mathematical literacy. It is the response of the mathematics education community to the call for reform in the teaching and learning of mathematics (National Commission on Excellence in Education, 1983). It is unique in that it reflects a concerted effort by classroom teachers, supervisors, educational researchers, teacher educators, and university mathematicians to revise the school mathematics curriculum. It has not always been the case that university mathematicians worked hand in hand with classroom teachers. The *Standards* is also unique in that it creates a vision of what it means to be mathematically literate in a rapidly growing technological society. Thus, for the first time in the history of mathematics education, we witness an attempt to define the goals of mathematics education in terms of both society's needs and the discipline of mathematics itself as practised by mathematicians.

In this chapter, I will examine the tension that has existed in the last century between society and the mathematician with respect to the mathematics education of our youth, and then go on to show how the literacy aims of the *Standards* are a courageous break with the past. The second part of the chapter suggests a particular approach to developing mathematical literacy that is in line with the problem-solving vision espoused by the *Standards*, but one which was not specifically pointed to in the *Standards* and one which has also been found to avoid many of the difficulties inherent in traditional approaches to problem solving in the classroom.

A History of Conflicting Needs and Goals

At times, mathematics education in North America has been influenced by mathematicians and, at other times, by society. Examples drawn from school algebra programmes will be used to illustrate this point.

In the 1880s, only one 14-year-old in ten attended high school. Algebra was a required course of study in the first year. The topics generally included operations with literal expressions, the solving of both linear and quadratic equations, the use of these techniques to find answers to problems, and practice with ratios, proportions, powers, and roots. However, the algebra curriculum during this period varied from one school to another because each college and university had its own individual entrance examination and thereby dictated the school syllabus to be followed by prospective students. Although the situation changed in 1900 when the College Entrance Examination Board (CEEB) was set up to work on syllabi that would be the basis for uniform, nationwide algebra examinations, it was still the mathematician who influenced the content of school mathematics. During the first decade of the 20th century, however, undercurrents of protest began in favour of a more practical approach to the teaching of mathematics. By the early twenties, the forces of change were too great to be ignored, forces such as a surge in school enrolment and cries for a more vocationally oriented curriculum. In parts of the country, child-labour laws and compulsory school attendance laws kept students in school for at least ten years. Thus, farm youths who had hitherto stayed away from any form of secondary education were now taking algebra. The proportion of students attending high school grew from 1 in 10 to 1 in 3.

This change in the school population led to changes in emphasis in the algebra curriculum. The traditional, formal approach—in which algebra was taught as a purely mathematical discipline, with no emphasis on understanding—survived a while longer in the CEEB examinations but was considered a thing of the past among leaders in the teaching of mathematics. The newer, more practical approach to algebra that had taken hold in England was beginning to appear in many of the algebra textbooks in Canada and the United States. Eventually, the College Entrance Examination Board called a group of educators together to consider modifying its algebra syllabi. Yet the hold of the CEEB on the formal algebra curriculum was not broken until 1930 when the Great Depression precipitated renewed attacks on education in general, and mathematics in particular, for being so far removed from everyday life.

During the period from 1930 to 1950, the main influence on the teaching of school mathematics was the socioeconomic conditions produced by the Great Depression and World War II. Preoccupation with issues of existence and survival led to the entrenchment of a kind of mathematics that was practical and vocationally oriented. The progressive education movement and the growing interest of psychologists in the study and measurement of individual differences contributed to an increasingly child-centred focus in the classroom. Moreover, compulsory school attendance had become universal, so high schools were faced with the prospect of educating everyone. They responded by lessening graduation requirements and developing many elective courses. Enrolments in the traditional mathematics courses declined precipitously, and curriculum innovators developed new courses, like consumer mathematics, to appeal to the majority of the population. University mathematicians, of course, had little interest in such developments.

The child-centred focus in mathematics classrooms began to shift in the 1950s. World War II had demonstrated how inadequate our mathematics preparation was, relative to the needs of a military power. After the war, the requirements of industry in engineering, the sciences, and mathematics escalated dramatically. The gap between the mathematics taught in high schools and the mathematics required for postcollege jobs in such fields as nuclear physics, space exploration, communications, and computers grew wider year by year. Cold War fears fuelled concerns about our preeminence in mathematics, science, and technology. The appointment in 1955 of the CEEB Commission on Mathematics, the launching in 1957 of the Soviet Sputnik, and the founding in 1958 of the School Mathematics Study Group marked the beginning of an era in which the voices of mathematicians would, once again, predominate.

In addition to major technological advances, significant developments had been occurring in mathematics itself over the past century or so. Thus, it was not difficult to find support for the idea that the mathematics taught in school should reflect the new ideas that mathematicians were finding so useful and powerful. The emphasis in a revised school mathematics program was to be on deductive reasoning, inductive discovery, and precision of language. The main objective was the development of ideas and understanding rather than merely computational skill and the recall of seemingly unrelated facts. Algebra in the new curriculum was to incorporate new topics like inequalities, emphasize unifying concepts like *set* and *function,* and be taught so that its structure and deductive character were apparent.

Despite the reforms of the new-math movement, the great educational rewards that were expected never came about. Enrolment in upper division, college mathematics courses decreased by more than 32% in the first half of the 1970s, while there was an 11% increase in the number of full-time equivalent students in four-year institutions (Fey, Albers, & Jewett, 1976). Enrolment in introductory mathematics courses on most campuses fell behind the enrolment gains registered by colleges overall. And many of the students who *were* taking mathematics were still reported to be poorly prepared. High school students' SAT scores were dropping. The public image of mathematics was down. The result was a back-to-basics backlash.

The mathematical skills that were considered important during the back-to-basics movement can been seen from the several studies of the mathematical needs of different sectors of society that were carried out in the 70s. For example, 100 employers from a variety of industries, responding to a questionnaire asking them to rate the importance of several mathematical competencies, regarded as essential the following activities: computing with whole numbers and decimals, adding and subtracting money amounts and fractions, calculating mentally, using tables, measuring length and weight, and using SI units (McIntosh, 1976).

Although most of the references to set theory and structure that were prevalent in school mathematics during the new-math movement of the 60s and early 70s were no longer seen in the textbooks of the decade following, there was no systematic emphasis on practical, real-life situations entirely in evidence either. Despite the stress on developing computational skills and attempts at integrating problem-solving activity, much of the mathematics taught in schools in this decade reflects, even if only vaguely, some of the traditional values of the mathematics education community, for example, the learning of generalizable problem-solving procedures and algorithms. However, Popkewitz (1988) has pointed out that there are other factors that enter into the formation of the mathematics curriculum that have more to do with the social history and imperatives of schooling than with the patterns of work, dispositions, and knowledge found in the scholarly community of mathematics. Yet even Popkewitz has to admit that mathematics and mathematics in schools "in creating anonymous and abstract relations is part of a modern social consciousness that has been called 'the homeless mind'" (p. 235).

The result is that much of school mathematics makes little serious contact with the real world. Consequently, the popular view of mathematics is a mixture of mystery, dislike, and even fear. Many people's relationship to mathematics is governed by what happened to them in school—usually a negative experience that begins quite early. The spontaneous learning of children, before they go to school, often gets repressed as soon as written symbolism is used to represent the operations they could normally carry out orally (Carraher, 1988). The mathematics that is learned in school becomes decontextualized from the real world. Learning school mathematics becomes, for most children, the learning of a set of rituals required to manipulate meaningless symbols. Those who succeed are usually those who manage to memorize the rituals.

In the past few years, school mathematics has evolved into a state where it now satisfies neither the needs of society nor does it correspond with the mathematical activity and goals of the community of mathematicians.

The Mathematics of Society

A comprehensive perspective on the mathematical needs of society is provided by a recent report written by a Canadian mathematics educator (Hope, 1986). After reviewing several research studies dealing with the mathematical demands of everyday life, as well as a variety of curriculum guides, Hope identified a set of quantitative tasks which, regardless of future advances in technology, he considered that all members of society should be able to perform:

(a) carry out the mathematical routines necessary for wise consuming—reading prices, calculating costs, handling money, . . . writing cheques; (b) carry out the mathematical routines necessary in homemaking—measuring, reading and following recipes, . . . planning renovations and repairs; (c) function in most non-technical work settings—handling instruments and reading their settings, reading and completing forms, . . . reading and following directions; (d) read and interpret quantitative information found in newspapers, popular magazines, government, political and business publications and to evaluate arguments based on such information—working with graphs, charts, and tables, . . . understanding the fundamentals of surveys and polls; (e) know sufficient mathematics to use and work with commonly seen technological devices—driving a car, working with tools, calculators, and simple appliances, running simple computer software programs; (f) participate and enjoy leisure activities, games, and sports—using scoring schemes, understanding simple statistics; (g) adapt to new mathematical demands as needed—learning new employment skills, using instruction and training manuals. (Hope, 1986, pp. 49-50)

Hope then determined five categories of mathematical understandings and competencies that he considered essential for handling the above real-world tasks:

1. Knowing how to use mathematics to solve problems;

2. Knowing how to perform calculations;

3. Knowing how to measure;

4. Knowing how to work with space and shape;

5. Knowing how to analyze and interpret quantitative data and arguments based on this information (p. 50).

However, it is important to note that the above characteristics of mathematically literate behaviour are viewed by Hope as being only part of the goals of mathematics education. He does not exclude from the K-12 mathematics curriculum some of the more traditional content areas, although his report does not specify what these might be. More importantly, he does cite evidence to support the notion that schools have not, to date, been able to succeed in developing these basic mathematical competencies and understandings in our students. (See also Stage, 1988.)

In-School Versus Out-of-School Mathematics

Research evidence has shown that, because much of the mathematics that is taught in schools is disembedded from the real world, many students are unsuccessful in their attempts to make sense of in-school mathematics. In contrast, several studies have documented that, in out-of-school situations, people can be quite skilled in their use of mathematics. Lave, Murtaugh, and de la Rocha (1984) compared shoppers' arithmetic in the supermarket with their performance on a paper-and-pencil arithmetic test covering integer, decimal, and fraction arithmetic, and using addition, subtraction, multiplication, and division operations. The twenty-five shoppers varied in the amount of their schooling and in the time since their schooling was completed. Twenty-two were female, and all were native speakers of English whose schooling took place in United States' public schools. Their scores averaged 59% on the arithmetic test, compared with 98%—virtually error free—in the supermarket, in spite of the fact that a number of the problems on the test were constructed to have exactly the same arithmetic properties as the problems grocery shoppers solved successfully in the supermarket.

Arithmetic problem solving in test and grocery shopping situations appears quite different. According to Lave et al., the supermarket study demonstrated that calculating occurred in several stages or "rounds". A process of gap-closing took place—gap-closing between the expected shape of the solution and the information and calculation devices available. In real-life problem solving, Lave et al. claim that a situation becomes a problem in the course of activity in a particular setting; people and settings simultaneously create problems and solution shapes. Even though there are frequent errors in early rounds of supermarket calculation, the researchers point out that the end product tends to be accurate because the juxtaposition of problem, solution, and checking makes powerful monitoring possible. Furthermore, since the process of problem generation is under the control of the problem solver, the solution shape is generated at the same time; the problem solver may exercise options other than calculation. This is in contrast with school mathematics tests in which the problem solver has little control over problem generation and solution; both are constrained according to a structured sequence and the problem solver has little to say about the terms.

Lampert (1988) has argued that an additional factor helps to explain the differences between supermarket and school results:

> In the grocery store, the shoppers had more courage to use their mathematical intuitions, *to make conjectures about what sort of mathematical tools might be appropriate*, than they did in the more school-like interview setting. In school, or in relation to an interviewer, we are accustomed to believing that the person who sets the problem knows the right answer. Thus, instead of feeling confident to test out our thinking in relation to the problem, and developing refined and reasonable conjectures, we work in apprehension of our intuitions being judged by someone in authority to be inappropriate. (p. 18)

Other studies that contrast the differences between in-school and out-of-school mathematics have been carried out by Carraher and her colleagues in Brazil. In one of their research investigations, Carraher, Carraher, and Schliemann (1985) compared the competence of working-class children in their everyday life of helping the family economy by selling fruits, vegetables, and refreshments in the streets with their competence in a school-like situation. Of the 63 problems presented to the children in the streets, 98% were correctly solved. A week later they presented the children with problems using the same numbers and operations but in a school-like manner. Two types of school-like exercises were presented: word problems and computation exercises. The children were correct 73% of the time in the word problems and 37% of the time in the computation exercises. In school-like situations, particularly in computation exercises, children appear to believe that written mathematics is called for and try to use it, even though they are less able with written than with oral mathematics. In out-of-school situations, children use oral mathematics, which is a usual form of computation in street markets. Children's computation strategies in the oral mode contradicted their apparent lack of ability when they worked in the written mode. Similar results were found with adults (Carraher, 1985).

Carraher (1988) points out that although street mathematics and school mathematics are based upon the same mathematical properties, there are differences in the ways subjects represent numbers and solve problems across situations. In oral mathematics, the relative meaning of the symbols is preserved, while in written algorithms this relative meaning is set aside. For example, in oral mathematics, calculation tends to run from hundreds to tens to units, while in written mathematics calculation tends to go from units to tens to hundreds, with the exception of the division algorithm. These differences can be understood, according to Carraher, as reflecting different processes for generating solutions to problems; while oral mathematics generates computation strategies on the basis of semantic relations, written mathematics generates solutions on the basis of rules for exchanging values from one column to another. These rules are in a sense similar to syntactic rules (like word order), but they are in some sense also different from syntax because they work in ways that are detrimental to meaning.

We have seen in this section that problem-solving activity outside of school seems to be based on processes that are different from those used in much of the problem-solving activity in school. We shall look next at some of the parallels between problem solving out of school and the kinds of activity practised by the community of mathematicians.

The Mathematics of Mathematicians

Mathematics requires, at times, a "talent of drawing pictures, of juggling symbols, of picking the flow in an argument", and of using "guesswork, analogy, wishful thinking" (Gian-Carlos Rota in Davis & Hersh, 1981, p. xviii). It is also the construction of models, hypothesis testing, proving, and the use of formal language as both a thinking and recording tool. What mathematicians actually do seems far removed from the mathematics that is taught in schools. According to Powell, a professor of mathematics at Rutgers University, mathematics should be viewed as "a way of thinking" that is in continual flux. He points out, however, that

> most teachers view it as a static subject, a set of rules that divides answers strictly into right and wrong. But real mathematics should challenge students to predict outcomes, look at alternatives and propose theories— all of which require discussion and involve ambiguities. (Staff, 1988, p. 3)

Lampert (1988) has suggested that what mathematicians know and the mathematics they have done over centuries is much more like the everyday thought and knowledge-in-action of Lave et al's (1984) grocery shoppers than popular notions would have us believe. She has emphasized that mathematicians act much like grocery shoppers, inventing their problems and their methods, and being invented by them as they pursue their goals.

In grocery shopping

> goals are not exogenous to the constitution of problems [and so] a problem
> is not structured as an end in itself or by a goal set elsewhere and presented
> to problem solvers by problem givers. A problem is a dilemma with which
> the problem solver is emotionally engaged. . . . Processes for resolving
> dilemmas are correspondingly derived of their assumed universalistic,
> normative, decontextualized nature. (Lave, 1988, p. 175)

Whereas, in schools,

> algorithmic problem solving is assumed to be the ideal model for the
> cognitive procedures employed to solve questions of fact in the service of
> goals exogenous to the process under study. (Lave, 1988, p. 174)

It is rather ironic that, over the past century, there has been the tension
between mathematicians and society over what is important in school
mathematics, considering that the actual practice in schools—even when
the mathematician had some influence—was quite unlike the practice
of mathematics in the professional community of mathematicians. As
well, school mathematics was also far removed from the activity and
needs of society in general—even when society had some influence.

Linking the Mathematician and Society

One of the particularly groundbreaking features of the *Curriculum and
Evaluation Standards for School Mathematics* (NCTM, 1989) is the
implicit attempt to bridge the mathematical goals of society with the
constructive, problem- and method-inventing activity of mathematicians. Even though this is not stated as an explicit goal, both the
composition of the working group and the vision that they have proposed
suggest that the *Standards* can be viewed as a means of incorporating
what mathematicians do with *what society, in general, does* with respect
to mathematics. School mathematics is being focused on the similarities
in everyday thought and knowledge-in-action between mathematicians
and, say, grocery shoppers. Some excerpts from the *Standards* may
illustrate this point:

> Students should be exposed to numerous and varied interrelated experien-
> ces that encourage them to value the mathematical enterprise, to develop
> mathematical habits of mind, and to understand and appreciate the role of
> mathematics in human affairs; that they should be encouraged to explore,
> to guess, and even to make and correct errors so that they gain confidence

in their ability to solve complex problems; that they should read, write, and discuss mathematics; and that they should conjecture, test, and build arguments about a conjecture's validity. (p. 5)...

"Knowing" mathematics is "doing" mathematics. A person gathers, discovers, or creates knowledge in the course of some activity having a purpose. This active process is different from mastering concepts and procedures. (p. 7)

Toward this end, classrooms are seen as places where interesting problems are regularly explored using important mathematical ideas. Problem solving is, in fact, proposed as a vehicle for achieving the goals of the *Standards*. A genuine problem is defined as "a situation in which, for the individual or group concerned, one or more appropriate solutions have yet to be developed" (p. 10). "Some problems also should be open-ended with no right answer, and others need to be formulated" (p. 6).

Some of the difficulties inherent in presenting problem situations to pupils in a school context were discussed in an earlier section (e.g., Carraher, Carraher, & Schliemann, 1985; Lampert, 1988; Lave, Murtaugh, & de la Rocha, 1984). It was pointed out that when pupils have little control over problem generation and solution, they are often unable to be successful. Furthermore, when pupils believe that the person who sets the problem knows the right answer, they do not feel confident in testing out their own thinking in relation to the problem. Thus, the problem-solving goals as set forth in the *Standards* could be difficult ones for teachers to achieve.

I suggest that a particular use of the computer could help teachers meet some of these goals. Although the computer is recommended in the report for its ability to process large sets of information, very little use is proposed with respect to the development of problem-solving abilities. I believe that the computer has the potential of rendering explicit some of the similarities between the everyday quantitative problem-solving activity of society and the pursuits of the community of mathematicians. Furthermore, the particular usage I am proposing is not fraught with the same kinds of learning difficulties that are inherent in the more traditional problem-presentation approaches described above.

One of the principal characteristics of a computer is its programmability. At a certain level, programming is the task of a professional. Why then talk of programming by the non-initiated, let alone by school children?

In many schools today, the phrase "computer-aided instruction" means making the computer teach the child. One might say the *computer is being used to program* the child. In my vision, *the child programs the computer* and, in doing so, both acquires a sense of mastery over a piece of the most modern and powerful technology and establishes an intimate contact with some of the deepest ideas from science, from mathematics, and from the art of intellectual model building. (Papert, 1980a, p. 5)

Programming is within the reach of elementary school age children and constitutes an activity that is rich in educationally unique possibilities:

1. To program is to model—a complex action must be described by a language in such a way that a new representation of the situation will result;

2. To program is to represent a sequence of actions and to predict the result;

3. To program is to compare what was predicted with what results, and to adapt and correct the model created against the reality that results;

4. To program is to use a mathematical formalism—but not the kind of formalism that represents the structure of a situation, rather the kind of formalism that describes the underlying process, that is, how an action is to be carried out by the machine;

5. To program is to generate one's own problem and the form that the solution will take in an environment requiring formal representation.

In order for programming to have these qualities and be accessible even to the young, it is necessary that the language used have certain characteristics.

Logo is a programming language that is a simplified version of LISP, a language used in applications of artificial intelligence. To this simplified version of LISP, the creators of Logo (Feurzeig, Papert, Bloom, Grant, & Soloman, 1969) added a computer-controlled "turtle"—a kind of robotic creature that moves along the floor, leaving a trace of its path. For practical reasons, the turtle became integrated with the screen in the form of a small, oriented triangle. The commands that direct the turtle are extremely simple: It suffices to command the turtle to go forward a certain number of steps, or to turn a certain number of degrees. The strength of Logo is derived from the power of LISP and the simplicity of the commands that direct the turtle.

Logo was designed by Papert and his colleagues initially as a means of understanding how children learn. The simple commands allow young children to manipulate the turtle. Furthermore, since Logo permits the user to define new commands, it was possible for Papert and his team of researchers to follow the evolution of certain kinds of knowledge among children. It was found that Logo supports a particular kind of learning that is the stuff of mathematicians (Papert, Watt, diSessa, & Weir, 1979). According to Papert, Logo puts "children in a better position to *do* mathematics rather than merely to learn *about it* "(Papert, 1980b, p. 177). In other words, in using Logo we are "teaching children to be mathematicians" rather than "teaching about mathematics".

The ability to describe processes plays a fundamental role in mathematical learning and the development of intelligence. The activity of describing to someone else how to construct, for example, a certain figure carries with it the possibility of discerning whether our description has been understood by another. The turtle is this "other" to whom we propose a certain description of a process and ask that it be executed according to our description. If, based on our description, the turtle does not draw what we had intended, then the description is insufficient. The turtle is thus the mirror of what we are capable of doing and of thinking.

The description that we give the turtle is a kind of *construction hypothesis*. The computer, through the intermediary of the turtle, allows us to verify this hypothesis. If the hypothesis is incomplete or false, we can see it immediately; the "error" made by the turtle becomes a new problem that must be solved. Thus, to program the turtle consists of presenting and verifying hypotheses. Children are thereby engaged in a process of knowledge acquisition that is familiar to the scientific and research community for whom knowledge becomes elaborated by confronting hypotheses with experimentation.

There have been a number of longitudinal studies (e.g., Hoyles, Sutherland, & Evans, 1985; Noss, 1985; Papert et al., 1979) that have shown the opportunities afforded by Logo for using mathematics in a context that allows the subject to both pose problems and decide on the shape of the solution in a reasonably natural way. These studies have described how both children and adults engaged in various Logo environments switch between exploratory and problem-solving activities; they have also illustrated how Logo provides a rich environment for pupil-posed problems, as well as a wide range of contexts for spontaneous experimental activity and collaboration.

In summary, it has been suggested that programming in the Logo computer language is analogous to the constructive, problem- and method-generating activity of mathematicians. Because a Logo environment permits pupils to generate their own problems and forms of solution, it involves learners in a mathematical activity that has the characteristics of both "grocery shopping" and higher mathematics. In this way, it can be seen as a bridge between the activities of non-mathematicians and mathematicians. Furthermore, the processes of hypothesis generation and verification that are required by Logo programming are among the life skills which, according to the *Standards*, must be developed in all of our mathematics students.

Conclusion

The history of mathematics education bears witness to the existence in the past of two different perspectives on mathematical literacy—even if the term mathematical literacy was never used. On the one hand, there was the mathematics that was perceived by society to be useful and necessary for functioning on a day-to-day basis in the home, and inside and outside the workplace. On the other hand, there was the mathematics that was engaged in by the community of mathematicians. The school mathematics programme has, unfortunately, been the battleground where the tug-of-war between these two perspectives has been played out. The current situation in our schools is one in which the students are not mathematically literate according to either perspective.

The publication by the National Council of Teachers of Mathematics of the *Standards* offers the promise of changing this situation. For the first time in history, we have a vision of mathematical literacy that does not pit one perspective against the other. The *Standards* explicitly proposes one view of mathematical literacy for all:

> In developing the standards, we considered the content appropriate for *all* students . . . what we believe all students will need if they are to be productive citizens in the twenty-first century. If all students do not have the opportunity to learn this mathematics, we face the danger of creating an intellectual elite and a polarized society. The image of a society in

which a few have the mathematical knowledge needed for the control of economic and scientific development is not consistent either with the values of a just democratic system or with its economic needs. (NCTM, 1989, p. 8)

In its explicit description of a certain quality of mathematical literacy for all, the *Standards* implicitly merged the two historical perspectives that have raged in the history of mathematics education. In line with the vision espoused by the *Standards,* it was argued in this chapter that the use of the computer in selected programming environments could serve as another vehicle for empowering school mathematics to make closer contact with the quantitative activity of both society and the community of mathematicians. The kind of computer-based, problem-solving activity that has been described allows learners to explore, to conjecture, to reason logically, to generate their own problems, to decide on the form of the solution, and to feel confident to test their own thinking—features normally absent in problem-solving practice in schools—and thereby makes accessible to students a mathematical power that is at the core of mathematical literacy.

References

Carraher, T. N. (1985). The decimal system. Understanding and notation. In L. Streefland (Ed.), *Proceedings of the Ninth International Conference for the Psychology of Mathematics Education* (Vol. I, pp. 288-303). Utrecht, The Netherlands: University of Utrecht, Research Group on Mathematics Education and Educational Computer Centre.

Carraher, T. N. (1988). Street mathematics and school mathematics. In A. Borbas (Ed.), *Proceedings of the Twelfth International Conference for the Psychology of Mathematics Education* (Vol. I, pp. 1-23). Veszprem, Hungary: OOK.

Carraher, T. N., Carraher, D. W., & Schliemann, A. D. (1985). Mathematics in the street and in schools. *British Journal of Developmental Psychology*, *3*, 21-29.

Davis, P., & Hersh, R. (1981). *The mathematical experience* (Introduction by Gian-Carlos Rota). Boston: Houghton Mifflin.

Feurzeig, W., Papert, S., Bloom, M. Grant, R., & Solomon, C. (1969). *Programming languages as a conceptual framework for teaching mathematics* (Report 1889). Cambridge, MA: Bolt, Beranek and Newman.

Fey, J. T., Albers, D. J., & Jewett, J. (1976). Undergraduate mathematical sciences in universities, four-year colleges, and two-year colleges, 1975-76. In *Report of the Conference Board of the Mathematical Sciences Survey Committee* (Vol. V). Washington, DC: Conference Board of the Mathematical Sciences.

Hope, J. A. (1986). Numeracy. Saskatoon, Canada: University of Saskatchewan, Department of Curriculum Studies.

Hoyles, C., Sutherland, R., & Evans, J. (1985). *The Logo Maths Project: A preliminary investigation of the pupil-centred approach to the learning of Logo in the secondary mathematics classroom, 1983-4.* London: University of London, Institute of Education.

Lampert, M. (1988, March). *Cognition in mathematical practice: A response to Jean Lave.* Invited address presented at the annual meeting of the American Educational Research Association, New Orleans, LA.

Lave, J. (1988). *Cognition in practice.* New York: Cambridge University Press.

Lave, J., Murtaugh, M., & de la Rocha, O. (1984). The dialectic of arithmetic in grocery shopping. In B. Rogoff & J. Lave (Eds.), *Everyday cognition: Its development in social context* (pp. 67-94). Cambridge, MA: Harvard University Press.

McIntosh, A. T. (1976). *Mathematical requirements of employers of lower ability school leavers.* Leicestershire, England: Leicestershire Education Department.

National Commission on Excellence in Education. (1983). *A nation at risk: The imperative for educational reform.* Washington, DC: U.S. Government Printing Office.

National Council of Teachers of Mathematics. (1989). *Curriculum and evaluation standards for school mathematics.* Reston, VA: NCTM.

Noss, R. (1985). *Creating a mathematical environment through programming: A study of young children learning Logo* (Doctoral dissertation, Chelsea College, University of London). London: University of London, Institute of Education.

Papert, S. (1980a). *Mindstorms: Children,* computers, and powerful ideas. New York: Basic Books.

Papert, S. (1980b). Teaching children to be mathematicians vs. teaching about mathematics. In R. P. Taylor (Ed.), *The computer in the school: Tutor, tool, tutee* (pp. 177-196). New York: Columbia University, Teachers College Press.

Papert, S., Watt, D., diSessa, A., & Weir, S. (1979). *Final report of the Brookline Logo* Project, Part 2. Cambridge, MA: Massachusetts Institute of Technology.

Popkewitz, T. S. (1988). Instructional issues in the study of school mathematics: Curriculum research. *Educational Studies in Mathematics, 19,* 221-249.

Staff. (1988, October). Myth #8: Reading is more important than math. *The Literacy Beat, 2*(8), 1-6.

Stage, E. (1988). *Can we stand and deliver?*—Mathematical literacy in the workplace. Washington, DC: Education Writers Association.

9

Scientific/Technological Literacy, Critical Reasoning, and Classroom Practice

Glen S. Aikenhead
University of Saskatchewan

"Scientific/technological literacy" is a slogan found in numerous education documents. Presumably, the phrase is intended to guide curriculum development and classroom practice, but slogans rarely do (Roberts, 1983). In an attempt to render the phrase useful to educators, this chapter postulates a coherence between current theoretical perspectives on literacy and specific practices in a science classroom.

The chapter explores scientific/technological literacy by first giving an historical overview of the emergence of an attentive public in North American society, and second by relating this emergence to the perspectives on literacy provided in other chapters of this volume. Implications for science education are then defined in terms of critical reasoning formulated in the notion of "a critical thinking disposition". The chapter ends with an illustrative account of classroom instruction that explicitly teaches critical reasoning and scientific/technological literacy.

An Historical Overview: A Social Context for Scientific/Technological Literacy

Recent scientific and technological development has had a profound influence on Canadian citizens. Research and development during and since World War II, for instance, aviation, communications, and nuclear power, has accelerated so quickly that our social values have scrambled to catch up. The norms of small-town postwar Canada contrast sharply with those of the global village of today. Largely because of the war effort, small science (low budget research projects) quickly evolved into big science (high budget, highly staffed research projects) in the large industrial nations (Price, 1963). The advent of big science required large capital funding, and created new partnerships among scientists in government labs, industry, and the universities (Krimsky, 1980). Moreover, the public's war time patriotic trust sustained a confidence in the emerging big science of postwar Canada. The minority who challenged this trust were dismissed as anti-democratic.

The United States' public confidence was temporarily challenged in 1957 by Sputnik I. But as a result of substantial investments in science and engineering, Apollo 11 landed on the moon. The Apollo program engendered public confidence in the program's massive technological fix. Meanwhile, patriotic confidence in science was being superseded by an economic-political confidence. At the same time, however, the 1960s brought advances in science and technology that had their share of negative impacts, and, in the case of big science the negative impact was much greater. Along with this bigger negative impact came the increased need for a more critical analysis by an informed public—a citizenry literate in science and technology.

The postwar exponential development of science and technology meant economic and political power for industrial nations. By 1960, however, this power seemed to have reached a sensitive limit. In the popular press, there was the chemical industry's DDT episode (Carson, 1962). Then, during the late 1960s and early 1970s, the growth of the emerging nuclear energy industry came under scrutiny by a minority of citizens (Bubb & Derion, 1978). Those who questioned the almost autonomous advancement of science and technology no longer carried an anti-democratic stigma. Instead, they became known as the attentive public. To them, unchecked exponential growth had become unacceptable. Pollution, unprecedented nuclear power development, and population growth rates ceased to be the metaphors of progress, and became instead the manifestations of our planet's natural limits.

An alternative to unchecked growth, harmony with nature, evolved from a poetic metaphor into the preferred economic reality. North American society was becoming increasingly conscious of the stewardship of the earth. Fringe elements went as far as idyllically returning to their "natural" roots of agrarian life. Most of the attentive public, however, contributed to government agency reports and engaged in public inquiries, community action programs, citizens' advisory boards, or personal discussions with friends and colleagues. For the most part, the attentive public was not anti-science/technology. Rather, they represented an authentic desire to nourish the quality of life. The priority of their values differed from the priority of values held by industrial and political leaders who, through their desire to ensure a quality of life, valued economic growth more highly.

The attentive public asked for proactive involvement in science/technology policy decisions, not just reactive involvement in setting regulatory standards. However, except for some isolated cases in the 1970s, the attentive public did not have, and still does not have, a strong political voice in North America. It is often perceived as a counter-elite in the economic-social infrastructure of our society (LaPorte, 1983). Its limited political and economic power is commensurate with its limited experience or savvy in dealing with the economic-social elite of North America.

In spite of its limited power, the attentive public's concern for the quality of life catalyzed the phenomenon of social impact assessment (SIA). By modelling government and industry's technocratic approach to policy making, the attentive public expected, via SIA, to increase its political potency. The number of Canadian social impact assessment studies increased dramatically from about 25 in the mid-seventies to over 3,000 in the late seventies (D'Amore, 1981, p. 366). This rise in the number of SIA studies documents in part the effect that an informed public, literate in science/technology, can have on its own destiny.

Scientific/Technological Literacy

The above synopsis of the social context for science and technology in postwar North America illustrates a goal of literacy described by Lloyd Brown (this volume) as the Bizzell radical view; that is, scientific/technological literacy empowers a group to gain control over its own destinies in dealing with the scientific and technological aspects of society. Literacy, as radical critical consciousness, leads to personal or social action (de Castell, this volume). Greenpeace is a prime example. Empowerment is thus one possible element of an attentive public's scientific/technological literacy.

A slightly modified element of literacy concerns the ability of individuals and groups to take control of their own lives in autonomous and responsible ways (Fleming, this volume). In this view, critical consciousness is tempered with *reasoned or justified* beliefs and actions, a notion that gives a fundamental place to critical reasoning (Norris, 1989). Empowerment from this viewpoint is the capability to construct reasoned justifications for one's beliefs and actions. Accordingly, membership in an attentive public does not require radical action, but a critical consciousness sustained by reasoned justifications. Empowerment gained through scientific/technological literacy, therefore, would allow one to handle challenges to one's beliefs brought about by science and technology.

There are three complementary and overlapping ways in which scientific/technological literacy leads to empowerment. When individuals are scientifically/technologically literate: (a) they explore, understand, and in some cases control their fate in a society increasingly shaped by science and technology; (b) they read science/technology text by integrating their relevant background knowledge with science and technology content in order to construct interpretations that more completely and more consistently explain the meaning of the text than alternative interpretations (Phillips, 1988); and (c) they possess the background knowledge and understanding of science and technology (the scientific cultural literacy) that permits them to interpret correctly the specific policies, practices, and activities of scientists and technologists (Blair, this volume).

Feeling at home in one's own culture is one educational aim. In a society increasingly shaped by science and technology, ignorance or fear of science and technology can enslave a citizen into a 20th century serfdom. "Techno-peasants" (Prewitt, 1983) are such people, bewildered or intimidated by the new techniques and languages of science and technology. Techno-peasants are outsiders in their own society because they are cut off (a) from exploring, understanding, and controlling their own fate with respect to science and technology; (b) from analyzing science/technology text information; and (c) from correctly interpreting policies, practices, and activities in which scientists and engineers engage. Therefore, techno-peasants are illiterate as judged by the three aforementioned characteristics of scientifically/technologically literate individuals.

In contrast to techno-peasants, scientifically and technologically literate citizens act upon a shrewd understanding of how the system works (Prewitt, 1983):

> The scientifically savvy citizen . . . is a person who understands how science and technology impinge upon public life. Although this understanding would be enriched by substantive knowledge of science, it is not coterminous with it. (p. 56)

Such citizens understand the social context of science and technology. They recognize that scientific/technological research is immersed in moral reasoning and political dynamics: research often competes for funding with other social activities; researchers' social goals are sometimes linked to corporate profits, political prestige, or to military strength; and the implications of research results often affect social policy. Thus, scientifically and technologically literate citizens will be as conversant in ethics as they are in politics.

All decisions arise from both knowledge and values. Informed citizens will make their decisions thoughtfully by bringing their pertinent knowledge into focus with the values that guide their decisions (Aikenhead, 1985; Gosling & Musschenga, 1985). Accordingly, the informed citizen will seek the values inherent in a scientific decision (Gauld, 1982; Holton, 1978; Hull, 1988; Savon, 1988), including the values of public and private science, and the values impinging upon science from other social institutions. The literate citizen (a) will be sensitive to the narrowing gap between basic research and its commercial implementation; (b) will have a sufficient grasp of science and technology to appreciate the communication conventions of science and technology, their assumptions, their key concepts, their beliefs, their human character, and their limits; and (c) will appreciate the ways in which science and technology inform government policy nationally, as it relates to economic growth, and internationally, as it relates to a nation's bargaining access to its scientific and technological knowledge.

> Neither science nor technology was neutral in the context of international diplomacy—indeed, . . . conflicts over access to science and technology were becoming *the* central conflicts over economic growth and development strategy. (Dickson, 1984, p. 196)

A scientifically/technologically literate citizen will detect political motivation obscured by scientific and technological jargon, calculations, forecasting and policy development; will show an ability to influence the content of decision-making agendas and to influence the conditions of participation in social decisions related to science and technology; will develop an historical perspective that accounts for the evolving politics of science, such as the diminishing sovereignty of small science with the growth of big science, and the dramatic alteration in the social contract of pure science when it helps nations achieve economic, political, and military success.

In summary, the scientifically/technologically literate citizen values progress in science and technology, but is concerned with the problems of articulating and controlling the social goals of science and technology. He or she has a finely tuned "crap-detector" (Postman & Weingartner, 1969) that is street-wise to the social context of science and technology.

Scientific/Technological Literacy and Education

While empowerment is a consequence of scientific/technological literacy, a critical thinking disposition is a necessary co-requisite to scientific/technological literacy. A critical thinking disposition assumes an array of intellectual skills, conceptual knowledge, and especially a *predisposition* toward critical reasoning. To paraphrase Norris (1989), a person with a critical thinking disposition has a tendency to act in ways motivated and justified by educationally satisfactory reasons. Such a person does not depend on others to judge the adequacy of claims made. For instance, students with a critical thinking disposition in science/technology do not need to depend on their teacher to justify a statement in a science text. Such students work out the justification themselves. The concept of a critical thinking disposition is congruent with Scheffler's (1965) intellectual independence, recently recast for science education by Munby (1982). A person with such a disposition will independently decide whether a claim is warranted or not. To be intellectually independent is to assess, on one's own, the soundness of the justifications proposed for a knowledge claim. Intellectual independence is an explicit goal for science education.

In resonance with Blair's (this volume) view of cultural literacy, Norris' critical thinking disposition, and Phillips' notion that reading is constructing interpretations from text and background knowledge, Hurd's (1988) conception of literacy underscores the independent interpretative use of what is learned by students in science education:

> As a teaching goal science and technological literacy translates into the ability of a student to interpret science and technological achievements and deficiencies in terms of the human and social forces that generate and sustain them. (p. 4)

Hurd warrants his claim with the techno-peasant argument:

> Students who are illiterate concerning the interaction of science, technology, and society are doomed to live isolated from the culture that surrounds them but which they cannot fully experience. (p. 4)

The independent *interpretative* use of conceptual knowledge is vital to the domain of thoughtful decision making (Broudy, 1969; Science Council of Canada, 1984). Thoughtful decisions are (a) initiated by a predisposition to reason critically, (b) guided by an explicated set of values, (c) informed by pertinent scientific and technological knowledge, and (d) informed by the epistemological and social status of that knowledge (Aikenhead, 1985). The epistemological and social *status* of scientific and technological knowledge is far more significant to decision making than is the scientific and technological knowledge itself (Aikenhead, 1980; Prewitt, 1983). Thoughtful decisions are permeated by critical reasoning; thoughtful decision makers possess a critical thinking disposition; informed citizens participate in their culture by exercising a critical thinking disposition in concert with their scientific/technological literacy for the purpose of making thoughtful and wise decisions.

As an educational goal, scientific/technological literacy guides the conceptualization and development of classroom materials. When a critical thinking disposition becomes an essential ingredient to these classroom materials, the marriage of critical reasoning and scientific/technological literacy occurs. This marriage will be explicated by considering a specific example of classroom practice. The case of *Logical Reasoning in Science & Technology* (LoRST) is described below; first in terms of its general characteristics and content (for the purpose of familiarizing the reader with the material), then in terms of the marriage of critical reasoning with scientific/technological literacy. The reader will see in LoRST the explicit training for an informed citizenry.

Classroom Practice

Logical Reasoning in Science and Technology

Logical Reasoning in Science and Technology (Aikenhead, 1989) teaches scientific facts and principles along with critical reasoning to a target audience of grade ten students of average academic ability. An outline of the book is found in the Appendix. The science instruction takes place within the social context of drinking and driving, and within the technological context of the Borkenstein breathalyser. Students learn scientific facts and principles in a way that connects the facts and principles with the everyday world in Canadian society.

Specific critical reasoning skills are taught in The Logic Game unit and then applied throughout the book. This application of reasoning skills from an everyday familiar domain to a science/technology domain provides students the opportunity to learn to transfer their reasoning skills; a difficult but nevertheless possible achievement according to Blair (this volume). More important than the individual reasoning skills themselves, however, is the increase in students' *predisposition* to analyze, to question, and to articulate a reasoned argument.

Goals

LoRST's ultimate goal is to significantly improve the scientific and technological literacy of students, so they can explore, understand, and in some cases justifiably control their own fate in a society increasingly shaped by science and technology. Because literacy requires the empowerment to interact meaningfully with one's environment (textual, cultural, or otherwise), LoRST was designed to train students to develop a personal meaning (in the sense of Polanyi's personal knowledge) of their world related to science and technology. Within the perspective of the learning theory called "constructivism" (West & Pines, 1985), students are said to learn meaningfully when they construct their own meaning of an event. Thus, a constructivist learning theory (assumed in LoRST) is related to empowerment (the ultimate goal of LoRST).

Closely aligned with the goal of literacy is the goal of achieving a critical thinking disposition (or intellectual independence). LoRST encourages students to develop a critical thinking disposition by training them to construct their own logical arguments for events and to critically analyze the arguments of others, that is, to acquire "argument competence" (Blair, this volume). For example, authentic conflicts between scientific experts are studied in LoRST as a method of honing critical reasoning skills, and as a way of understanding the epistemology and sociology of science.

Features

Although LoRST does not "cover" as many science facts as science courses that are dedicated to covering an encyclopedia of correct answers and showing the structure of a particular science discipline, LoRST content is learned in greater depth and with greater critical thought. Students are expected to *construct* their knowledge for personal use in their everyday lives, rather than memorize isolated bits of information for tests and course credits. Constantly, students are asked: How do you know? What does it mean? How does it help you make sense out of such and such? How is science used socially? For whose purpose is science used? Consequently, science topics in LoRST tend to receive an in-depth treatment. Time is taken to assure that students apply ideas to the complex everyday world (e.g., analyzing newspaper articles); and achieve a firmer grasp of the topics, that is, engage in higher order thinking.

The intellectual skills and background knowledge needed for success in university science and engineering courses are developed systematically in LoRST. Mathematical problem solving skills are emphasized. But in addition, written and oral language skills are developed explicitly. The requirement to express oneself clearly and logically in prose lends a literacy rigor to LoRST not normally found in science courses.

The more difficult intellectual skills associated with LoRST (e.g., applying and interpreting scientific knowledge) tend to be demanding. Higher student motivation often compensates, however. The book was developed for average academic students and contains enrichment for academically talented students as well.

Young women are encouraged in LoRST to do well in science and math. The book offers a balance of socially traditional male and female contexts in which to learn and apply the book's content. In addition, the "jobs" columns found throughout LoRST describe career opportunities in science and technology in a way that encourage both men and women.

LoRST requires about 70 hours of instruction (70% to 80% of a school year). Student activities are integrated into the text. The activities range from traditional science labs, to analyzing the media, or making decisions on public policy related to science and technology. Many activities are structured so teachers easily can make choices, modifications, or substitutions to fit their class situation. The community, rather than the textbook alone, is a source of information for students.

The development of LoRST followed a multistage sequence which took advantage of the classroom realism well known to teachers and students. First, the author wrote and taught the first draft. Based on this classroom experience, the student manual was modified. Thus, the classroom materials evolved "in situ" with grade ten students; appropriate teaching strategies for a real classroom situation were identified; and the rough draft of the Teacher Guide was written. The second draft of LoRST was vetted in a field trial with volunteer teachers. Their classes were observed daily. In collaboration with students and teachers, appropriate teaching strategies were tested and the student materials modified. As a result, LoRST was polished into a third draft for extensive field testing in Saskatchewan.

The Socio-Technological Context

In LoRST, the social issue of drinking and driving creates the need to know the technology of the breathalyser, which in turn creates the need to know how science and technology interact with each other, and how they both interact with various aspects of society such as the law, moral reasoning, and public policy. In this realistic socio-technological context, students learn scientific content involving mixtures, concentration, chemical reactions, photometry, electrical circuits, and the biology of body cells and systems. Moreover, this scientific content is continually scrutinized by the critical reasoning skills developed early in and fostered throughout the book. The scientific content is explicitly related to the theme of drinking and driving, and to other social issues of current importance; for instance, the effects of smoking to one's health, and the effects of toxic chemicals on the environment. The skill at making thoughtful decisions (scientific, legal, moral, logical, and public policy) gradually develops with study and practice throughout the book.

The social issue of the hazards of drunk driving is critically relevant to grade ten students because many are just learning to drive. This social issue requires particularly realistic decisions by students, rather than the more idealistic, hypothetical decisions often associated with classroom exercises.

The general characteristics and content of LoRST described above create a context in which one may consider the marriage of critical reasoning with scientific/technological literacy. This marriage is discussed in the following section.

Reasoning, Scientific/Technological Literacy, and LoRST

LoRST enables a science teacher to focus on critical reasoning and scientific/technological literacy in an explicit and pervasive manner.

Reasoning

The first unit of LoRST, Science and the Law, motivates students into formulating arguments in a premises/conclusion format. Initial attempts at constructing arguments are later reworked when new ideas about logical reasoning are introduced; for example, when students are taught the criteria for making different types of decisions—legal, scientific, and moral. The seeds of the ability to detect invalid arguments are planted by examining controversial results from scientific research, and by comparing the epidemiological and etiological strategies used to obtain those results.

The Logic Game unit challenges students to scrutinize statements. Basic assumptions are explicated and the relationships between arguments/assumptions and decisions/values are introduced. These ideas are continually developed in various science and social contexts throughout LoRST. Students learn to treat basic assumptions and values as normal constituents of knowledge claims and thoughtful decisions. Students also develop the habit of looking for underlying assumptions.

The Logic Game, as the title suggests, treats logic in terms of a set of rules: conditions of truth for premises, symbolic logic, and truth functional analysis. Most tenth grade students are pleasantly surprised at their excellent achievement with these basic rules for reasoning. *Soundness* of arguments is a concept students incorporate easily into their lexicon. Building on initial student success, the more intriguing though more challenging fallacious arguments are introduced as typical *invalid* arguments. Six common fallacies were chosen based on their appearance in scientific discourse. The fallacy of false cause is given special attention as it represents the quagmire of scientific induction.

Because reasoning follows two different sets of "rules", inductive and deductive, the two are taught to students in the context of discussing the nature of proof. For example, how many ampoules of potassium dichromate in a shipment must be tested before a breathalyser technician concludes that the whole shipment is accurate? The problem itself not only illustrates induction, but it defines the need to understand statistics and measurement errors, topics which are taken up at appropriate places later in the text.

Every rule to The Logic Game is not only verbalized by students, it is applied to common everyday events. For instance, students are evaluated on their ability to articulate the fallacy which explains the humor in a cartoon. Marks are given not for picking the "right" fallacy (students interpret cartoons very differently), but for the *soundness* and *validity* of their argument that warrants their claim. Time and time again, the content of LoRST is turned upon itself. A teacher must be precisely logical in the wording of examination questions, otherwise the rules of logic are applied by students to pick apart an unacceptable test question.

Two weeks of The Logic Game raises many students' *predispositions* to analyze claims by searching for assumptions, by casting explanations in terms of premises/conclusion, and by recognizing a correctly used truth condition or a broken rule of logic. The occasional, highly enthusiastic student must be cautioned against using critical reasoning with teachers in other classes who are not prepared to allow for the intellectual independence that comes with knowing The Logic Game.

The book provides students with an explicit, simple rationale for studying logic: empowerment and intellectual independence. This justification appeals particularly to those students who see themselves as academic underdogs. "The more you learn to recognize good and poor logic, the more power you will have to make your own informed decisions" (Aikenhead, 1989, p. i).

Scientific/Technological Literacy

LoRST attempts to educate a student for the role of scientifically and technologically literate citizens. The book's content requires the reader to address the fact that science and technology exist in a social context. For example, the logic of scientific inferences is introduced in a situation of conflict over the safety of the pill (epidemiological studies). Classification of mixtures is communicated through the "technology" of salad dressings. Concentration problems are cast in the world of recipes, court cases, false liquor advertisements, and toxic chemicals. Electricity concepts are bound up with home appliances used by adolescents (hair blowers), and with household electrical consumption as a function of life style. Equilibrium is taught when students need to know details about how and why blood alcohol content varies with time, and how this relates to being over .08 on the breathalyser. Henry's Law is presented as the key premise—a key logical link—in the logic of the breathalyser. Henry's Law links a person's *blood* alcohol content with his or her *lung* alcohol content analyzed in the breathalyser. At the same time, in vitro and in vivo empirical data are compared in terms of evidence beyond reasonable doubt in court. Scientific assumptions about models are seen to have technical and legal implications. Statistical reasoning and measurement errors are studied when students analyze survey data they collect in the community. Risk analysis logically follows from discussions about predicting the relative effects of alcohol on men and women. Basic assumptions play a major role in risk analysis, as does the truth-condition rule. Neurological facts are explored through a study of the mechanical effect of alcohol on neurotransmitters, and the social consequences of Hoffman La Roche producing a "sobering up" pill.

Not only are scientific concepts introduced and applied in a social context, students are also required to reflect upon the interrelationships between science and other social institutions—technology, law, ethics, politics, and economics. Students draw diagrams that conceptualize legal and moral reasoning, and they sketch the possible contribution of science and technology to those legal and moral decisions.

Students are trained to be vigilant in detecting human consequences hidden in scientific decisions; human consequences such as prestige, credibility, and financial security. The values guiding scientific decisions are given explicit treatment, first in the introductory unit, and then each time an issue arises. For instance, the value of a "technological fix" is given special consideration in the context of how to keep drunk drivers from driving, and in former President Reagan's famous "star wars" speech. Students learn to conceptualize scientific activity in terms of *public* science (science reported in journals, conference proceedings, and textbooks) and *private* science (science done in labs and communicated in personal notebooks, letters, and conversations) by identifying the norms and counternorms associated with each (Holton, 1978). The political nature of Research and Development in Canada comes under scrutiny, as well as the narrowing gap between basic research (academic science) and its commercial exploitation (technological implementation). Students analyze such questions as: "Technology can design or produce marvellous things, but for whom? Who benefits?"

Traditional science and technology topics are studied in two units, The Breathalyser and How Alcohol Affects Your Body. These units familiarize students with many of the basic communication conventions, key concepts, and problem-solving skills that are needed to participate in a dialogue with scientists and technologists, or to interpret news items on TV or in newspapers (in other words, the decoding, comprehending, and interpreting skills of text literacy). For example, the technology of burning PCBs is learned while detecting fallacious arguments in statements uttered by a TV reporter and a company manager during a program critical of the company. The manipulation of scientific data and the explanation for why scientists fudge data become evident during the analysis of a research report on the rate at which blood alcohol concentration decreases in the body.

The human character of science is given explicit attention by treating scientific decisions as consensus making, and by delineating the implications of that viewpoint; for instance, the provisional status of knowledge thus produced. Students experience the social dynamics and subjectivity involved in constructing scientific knowledge. They reflect upon these experiences during classroom discussions that articulate the nature of consensus making in science. The discussions are followed by an analysis of subjectivity versus objectivity applied to a wide variety of areas, from mathematics to aesthetics.

The role that assumptions play in science is an epistemic essay topic for students when they explore why scientific assumptions need not be true in order to be useful, as illustrated by Dalton's assumptions about atoms. Dalton made three basic assumptions about atoms: (a) an atom is the smallest unit of matter; (b) the weight of one atom of an element is the same as the weight of any atom of the same element; and (c) the weight of an atom of one element is different from the weight of atoms of other elements. Based on these assumptions and on experimental evidence, Dalton used deductive and inductive reasoning to explain many chemical changes. Today, a scientist would recognize that all three of Dalton's assumptions are false. Nevertheless, Dalton got the whole field of chemistry started. Progress in science does not require the truth of assumptions.

Question: Dalton's assumptions were not true. What value are scientific assumptions then, if their truth doesn't mean all that much?

The epistemological status of laws, theories, and hypotheses are mentioned continually throughout LoRST. Knowing whether a scientific statement is meant to describe or explain tends to clarify the logical content of the scientific statement.

Technological literacy is explicated in LoRST by presenting a case study of Robert Borkenstein, the inventor of the Borkenstein breathalyser. The socio-technological dimensions to technological literacy are the subject of student essays; for example, essays are required on the introduction of the automobile, and on the artificial heart.

Conclusion

In several ways, LoRST encourages the empowerment of students by teaching them to participate in their society as informed citizens. The scientific and technological knowledge students acquire from LoRST is seldom the isolated, idealistic content commonly found in science textbooks. Isolated knowledge has little empowerment value. Knowing *how* to use the knowledge does have empowerment potential. In LoRST, students apply scientific and technological knowledge in concert with logical reasoning skills, to make their own meaning out of such social issues as drinking and driving. Students also exercise their literate dispositions and their scientific/technological literacy capabilities by exploring the logical, social, and human limits to scientific knowledge.

The marriage of scientific/technological literacy with critical reasoning can take place in the milieu of classroom practice. Scientific/technological literacy can be more than a slogan when conceptualized in terms of the empowerment perspective on literacy: (a) to explore, understand, and in some cases justifiably control one's own fate in a society increasingly shaped by science and technology; (b) to integrate science/technology text information and one's relevant background knowledge of science and technology, in order to construct interpretations that more completely and more consistently explain the meaning of a text than alternative interpretations; and (c) to interpret correctly the specific policies, practices, and activities engaged in by scientists and technologists. Scientific/technological literacy can guide the development of curriculum materials, as evidenced by *Logical Reasoning in Science and Technology*.

References

Aikenhead, G. S. (1980). *Science in social issues: Implications for teaching.* Ottawa: Science Council of Canada.

Aikenhead, G. S. (1985). Collective decision making in the social context of science. *Science Education, 69,* 453-475.

Aikenhead, G. S. (1989). *Logical reasoning in science & technology.* Rexdale, Ontario: Wiley.

Broudy, H. S. (1969). Science and human values. *The Science Teacher, 36*(3), 3-28.

Bubb, I.C., & Derion, J. C. (1978). *Light water: How the nuclear dream dissolved.* New York: Basic Books.

Carson, R. (1962). *Silent spring.* Greenwich, CN: Fawcett.

D'Amore, L. J. (1981). An overview of SIA. In F. Tester & W. Mykes (Eds.), *Social impact assessment: Theory, method and practice.* Calgary: Detselig Enterprises.

Dickson, D. (1984). *The new politics of science.* New York: Pantheon Books.

Gauld, C. (1982). The scientific attitude and science education: A critical reappraisal. *Science Education, 66,* 109-11.

Gosling, D., & Musschenga, B. (Eds.). (1985). *Science education and ethical values.* Geneva: WCC Publications.

Holton, G. (1978). *The scientific imagination.* Cambridge: Cambridge University Press.

Hull, D. L. (1988). *Science as a process.* Chicago: University of Chicago Press.

Hurd, P. (1988, February). *The emergence of a new synthesis for biology education.* Paper presented to the 3rd National Science, Technology and Society Conference, Arlington, VA.

Krimsky, S. (1980). Public participation in the formation of science and technology policy. In D. Wolfe, A. W. Branscomb, & B. M. Casper (Eds.), *Public policy decision making and* scientific literacy: Information needs for science and technology. (Report No. NSF-80-21-A6). Washington, D.C.: National Science Foundation.

LaPorte, T. (1983). Provisional model of technology and social change. (Political Science 188) Unpublished manuscript, University of California at Berkeley, Berkeley.

Munby, H. (1982). *What is scientific thinking?* Ottawa: Science Council of Canada.

Norris, S. P. (1989). Can we test validity for critical thinking? *Educational Researcher, 18*(9), 21-26.

Phillips, L. M. (1988). Evaluating and improving inference ability in reading comprehension. *Journal of College Reading and Learning, 21,* 137-150.

Postman, N., & Weingartner, C. (1969). *Teaching as a subversive activity.* New York: Delacorte Press.

Prewitt, K. (1983). Scientific illiteracy and democratic theory. *Daedalus, 96* (Spring), 49-64.

Price, D. (1963). Little science, big science. New York: Columbia University Press.

Roberts, D. A. (1983). Scientific literacy: Towards balance in setting goals for school science programs. Ottawa: Science Council of Canada.

Savon, B. (1988). *Science under siege: The myth of objectivity in scientific research.* Toronto: CBC Enterprises.

Scheffler, I. (1965). *Conditions of knowledge.* Chicago: Scott, Foresman.

Science Council of Canada. (1984). *Science for every student* (Report No. 36). Ottawa: Science Council of Canada.

West, L. H., & Pines, A. L. (Eds.). (1985). *Cognitive Structure and Conceptual Change.* Toronto: Academic Press.

Appendix

Outline of Logical Reasoning in Science & Technology

I. SCIENCE AND THE LAW

Drinking and driving tragedies

Court cases on impaired driving

Making decisions (legal, scientific, moral)

Scientific decision making

(These topics create the need to know more about logical reasoning, the breathalyser, science concepts, and decision making. The social construction of scientific knowledge is introduced in simulations of scientific consensus-making).

II. THE LOGIC GAME

Basic assumptions and values

Some rules of logic

Arguments in general

Deduction and induction

(Topics include: How do you know what is true? What are the rules for correct reasoning? What are common mistakes in logical reasoning? How do you apply all of this to real situations reported in the mass media?—e.g. conflicts between epidemiological and etiological studies.)

III. THE BREATHALYSER

Robert Borkenstein

Science, technology, research and development

Mixtures

Concentration

Body respiratory system

Henry's law

Mechanics of the breathalyser

Chemical changes

Photometry

Current electricity

(The sequence of these topics is defined in a natural way by the sequence of events in using the breathalyser. Quantitative problem solving dominates many of the sections. Hands-on activities involve students with the phenomena under study. The activities demand that students apply "The Logic Game". A significant amount of content is introduced in the student activities, rather than being presented in the text.)

IV. HOW ALCOHOL AFFECTS THE BODY

Digestive system

Liver

Circulatory system (Equilibrium)

Brain

Cells

Risk assessment

(Through "The Fantastic Voyage" metaphor, students follow ethanol molecules around a body as ethanol is absorbed, distributed and eliminated. Biochemistry is introduced on a need-to-know basis. Molecular changes are correlated with behaviour changes and breathalyser readings. Quantitative and logical analysis continues to be applied to most topics. Activities involve collecting and analyzing survey data, discussing media clips, and scrutinizing research data.)

V. DECISION MAKING

Types of decisions

Technological fixes

A decision-making guide

(Students work through simulations and case studies that require different types of decisions—scientific, legal, technological, moral, and public policy—and that require a rigorous application of the book's content. Thoughtful decision-making skills are emphasized.)

10

Literacy Theories Informing the Teaching of Reading: the Transition to Whole Language Instruction

Mona J. Beebe
Memorial University of Newfoundland

A major issue in teaching reading in the elementary schools is whether to use a skills approach or use a whole language or holistic approach. The skills approach has been firmly entrenched for years. However, beginning in the mid-sixties and mushrooming in the seventies the idea emerged that fractionating the reading process into a series of discrete skills interfered with the essential purpose of reading—the understanding of printed text. The skills approach to reading tends to treat the reading of print as an exercise in the identification of letters and words. The whole language approach, on the other hand, is based on the assumption that reading involves processing all the information available to readers as they attempt to construct meaning from printed material.

In the initial sections of this chapter, criticisms of the literacy theories of the 1960s and 70s will be used to highlight the presumed advantages of whole language theory. The final sections of this chapter will discuss several ways in which whole language theory is used to inform teaching practice in the elementary school, and point to a series of potential misconceptions about whole language instruction which could undermine its goals.

Background to the Skills Approach

The debate as to whether or not reading should be taught as a fractionated, compartmentalized, set of skills goes back more than one hundred years. The alphabetic method of teaching reading was used almost universally, not only in Greek and Roman times, but also in

Europe and the United States until well into the nineteenth century. In the ABC, or alphabetic method, the child learned first to name the letters. It was held, albeit erroneously, that when children had mastered the letters by name they had also mastered the sound and should, therefore, be able to read (Mathews, 1966, p. 23). After adequately learning the letter names, nonsense syllables such as 'ab', 'ib', and 'ob' were introduced. The beginning reader first spelled each syllable and then pronounced it, even though there was often little relationship between the letter names and the sound associated with the syllable. Children subsequently progressed to three letter nonsense syllables, one syllable words, two syllable words, and so on up to as many as five and six syllable words. Eventually, the child was allowed to read sentences but not without first naming the letters of each word.

Those children who learned to read did so by saying the words in sequence. In effect, the reader memorized the words, but the technique of naming the letters in the words only helped the reader to remember what the word looked like rather than to sound out the word. Naming the letters did not serve its ultimate purpose of helping children make the best of the religious selections in their readers!

During the early nineteenth century, exercises and rules for pronunciation and enunciation were included in the readers. Lists of words were provided according to the number of syllables the words contained and their similarity in sound. Noah Webster's Blue-Backed Spellers attempted to introduce the teaching of the sounds of letters as well as their names in order to aid children in their pronunciation. This set the stage for the latter half of the nineteenth century when fluency in oral reading was the focus of reading instruction.

Given this emphasis on oral fluency, a few teachers began to experiment with easier ways to teach reading. Samuel Worcester, for example, introduced the idea of the whole word method. He believed that it was not necessary for children to know the letters before they began to read. Rather, children could learn to read words by seeing them, hearing them pronounced, and by having their meanings illustrated. Only later, he argued, was it necessary for children to learn how to analyze the sounds and name the letters in the words (Smith, 1965, p. 86).

During the era when the emphasis on oral fluency reached its pinnacle (1840-1925), three important developments occurred which supported the principle that learning to read involved a carefully sequenced set of simple-to-complex skills. First, beginning about 1840, a graded school system was established. Accompanying the grade structure were graded readers. Thus, heightened attention was given to the progression of increasingly complex skills which had to be mastered at each grade prior to promotion to the next grade. Without a doubt, the most popular series was the *McGuffy Readers* which were widely used for the next forty years.

Second, as new basal readers appeared, the subject matter reflected a new emphasis in education—the importance of the acquisition of knowledge and of capturing and maintaining the child's interest. Patriotic selections virtually disappeared and moralistic stories dwindled as basal readers in the upper elementary grades expanded their scope to include informational selections on nature stories, healthful living, and biographies. Comprehension, then, became a major concern and by the end of the nineteenth century was seen as more important than the mechanical ability to read. It should be pointed out, however, that expressive oral reading was still very much "the order of the day".

The shift from oral to silent reading instruction represented the third major development in the way reading was perceived. The era from 1910 to 1925 marked the beginning of the scientific movement in education when psychological studies in reading clearly indicated the superiority of silent over oral reading. Reading now came to be seen as a psychological, thoughtful activity that depended on underlying skills and abilities. Proficiency in speed and comprehension were found to be largely responsible for reading ability, although the skills that were involved in both components remained unknown. There were, however, attempts to evaluate the proficiency of these unidentified subskills through the use of follow-up activities and questions after passages were read.

The new emphasis on the acquisition of comprehension skills was not based on scientific verification of what subskills constituted comprehending ability. Rather, it was based on the intuitive judgements of educational leaders. McKee (1934) lamented on the fact that research had not kept up with the demands of the school.

> Ideally the selection of methods and materials should be determined by findings of experimental research . . . The results of such research mature too slowly, however, and the school cannot wait. Consequently, most methods and materials must be chosen by sound educational experience and critical judgement. (p. 74)

What was required was research that identified the presumed components of comprehension and which, if possible, verified the new approaches to teaching reading adopted by the more progressive and innovative teachers on the basis of trial and error. Such research, however, had to wait until the early 1940s and the application of new multivariate techniques such as factor analysis to reading research.

Delineation of Comprehension Skills

By the 1940s the consensus was that reading is a complex process and that gaining meaning during reading was central to the activity. Statements like the following started to appear:

> Reading is not a simple, mechanical, mental process of recognizing words visually, but a very complex intellectual activity, which in and of itself provides for the development as well as the enrichment and refinement of ideas, and the operation of all the subtest types of reasoning, imagining, judging, evaluating, discriminating, problem-solving, thinking. Many educators go further than this. They assert that reading is one of the best means of broadening and enriching experiences. (Gates, 1937, p. 382)

Gates believed that it was important to determine precisely what skills were involved in the reading process. This meant delineating the underlying skills of comprehension. Teaching procedures could no longer be based upon and limited to the armchair analysis of reading, as was the case in the past.

Davis' (1942, 1944) research in the factor analytic tradition was extremely influential. It had a profound effect on the way teachers perceived the structure of reading comprehension. Davis first surveyed the literature to determine the skills involved in reading comprehension that were considered to be the most important by authorities in reading. He then designed the *Cooperate Reading Comprehension Tests* to measure each of these skills. The subsequent factor analysis of the data from a sample of 421 college students generated a nine-dimensional measurement model of reading comprehension by which the numerous test items in his comprehension test were largely explained. The dimensions were: word knowledge, reasoning, attention, purpose, context, literal sense, structure, literacy devices, and synthesis.

As a result of these analyses, Davis indicated that it was not sufficient to assign learning exercises in reading that consisted of only factual questions to be answered after reading a passage. Such narrowly conceived procedures would not call attention to, nor give sufficient practice in, the separate and essentially unrelated skills of reading implicit in the nine factors.

Finally, it seemed, research was "discovering" the basic psychological processes in reading that educators and psychologists had been unable to identify with certainty. The reasoning component together with the word knowledge component accounted for 89% of the variance in ability to comprehend. Such results simply could not be ignored by the authors and publishers of basal readers. If the ability to comprehend was to be developed, the basic skills had to be taught in an efficient and sequential manner.

During the 1940s, the number of teachers' manuals for a reading series increased, as did the number of pages each manual contained. The topics covered in the manuals, or Teachers' Guides as they were then called, broadened to include treatment of what should constitute a balanced program: word recognition, comprehension, evaluation, and enrichment activities. Perhaps the most important inclusion was the set of skills charts which gave a listing of the skills that were to be taught for each passage in the basal reader. Included in the teacher's manual were instructions for teaching the skills associated with specific pages in the basal. Publishers and authors of basal series had become more concerned with assisting teachers in the methods for developing reading efficiency.

Two reading series that developed during this time were particularly innovative. The *Learning to Read Program* prepared by Nila Banton Smith provided, for the first time, social studies and science content that was designed to accompany topics in these content fields. This, of course, was an attempt to extend the development of comprehension skills into other areas of the curriculum. A second set of readers, the *Ginn Basic Readers,* was produced by David H. Russell and several others in the late 1940s. The distinctive feature of their program was the vertical arrangement of the reading skills. This meant that specific skills were introduced across grade levels to ensure continuity. Thus, a child could learn to pick out the main idea and the supporting details in one grade level, but the concept would be reinforced at a higher grade level where the reader would be required to infer the main idea from the supporting details (Smith, 1965, pp. 280-287). In almost all series the skills were presented under headings such as vocabulary skills, selecting and evaluating skills, organizing skills, and appreciating skills.

The use of context clues and structural analysis appeared for the first time as techniques that needed to be taught as aids in figuring out the pronunciation of unrecognized words. The child was encouraged to utilize these techniques before resorting to "sounding out" (Smith, 1965, p. 290). This emphasis on meaning in reading even influenced word identification techniques.

These innovative skills-based programs enabled teachers to use procedures that were far more systematic than those used previously for teaching reading. Furthermore, they were based on seemingly irrefutable scientific findings. Their utility, therefore, was unquestioned and their widespread use was reinforced by the social forces of the post-war era.

Entrenching the Skills Approach in Basal Readers

Two major societal influences shaped reading instruction during the 1950s and 60s: expanding knowledge and technological change. A rapidly increasing knowledge base made it possible for technology to produce machines that replaced many unskilled jobs. Consequently, many workers found themselves jobless. Education came to be seen as a necessary prerequisite for holding jobs, for climbing the job ladder and for obtaining prestigious and well-paid employment. Proficiency in reading was considered to be the basic requirement for schooling achievement and, as a result, even greater emphasis was given to reading skills.

By 1960, Gray had established his hierarchy of reading comprehension skills. The skills ranged over three levels: (a) the literal level which concerns the basic question, "What does the passage say?" (b) the inferential level where the "reader seeks to secure a fuller more penetrating grasp of the message . . . [by] sensing the meanings implied but not stated by the author"; and (c) the interpretive level where the reader "focuses on the significance and implications of the author's ideas" by reflecting on what the author has said (pp. 13-17). Gray referred to these three levels of skills as the abilities to "read the lines, to read between the lines, and to read beyond the lines" (p. 17). Further, he urged vigorous emphasis on both the materials and the methods for teaching reading.

In 1968, Barrett constructed a taxonomic model of reading which defined and classified comprehension into five major abilities or levels. It was intended as a teaching tool, rather than a complete classification of comprehension skills and tasks. The five levels are: literal, reorganizational, inferential, evaluative, and appreciative. In the same year, Davis (1968) conducted a second factor analytic study on comprehension in order to overcome criticisms levelled against his 1944 study. This time he collapsed two skills into one (the attention and literal factors became "understanding content stated explicitly"). Davis states that the implications of his research for teaching were clear. He argued in favour of systematic and carefully planned learning experiences of appropriate grade level difficulty. In particular, he recommended three types of learning activities: (a) actively promoting vocabulary learning; (b) providing opportunities for drawing inferences from reading material; and (c) directing students' attention to the structure of passages and their literary features such as tone, mood, and purpose.

Teachers' manuals were increasing in number as more reading series were published. Skills emphases mounted in intensity through the 1960s. New series competed with earlier series for more complete coverage of the comprehension and word recognition skills—especially phonics, structural analysis, and whole-word identification. The suggestions in the manuals were clear and practical. They covered three areas: (a) teacher-directed activities; (b) independent work exercises; and (c) extended activities. In addition, some programs were now extending their basal series through the seventh and eighth grades, which meant that increased attention could be given to the development of study skills for the purpose of reading in the content areas. These skill programs were sequentially planned and the skills acquired at each grade were reinforced through practice at the next grade. Notwithstanding these developments, some children remained unresponsive to the skills emphasis and a new generation of researchers began to question the logic of the skills approach.

Criticisms of the Basal Reader
Skills Approach to Reading

The teaching of reading by a skills approach has a long history, culminating in extensive hierarchies of skills to be developed across the first six or eight years of schooling. During the 1970s and 1980s, reading researchers shifted emphasis and attempted to look at reading, not as a series of discrete sequential skills to be taught, but rather as a highly-complex, multi-faceted, and integrated process. Researchers are now concerned with understanding how children learn to read, rather than with specifying *a priori* what decoding and comprehension skills readers should be taught.

Because of this shift, basal readers have been criticized considerably. Newman (1985) draws attention to two weak assumptions inherent in traditional basal reading programs. First, these programs assume that the complex processes of reading have to be broken down into their most basic components. Second, they assume that if students are taught these skills sequentially, they will eventually become proficient readers. These assumptions are not necessarily true. For example, while some students become adept at correctly completing worksheets on particular skills, they may not be able to read a passage with satisfactory comprehension.

Such doubts about the effectiveness of basic skills approaches to the teaching of reading have given rise to new explorations of the reading process. The formal mathematical modelling of the factors or abilities of reading comprehension gave way in the late 1960s to new research based on the painstaking analyses of the errors or miscues that children make when they read. This psycholinguistic research was complemented by experimental research on concept development and schema acquisition by cognitive psychologists. A third research tradition has examined the relevance of the reader's awareness or perception of the strategies that are used when reading. This new and rapidly growing body of knowledge about how reading and other language processes work has already had profound effects on how reading and writing should be taught.

These new lines of research provoked critical analyses of the basic skills approach and the major vehicle of this approach—the basal reader series. The criticisms of theorists such as Doake (1985), Goodman (1986), Holdaway (1979), Huck (1977), Newman (1985), and others may be summarized as follows:

> 1. Basal readers place undue emphasis on isolated parts of language: letters, letter-sound relationships, words, sentence fragments, or sentences. This emphasis encourages readers to perceive reading as a word-naming activity instead of a meaning-making activity, in which sense is made of stories and expository passages.

2. Basal readers introduce arbitrary sequences of skills which too often lead to learning these skills as ends in themselves, rather than to learning *how* and *when* to use the skills in meaningful reading situations.

3. Basal readers often contain artificial-language passages, by controlling vocabulary, by building around specific phonic relationships or word-attack skills, and by using readability formulae to create selections written to a specific reading level.

4. Basal readers minimize the time spent on reading real stories by monopolizing the time with skill exercises. This is particularly true when workbooks are used extensively. In the report *Becoming a Nation of Readers* (Anderson, Hiebert, Scott, & Wilkinson, 1985), it is claimed that up to 70% of the time allocated for reading is spent in independent reading practice or seatwork. Most of that time is spent on workbook and skill sheets directly related to the basal program in use. Yet, classroom research shows that the amount of time devoted to worksheets is unrelated to year-to-year gains in reading proficiency (pp. 76-79); indeed, the amount of time spent on worksheets may be inversely related to reading gains.

5. Basal readers contain some children's literature selections which are often modified either by simplifying the vocabulary or by rewriting them to accommodate the development of particular skills. Similarly, overly short selections from children's literature are often included that lack the integrity and the unimpaired context of the original.

6. Basal readers represent a substantial financial commitment for school boards. Sometimes few funds are left over for the purchase of library books and other authentic reading material which children need in order to practice the skills they are taught.

Theories and Processes of Learning to Read Naturally

During the 1960s and 1970s, as the basal-reader approach became more and more unacceptable to many educators, researchers turned their interests from prescribing what skills ought to be taught to describing how children learn to read. They looked in two directions: (a) how language is learned and how this applies to learning to read; and (b) how some preschoolers have learned to read on their own. It was believed by researchers such as Yetta and Kenneth Goodman (1979) and Frank Smith (1973) that, since reading is a language process, it could be learned in much the same manner as children learn to speak and listen. Perhaps then, the search for understanding should begin by studying how children learn to speak at home. Could these natural learning conditions be applied to learning to read in the school?

One of the best ways to assess how the transition from speaking to reading occurs is to find out how early readers have learned to read prior to attending school. Generally, the research has examined (a) how children learn to interact with print in the real world, (b) what developmental patterns are involved in reading acquisition, and (c) what significant features of written language children notice. These matters are addressed in the following three sections.

Learning to Speak

Parents speak to their children from the day they are born. They act as models of the language to which the child is being introduced. The home setting provides a context which enables children to understand the meaning of words. The language heard is varied and vast. All kinds of sentence structures are used and no limits are placed on the vocabulary. Children generate and apply the rules of language through trying it out for themselves. They receive feedback as they expand, elaborate, and model the language. Preciseness in language usage comes later, since children are first and foremost trying to convey meaning—for wants, needs, and interests.

Pre-School Reading

The first studies done on early readers (Durkin, 1961; 1966; Plessas & Oakes, 1964; Torrey, 1969) described the children's characteristics and their home environments. Most of the children learned to read without instruction. The three common factors identified to explain this achievement were: (a) exposure to a wide variety of print material, especially children's books; (b) parents' reading to the children; and (c) opportunities for children to ask questions about reading and writing. Later research by Doake (1981), Forester (1977), Goodman (1980), and Holdaway (1979) led to the general agreement that children learned to read on their own in a manner that paralleled learning to speak. Oral language learning takes place in an environment where the child is immersed in language that is used purposefully. Readers who learned to read themselves also were found to be immersed in environments in which print and books were used with the child in imaginative and meaningful ways. In both learning to speak and to read, the environment was found to be emulative rather than instructive, and continuous reinforcement was given for closer and closer approximation by the child to accurate speech and reading-like behaviour.

Doake (1981, 1985) identified four stages that preschoolers go through in acquiring early literacy. First, they develop positive and powerful attitudes toward books because they are read to and they see the use of books within the home. Second, they gain control over the oral dimensions of written language. They do this by asking for favorite stories to be read and reread. Each time the story is reread, these children join in with the reading whenever possible and before long they can reproduce the story, first in their own words and later with considerable accuracy. During the third stage, children show an increasing awareness of the print and begin to match their voicing of the words in the story with the words on the page. The fourth stage occurs when children integrate their perceptions of words with their knowledge of the story. Now, rather than relying only on memory in order to "pretend" to read the words, the reader is actually reading the words and using background knowledge to reject or confirm the accuracy of the reading.

The Cognitive Basis for Reading Acquisition

The research described in the previous sections indicates that the influence of home socializing factors plays an important part in how and when children acquire reading ability (Durkin, 1966; Goodman, & Haussler, 1986). Underlying home environment factors, though, are cognitive considerations that allow children to acquire literacy.

Research in the 1960s and 1970s shifted from the skills approach, which focused on the teacher and the *teaching* of reading, to a language approach, which focused on the reader, the reader's language resources, and the *learning* of reading. The Goodmans in the late 1960s were among the first to point out that reading involved more than simply learning how to identify words and letters in a precise and sequential manner. Rather, they claimed that reading involved the processing of all information available to readers as they attempted to construct meaning from print. This information included: (a) the configuration of letters in a line of print, sentence, or paragraph; (b) the syntactic, or grammatical cues inherent in that line, sentence, or paragraph; (c) the semantic, or meaning cues associated with the reading material; and (d) the interrelationship among (a), (b), and (c) within the reader's repertoire of prior knowledge, including knowledge about language. These sources of information allowed the reader to react to printed words in numerous ways through making inferences, evaluating, checking validity, and drawing conclusions.

In other words, by using thinking and reasoning processes, readers drew upon their familiarity with language and upon the general knowledge they had acquired to associate the letter-sound relationships that they learned in school with what appeared on the page. It was the interaction between what was in the head and what was on the page that allowed a reader to understand; not the learning of a fragmented set of skills. And what was in the head was knowledge of language and knowledge of the world.

Teachers had become reasonably proficient in teaching skills to children. The newer approach, however, stressed helping readers learn to combine prior knowledge with knowledge of letter-sound relationships in order to understand print. Usually good readers could figure this out for themselves, but all too often weaker readers believed that reading was just knowing how to pronounce the words. It seemed, then, that too many children did not understand that reading was a meaning-getting activity and that there was more to reading than sounding out words. Advocates of the newer approach to reading believed that the language children already knew had to be kept whole if it was to promote reading improvement. This meant rejecting the earlier tradition of fragmenting language; that is, learning it as letters, then words, followed by phrases, and finally sentences. Consequently, the term "whole language" came into being.

Whole Language Classrooms

Whole language teaching focuses on all aspects of language (speaking, listening, reading, and writing) in an interrelated way as the child learns to read and write. The way in which this is usually done is through the use of themes, whereby a topic is selected and all four language activities are utilized with material related to the topic. This means that from the beginning young children not only engage in reading, listening, and speaking, but in writing as well—a long-neglected area in our curriculum. Durkin (1966) found that many preschool children show interest first in writing words, and that this interest supports their efforts in teaching themselves to read. Teachers using the whole language approach capitalize on this interest by encouraging children to write from the very earliest grades. The children sound out the words they need and spelling approximations are readily accepted. Through individual conferences, teachers work with children to help them clarify the meaning of their stories and then move gradually toward more conventional spelling and structures—a pattern of interaction very similar to a parent assisting a toddler as he or she tries to communicate orally. Children have to be encouraged to take risks in their reading and writing by saying what they think the word might be or how it might be spelled. In contrast, if perfection or correctness is always demanded, many children will not try unless they know they are correct.

Whole language classrooms are supposed to be exciting and supportive learning places. Language experience charts, poetry, captions, labels and, most importantly, the children's productions cover the walls. The shelves and display cabinets are filled with trade books, big books, predictable books, as well as books the children have authored. A whole language classroom is a print-filled environment. The children's desks are grouped to facilitate verbal interactions as they discuss with one another or read to each other what they are writing or reading. An area is set aside in each class where all children can gather for stories and other shared activities. Many different kinds of language activities take place including choral reading, shared book experience (class reading of big books), writing workshops, reading one's writing from the author's chair, creating language experience charts, writing in journals, USSR (uninterrupted, sustained, silent reading), reading aloud to children, and participating in individualized reading programs.

All of this is not to say that teachers cannot and do not use basal readers in a whole language classroom. Most whole language teachers begin by incorporating whole language activities into their basal reader programs. As they become more comfortable with the language activities, they are usually less inclined to adhere closely to the basal reader. After two or three years, the importance of the basal tends to decline to the point where teachers incorporate some of the basal suggestions into their themes.

Whole Language Metamorphism

This chapter began by drawing attention to a dilemma faced by reading teachers: namely, whether to continue using a skills approach or whether to change emphasis and use a whole language approach. Following a discussion of the origins and theoretical underpinnings of the basal reader orientation to the language arts, some of the acknowledged limitations of the method were identified. The theory underlying the naturalistic approach to the pedagogy of early reading was described, followed by a discussion of the cognitive underpinnings of reading acquisition and of how this theory was being translated by teachers in whole language classrooms.

In this section of the chapter, it is emphasized at the outset that the intent of the foregoing discussion was to show in what respects the holistic or naturalistic theories of early reading were responses to two conditions: (a) the basal reader approach became excessively rigid and inflexible and basic skills came to be taught in a mechanical fashion without adequate concern for meaning; and (b) instruction in the schools mirrored the technological and socioeconomic changes occurring in the wider society. Thus, whole language teaching might best be viewed as a change attributable largely to adaptations or theoretical revisions stemming from new conceptions about reading and writing processes which have been validated by research.

Such change is ongoing. While whole language procedures can help children understand the intent of reading and provide strategies for helping children gain meaning during reading, there are, however, certain pitfalls in the approach. Misconceptions about whole language teaching can arise if teachers do not understand the theoretical rationale upon which whole language activities are based. Without a good understanding of the origins of whole language, teaching activities can become just another set of "good ideas". Many whole language activities involve considerable reading and writing, and reading and writing take time. Some teachers might believe that the activities waste valuable teaching time that could be utilized better in conveying knowledge to the children and having them complete workbook or worksheet activities which produce more short-term tangible results. Unfortunately, such teachers would fail to realize the importance of providing ample time for reading and writing practice. The desire and the ability to read and understand content material or storybooks is not likely facilitated by completing workbook assignments related to a basal story. Nor is the motivation and ability to write letters, stories, reports, or poems likely to occur when children are asked to answer questions on worksheets that require merely one-word, one-phrase, or one-sentence answers.

Another misconception that may surface is that in whole language one does not teach letter-sound relationships, nor any of the comprehension skills. It might be believed that young children will acquire a knowledge of phonics without any teaching. However, most will not. Phonics and structural analysis need to be taught within the context of natural reading situations. This means that as opportunities arise within the stories being read, the teacher must seize the opportunity to teach the skill and to show children how to use it in conjunction with the context of the story and in association with their already existing background knowledge.

Similarly, a comprehension skill such as finding the main idea, may be taught by asking the child to predict what a story or selection in a subject area text is about, based on their background knowledge, the title, and any pictures. As the children read the selection they can confirm or reject their prediction and revise their prediction as the story unfolds or as new information in a passage becomes available. Here again, the skills are taught within the confines of a meaningful reading task.

A third possible misconception is that children do not need to be shown how to focus on individual words or letters. Since whole language advocates insist that language should not be broken down into discrete parts and taught in a series of steps, teachers might conclude that there is no need to select and focus on individual words or letters. Consequently, young children would not learn that at times they need to look at individual words or letters within words. As a result, when they read a story they may give a memorized version or the gist of the story and not actually read the words. Again, what teachers need to do is to show children how to focus on letters and words within a meaningful reading situation.

These potential problems with the whole language approach suggest two things. First, teachers who use this approach need to become familiar with the theory underlying whole language activities. Second, for those teachers who were schooled in the skills tradition and who are reluctant or even hostile toward the idea of changing their views and approach, it might be prudent to allow them to change gradually, rather than introducing a new program all at once.

Conclusion

Although it appears that the skills approach and the whole language approach are discrete movements in the reading field, they are based on related theories of literacy development. The former grew out of efforts to discover the skills that constitute good reading, and thus breaks reading into sets of discrete, identifiable skills. Many children, especially good readers, learn to read using this teaching technique. Weaker readers, however, often have a difficult time with this approach. The good readers learn intuitively how to transfer the skills taught to real reading situations. Weak readers are often unable to make the transfer and, consequently, are inclined to view reading as saying the words in sequence and completing skills worksheets. Reading for them is not a meaning-getting activity.

The whole language approach is an informed and logical response to these limitations of the skills tradition. It is based on the perception that good readers seem to convert skills into effective strategies for understanding print. It follows, then, that if language is kept *whole,* and if increased emphasis is placed on the development of effective reading strategies such as predicting, confirming meaning, and inferring through the application of background knowledge, that all readers might eventually be able to read for meaning.

Perhaps, rather than simply facing teachers with seemingly competing literacy theories, an analysis of these theories, as has been done in this chapter, may provide a basis for both understanding and consensus in the teaching of reading.

References

Anderson, R. C., Hiebert, E. N., Scott, J. A., & Wilkinson, I. G. A. (1985). *Becoming a nation of readers.* Washington, DC: National Institute of Education.

Barrett, T. A. (1968). A taxonomy of cognitive and affective dimensions of reading comprehension. Outlined by Clymer, T. C. What is reading?: Some current concepts. In H. M. Robinson (Ed.), *Innovation and change in reading instruction.* NSSE 67th Yearbook, Part II. Chicago: University of Chicago Press.

Davis, F. B. (1942). Two new measures of reading ability. *Journal of Educational Psychology, 33,* 365-372.

Davis, F. B. (1944). Fundamental factors of comprehension in reading. *Psychometrika, 9,* 185-197.

Davis, F. B. (1968). Research in comprehension in reading. *Reading Research Quarterly, 3,* 499-545.

Doake, D. B. (1981). Book Experience and Emergent Reading Behaviour in Preschool Children. Unpublished doctoral dissertation, University of Alberta.

Doake, D. B. (1985). Reading-like behaviour: Its role in learning to read. In A. Jaggar & M. T. Smith-Burke (Eds.), *Observing the language learner.* Newark, DE: International Reading Association.

Durkin, D. (1961). Children who read before grade one. *The Reading Teacher, 14,* 163-166.

Durkin, D. (1966). *Children who read early.* New York: Teachers College Press.

Forester, A. (1977). What teachers can learn from "natural readers". *The Reading Teacher, 31,* 160-166.

Gates, A. I. (1937). The measurement and evaluation of achievement in reading. In *The teaching of reading: A second report* (Thirty-sixth Yearbook of the National Society for Studies in Education, Part I). Bloomington, IL: Public School Publishing.

Goodman, K. (1986). Basal readers: A call for action. *Language Arts, 63*, 358-363.

Goodman, K. S., & Goodman, Y. M. (1979). Learning to read is natural. In L. B. Resnick and P. A. Weaver, (Eds.), *Theory and practice in early reading*. Hillside, NJ: Erlbaum.

Goodman, Y. M. (1980). The roots of literacy. In P. D. Malcolm (Ed.), *Claremont Reading Conference, Forty-fourth Yearbook.* Claremont, CA: Center for Developmental Studies, Claremont Graduate School.

Goodman, Y. M., & Haussler, M. M. (1986). Literacy environment in the home and community. In D. R. Tovey and J. E. Kerber (Eds.), *Roles in literacy learning: A new perspective.* Newark, DE: International Reading Association.

Gray, W. S. (1960). The major aspects of reading. *Sequential development of reading abilities.* Supplementary Educational Monographs, No. 90. Chicago: University of Chicago Press.

Holdaway, D. (1979). *The foundations of literacy.* Sydney: Ashton Scholastic.

Huck, C. S. (1977). Literature as the content of reading. *Theory into Practice, 16*, 363-371.

Mathews, M. M. (1966). *Teaching to read: Historically considered.* Chicago: University of Chicago Press.

McKee, P. (1934). *Reading and literature in the elementary school.* Cambridge, MA: The Riverside Press.

Murray, D. (1968). *A writer teaches writing.* Boston: Houghton Mifflin.

Newman, J. (1985). Whole language: Theory in use. Portsmouth, NH: Heinemann.

Plessas, G. & Oakes, C. (1964). Prereading experiences of selected early readers. *The Reading Teacher, 17*, 241-245.

Smith, F. (1973). *Psycholinguistics and reading.* New York: Holt, Rinehart & Winston.

Smith, N. B. (1965). *American reading instruction.* Newark, DE: International Reading Association.

Torrey, J. W. (1969). Learning to read without a teacher: A case study. *Elementary English, 46* , 550-556.

11

The Actualization of Reading and Writing:
Public Policy and Conceptualizations of Literacy

Stanley B. Straw
University of Manitoba

Olson (this volume) suggests that literacy has been "mythologized". We have conceptualized literacy in such a way that it does not define what people really need in order to carry out their daily lives, but what public myth has determined that people need. The call for universal functional literacy is so wide-spread that challenging it is almost heresy. However, in this chapter, I would like to question the validity of such conceptualizations of literacy and the need for generalized literacy in our present-day society.

Indicators of functional illiteracy in some ways are like the poverty line; they are only indicators of quality of life—not its definition. Illiteracy parallels poverty in that governments bemoan the existence of functional illiteracy without really suggesting reasonable solutions to the problem. Functional illiteracy is unlike poverty, however, for a number of reasons: first, literacy levels and literacy needs are not as well researched or understood as poverty; second, literacy operates in a vast number of currencies, whereas poverty operates within a limited number of currencies (primarily money); third, there are income statistics on all taxpayers of our society, but statistics are not available for everybody's literacy rate.

Olson points out that literacy has been mythologized or romanticized to the point that we have deluded ourselves on the kinds of literacy necessary for an acceptable quality of life for members of our society. Whenever a particular level of literacy has been defined as functional and that level has been approached, literacy has been redefined so that approximately 20% of the population falls into the functionally illiterate category. When literacy is defined in a consistent way, the literacy level of school students has not changed dramatically during this century. Tuinman, Rowls, and Farr (1976) state: "We believe that, from the information we are able to gather, we would conclude first that there is *no reason* for an *en masse* pessimism . . . We are convinced that anyone who says that he [sic] knows that literacy is decreasing is ignoring the data. Such a person is at best unscholarly and at worst dishonest" (p. 463). In the United States, literacy levels in general and literacy levels of disadvantaged groups in particular, have been rising over the past 20 years (Applebee, Langer & Mullis, 1985). Nonetheless, we are faced with reports (e.g., Hirsch, 1987) that use as evidence for a dropping literacy rate and a failure of schools to meet the needs of society, such facts as students' not knowing where Argentina is or who killed Millard Fillmore. Such reports fail to address whose needs literacy is supposed to meet and cast literacy as the accumulation of knowledge in decontextualized circumstances, such as those that can be measured by pencil-and-paper tests, rather than as the application of skill in day-to-day living.

Educators have been responsible in part for inflating the levels thought to be necessary to achieve functional literacy because, as long as there is a large segment of the population that has not achieved this rising level, the case can be made for additional funding, support, and recognition. Educators, have, thereby, lent their complicity to attacks on the school system by agreeing that if society would only commit the resources necessary, the goal of universal literacy could be achieved. Literacy has thus been a saviour of the schools. On the other hand, literacy has been the taunting devil, in that schools have come under attack for wasting funds, squandering resources, dropping standards, and shirking the ultimate responsibility to educate society to minimal levels of literacy.

Neither our schools nor the bureaucrats responsible for public literacy policy seem willing to identify their own conceptualizations of literacy and the bases for them. Furthermore, few address literacy from an actualization point of view—a view to be explained later. They define functional illiteracy in terms of standardized test scores that ask prison inmates to read bus and train schedules, women whose husbands have for thirty years paid the bills to explain how a check voucher should be completed, or citizens to choose from a multiple-choice list the correct meaning of a section of Canada's Charter of Rights.

These kind of tasks seem to take literacy to be the ability to deal with written language in unfamiliar, decontextualized circumstances. One must ask if prison inmates need to know how to read a bus schedule, or if knowledge about the richness of living in a free and democratic society can be tapped by selecting between (a) Everyone is equal in Canada; and (b) The law in Canada cannot favour one person over another, as an interpretation of the Charter of Rights (Calamai, 1988). Such questions imply that literacy is not a way of solving problems, not a means of thinking and learning, but rather the manipulation of textbook-like symbols with little real purpose associated with that manipulation.

Historical Development of Conceptualizations of Literacy

Three major notions—(a) locus of meaning in any literacy act, (b) *the nature of knowledge* presumed needed in order to operate in any literacy act, and (c) *the purposes for literacy*—combine loosely with larger conceptualizations of epistemology, philology (in its traditional sense as a study of the meaning of literature), and personal control to define five historical periods in the conventional conceptualizations of literacy and the literacy process: the Transmission, Translation, Interaction, Transaction, and Social Construction Periods.

The Transmission Period

The Transmission Period ran roughly from before the American revolution to the turn of the twentieth century, embodied what Gilbert (1987) has called "romantic expressivism", and was embodied in the literary criticism termed "historical-biographical" and "moral-philosophical" (Guerin, Labor, Morgan, & Willingham, 1979). It is the most conservative and historically resilient conceptualization of literacy in North America. In transmission, the overriding metaphor is literacy as a *conduit*. It is a conceptualization of literacy in which information, knowledge, or meaning are shunted from the author to the reader via the vehicle of text (Smith, 1984a). This conceptualization of literacy has been reinforced by conceptualizations of education as the movement of information or meaning from the teacher to a passive learner. Essentially, the transmission point of view is based on the Lockean idea that the student, reader, or recipient of information is a *tabula rasa* upon which the teacher, author, or sender of information may write knowledge. In the transmission conceptualization of literacy, the author is valorized as the source and locus of all meaning. Associated with this notion of literacy is the communication contract—that literacy, like all language, is part of an act of moving knowledge, whole and unchanged, from the author to the reader.

In the purest interpretations of the transmission model, the power of the author was absolute. All meaning and authority resided with the author. The most "successful" understanding of an author's message was indicated by the ability of a reader to memorize an author's work and recite it from memory. Text was equated with authorial intent and was seen as the vehicle or container through which that intent was moved from author to reader, from meaning-maker to meaning-apprehender.

In this conceptualization of literacy, the text was merely the vehicle for the movement of meaning. This communication/transmission notion of language is classical in that both Plato and Aristotle saw language as mimetic, with the power of communication residing in the power of the rhetoric —that is, the ability of the sender to shape the message so that it persuaded and moved the audience.

The importance ascribed to the author in the transmission theory was also reflected in the notions of a good reader. The good reader was one who could reproduce the author's intent. Therefore, readers needed to be aware of historical, biographical, moral, and philosophical information about the author (Guerin, et al., 1979). The procedures of reading and interpreting were not important; what was important was the knowledge, the declarative knowledge, that one had about the authorial context in order to find out the author's intent. The process of reading was defined by one's knowledge of the author and his or her most probable intents.

The Shift from the Transmission to Translation Period

The Industrial revolution in North America changed lifestyles tremendously, and had a concomitant effect on conceptualizations of reading and literacy. Literacy and general education became less exclusive and increasingly valued (Gere, 1987). Part of the consequence of this shift was that people either needed to read for their jobs, a change from prior to the turn of the twentieth century, or wanted to read for pleasure during their increased leisure time.

In reading theory, perhaps the most important hallmark of the change in conceptualizations of literacy was the appearance of the interest of psychologists in reading and in the underlying skills of reading. Gradually there was a change in the conventional notions of reading and literacy; authorial dominance began to be overshadowed by a new phenomenon, text dominance, and reading began to be conceptualized as *translation* rather than transmission.

The Translation Period ran from about 1900 to the mid-1960s, though there is evidence that this point of view has persevered into our own decade (e.g., Just & Carpenter, 1980). This point of view is held by many policy makers today, and is associated with New Criticism in literacy theory and with skills models of reading comprehension.

In response to the needs of readers with increased leisure time and limited education, more writing was done in the later nineteenth century to entertain as well as to inform and instruct. A variety of themes was present in the work. However, unlike the overt, Romantic, and superficial messages put forward in the period of transmission, these new themes were often implicit. The shift from the explicit message to the implicit message cast the reader in a very different role in terms of the act of reading. In the transmission era, readers were asked to decode authors by learning about an author's life, point of view, and philosophical stance. As the message of text became more implicit, the reader was reconceptualized as a translator of text into meaning—a decoder of text rather than a decoder of author. In the transmission point of view, the reader was expected to know the author in order to gain meaning; in the translation point of view, text was decontextualized from the author and seen as independent of the author. An "intentional fallacy" was articulated (Wimsatt & Beardsley, 1954 [reprint]), claiming that it was a fallacy to assume that the meaning of a text equalled the intent of its author. The translation point of view led to the reification of text as the place where meaning resided (rather than with the author). With this shift, the author disappeared from the communication contract, with the text taking over the role previously held by the author. There was a realization that the reader must bring some kind of skill to the act of translating text into meaning. The word "skill" became an important concept that ruled conceptualizations both of reading and teaching for the next half century (e.g., Davis, 1944; Gough, 1972; LaBerge & Samuels, 1974).

Readers began to believe that the message of a text dwelt within its structure and style, and that their task was to seek out that message. Instead of presenting students with pre-packaged meanings of texts, based on an author's life or philosophical point of view, instructors provided pupils with knowledge about reading and literature skills which they could then apply to a new selection in interpreting meaning.

The Interaction Period

Most reading theorists now accept a notion of interaction as a primary metaphor for the reading process. However, interaction is a relatively new phenomenon on the landscape of reading and language. The Interaction Period is associated with structuralism in literacy theory dating from the mid-1950s (e.g., Frye, 1957), and with psycholinguistic and interactive models of reading dating from the late 1960s (Goodman, 1970; Rumelhart, 1977). Hunt (1990) suggests that this shift can be dated from the appearance of Chomsky's *Syntactic Structures* in 1957 in which he presented a new conceptualization of language that called into question the notion of reading merely as translation or decoding. Chomsky's reconceptualization of language learning and use, paired with a renewed interest by cognitive psychologists in the application of psycholinguistics to reading, resulted in the development of interactive models. Here was a fundamental change from translation models, in that meaning was thought to be moulded in light of readers' background and knowledge. In some ways, this shift re-recognized the role of the author in the communication contract. Interaction suggested that the author and the reader could share knowledge and experience through reading and via the linguistic structures of the text.

Interactive models of reading were attempts to account for both the information encoded in the text and the knowledge and experience of readers as they decoded the text. Interaction theories have attempted to strike a balance between all three knowledge sources (author, text, and experience), such that neither is dominant in the acts of reading and processing text. Most interactive theorists would suggest that the closer the match between reader knowledge and authorial information as realized in text, the better comprehension is likely to be; the worse the match between reader knowledge and the textual realization of authorial information, the poorer the comprehension is likely to be. Although interactive theorists acknowledge that text gestures toward meaning in such a way that readers must "fill in the gaps" with their own personal experience, interactive models also suggest that meaning must ultimately be reconciled to the text itself (e.g., Rumelhart, 1985, p. 736). The good reader is the reader whose background knowledge most closely resembles the text itself or who can best reconcile personal experience with the text. It also assumes, because a reconciliation must take place, that meaning is determinate and determinable, based on some level of analysis of the structure of text.

The Transaction Period

The Transaction Period has roots that extend back to the middle 1930s, but has been recognized with the advent of reader-response criticism in North America (Rosenblatt, 1978; Tompkins, 1980), and with the advent of reception theory in Europe about 1970 (Holub, 1984). It may be the most widely held view among literacy educators at this time.

The shift from interactive notions of reading to transactional notions was a significant rethinking of literacy. All three of the prior notions of reading were grounded in a basic assumption that reading was communication, that reading was part of a larger language act that included the author as originator of meaning, the text as symbolic or representative of meaning, and the reader as receiver of meaning. Transmission theories valorized the author; translation theories reified the text; interaction theories celebrated the negotiation between reader knowledge and text structure. All, however, assumed the purposes of reading were inherently related to a communicative act. When the basic communicative assumption was questioned by theoreticians and researchers, the foundations upon which earlier models were built was undermined. Here is the essence of the shift presently being experienced in the area of reading and literary criticism.

In contrast to conceptualizations of literacy built on the communication model, transactional models suggest that literacy is a more generative act than the receipt or processing of information or communication. From the transactional point of view, both meaning and significance are constructed by the reader during the act of reading. The reader draws on a number of knowledge sources in order to create or construct meaning. The knowledge sources include the text itself, the reader's knowledge of language and language features, the background experiences of the reader, the world knowledge and world view of the reader. Harste, Woodward, and Burke (1984) suggest that these knowledge sources include the social as well as the literary experiences of the reader.

In contrast to theories based on the communication model, transactional theories suggest that meaning is created by the active negotiation of readers, their backgrounds, and the texts they are reading. Transaction is the generating of meaning in response to text. Transactional theories suggest that meaning is indeterminate because each reader brings a unique set of background experiences, world knowledge, social experiences, and social identifications to the act of reading (Straw, 1990). No two readers likely will ever generate exactly the same meaning from a single text, because they have different sets of background experience. By the same token, the same reader will never generate exactly the same meaning from the same text at two different readings, because at different times this reader's experiences will be different, if for no other reason than he or she will have experienced the reading of the text previously.

These assumptions about the generative nature of language and reading contrast with previous assumptions about comprehension—those that suggest that meaning is knowable in an objective sense, that comprehension is measurable, and that meaning is a static or determinate reality—all underlying assumptions of theories that accept that communication is the central purpose for reading.

Rosenblatt (1978) refers to the creation of the reader as "the poem" (p. 69). She describes the transaction as a dynamic: "The dynamics . . . include first the dialogue of the reader with the text as he [sic] creates the world of the text." (p. 69). Bogdan (1986) refers to these negotiations as a dialectic—a kind of conversation between text and reader which results in a constructed meaning—a synthesis between reader knowledge and text.

Tompkins (1980) describes Fish's transactional view of reading in this way:

> Fish makes the crucial move in reader oriented criticism by removing the literary text from the centre of critical attention and replacing it with the reader's cognitive activity. The decisive shift in focus opens a new field of inquiry. If meaning is no longer a property of text but a product of the reader's activity, the question to answer is not 'What do poems mean?' or even 'What do poems do?' but 'How do readers make meaning? (p. xvii)

This is the question that transactionalists are attempting to answer in investigating the reading process and is, perhaps, the first major step toward actualizing reading: that is, changing the underlying assumptions about reading from a communication model to an actualization one.

The Social Construction Period

The Social Construction Period is current. Its point of view, yet to be completely articulated, is associated with theories of Vygotsky (1978) in language and learning, with a group of literary critics loosely called social pragmatists (Hunt, 1990), and with re-emerging notions of top-down models of reading comprehension.

The social construction theory maintains that knowledge is socially patterned and conditioned, that coming to know is a result of social experiences and interactions, and that all knowledge and knowledge construction are essentially social acts. These hypotheses suggest constructionist notions of reading. The impact of these ideas on the literacy process is that reading and writing likely will be viewed as a single act of literacy, and that subsequent models of literacy will attempt to identify where knowledge comes from (from social interactions) and how coming to know is mediated by social experience. Much of the difference between the prison inmate and the Winnipeg traveller, in my ubiquitous bus schedule example, is related to social background and the social context for the act of reading. The work in social construction suggests that since all knowledge is socially constructed, and since knowledge of the literacy process is one form of knowledge, literacy is both profoundly constructive and profoundly social (Hunt, 1990; and Hynds, 1990).

Integration of Reading and Writing

Two major movements have led me to believe that the field of reading comprehension theory and literary critical theory are heading for a more constructionist notion of how reading processes take place. The first of these movements is the social construction movement just discussed. The second is a move toward the integration of our notions of reading and writing that will lead, I think, to a conceptualization of a single literacy process to account for both.

Since the appearance of transformational-generative grammar, the relationships between reading and writing have been seriously investigated. Up to now, researchers have found only weak correlations between the two (e.g., Dahl, 1981; Hopkins, 1981). However, as new models of the writing process are emerging (e.g., Flower, Hayes, Carey, Schriver, & Stratman, 1986), I have been struck by a similarity between descriptions of the two processes, not so much in their products—a focus on products was in some ways the problem with previous correlational research between reading and writing—but in how reading and writing operate. The similarity of processes has led me to investigate the application of compositional models to the reading process. I refer to this notion as "Reader as Rhetor, Text as Audience". In the Reader as Rhetor notion, I suspect that the hypothesis-generating/text-confirmation acts of reading are similar to, if not identical to, the discovery, organizing, and drafting/revising stages of the writing process as hypothesized by cognitive psychologists. I suspect that, although the specifics of the model changes, the constructive dynamic in the reading process is identical to the constructive dynamic in the compositional models of the writing process. The productive rhetorical nature of reading appears in the same general nature as the productive rhetorical nature of writing, although the specifics and products may look different.

This hypothesis is based on the assumption that both reading and writing are driven by basic personal purposes. The purpose of reading affects significantly both the reading process and the products generated (Tierney & Cunningham, 1984). Readers who are reading for one purpose employ different strategies than those reading for a different purpose. For example, readers who are reading to reinforce already-held beliefs read differently from those who are reading to create and capture a new experience. A prison inmate reading to complete a literacy test reads in a different fashion than the person attempting to catch a bus at night. So, instead of having any particular meaning, texts serve to constrain or contain the generative activity of the reader. In the same way, text possibilities or textual structures constrain the writer's ability to generate meaning. The recognition of these constraints highlights the inseparability of knowledge and language as hypothesized by Vygotsky (1978). I am suggesting that the basic underlying drive (purpose) is precisely the same in both reading and writing. In addition to being driven by purpose, both reading and writing appear to be informed by identical knowledge sources. Both draw on the background knowledge of language users, including their knowledge of the language system and the constraints of language.

The overriding "metaphor" of reading as writing cannot necessarily be applied at the letter-by-letter level, or even, probably, at the word-by-word level. Nevertheless, it is an appropriate metaphor. Since the primary purpose of reading is comprehension (Durkin, 1986), then models of reading need to be driven by the notion of meaning. However, researchers, theorists, and literacy policy makers have become embattled in discussions of decoding and recoding to the point that they have assumed that meaning is the *product* of reading rather than the single *purpose* in reading, and, therefore, the major activity in the act. Models of composition have placed decoding-like activities near the end of the description of the writing process. I think that such a placement should also be true of models of reading—that word and letter identification in reading are analogous to later-occurring revision and editing as these have been explained in the writing process. Readers should approach text as the primary activator, controller, and drafter of meaning possibilities.

Furthermore, both reading and writing rely on elaborate monitoring systems. Monitoring systems tell writers when the writing is or is not achieving their purposes, and give them information as to how to solve writing problems when they arise. In the same way, readers have monitoring systems that tell them when the reading is or is not achieving their purposes, and give them information as to how to solve reading problems when they arise. Although these processes result in different physical products, they result in similar or identical cognitive products—meaning.

This view of reading as writing suggests that the reader hypothesizes meaning and significance before encountering the reality and particulars of text, and that readers have drafts of meaning in their heads as they read. While reading, readers are constantly revising that draft in light of their audience—the text. This revising activity delays the particulars of word recognition, phonic analysis, and so on, until much later in the reading process than has been hypothesized before—it places decoding and recoding in the position of the editing stage in writing, rather than at the beginning of the process.

Such composing models of reading have been suggested by a number of authors in their attempts to account for the generative nature of reading. Wittrock (1984) states that "[g]ood reading, like effective writing, involves generative cognitive processes that create meaning by building relations between the text and what we know, believe, and experience ... When we read, we generate meaning ..." (p. 77). Hansen (1987) suggests that students learn to read effectively as they learn to write effectively, a point of view supported by Smith (1984b). Graves and Hansen (1984) state that "[w]e started by giving the same definition to both reading and writing: They are composing acts" (p. 70). One of the most completely articulated hypotheses about the similar natures of reading and writing has been generated by Tierney and Pearson (1984). They have suggested that reading and writing share the same dynamics of planning, drafting, aligning, revising, and monitoring. They have presented a convincing argument on the compositional nature of reading and have suggested that the rhetoric of writing is identical to the rhetoric of reading. Many authors use composition as a metaphor for reading; authors such as Tierney and Pearson extend that metaphor so that descriptions of both reading and writing look much the same.

Conclusion

The major conclusion I am able to draw from the review of the historical developments in literacy is that our policy-makers and those who decide funding for literacy hold essentially conservative views about literacy and functional illiteracy. The government and public at large conceptualize literacy as either transmission or translation. They still perceive the single purpose of language, written language particularly, as communication—that is, the shunting of information and knowledge from one source to another. They see the communication contract being fulfilled by the forms of language themselves, without taking into account the background knowledge or the literacy needs of the reader. Furthermore, they assume that the locus of meaning in any literacy act is either with the author (authorial intent) or within the text (textual intent). They do not accept the notion that readers are the most important players in any literacy experience, and that reading goes beyond skill in decoding text. Furthermore, they perceive the kinds of knowledge that readers need in any act of literacy to be either knowledge of the intents of the author or knowledge of the decoding skills of reading. They perceive the nature of meaning such that literacy is determinate, measurable, and decontextualized. Otherwise, we would not have policy-makers who define states of illiteracy by means of tests of declarative knowledge (such as where Argentina is) or of the skills of reading (as reflected in such things as reading comprehension tests).

In reference to the purposes of literacy, I believe that we must, both in our schools and in our public policy, abandon the notion that literacy is only a communicative act. There are times when literacy is a communicative act—but only when *both* the author and the reader choose it to be this. If an author chooses a purpose for using writing other than communication (such as for exploration), and a reader reads that writing as if the text were written for the purposes of communication, then the contract is undermined. By the same token, if a writer writes for the purpose of communication and a reader reads the writing for some other purpose (such as for pleasure), then the communication contract is also undermined. I do believe that at times literacy is, can be, and should be, a communicative act. However, I do not believe that it always is, or, for that matter, that it generally is. Communication is only one of a wide variety of purposes for literacy, and communication is a valid purpose of literacy only when both the author and the reader maintain the communication contract. If either of them employs reading or writing for some other purpose, and there are many, then communication breaks down. If we continue to conceive literacy as a route to communication, we will succeed in ignoring many, if not most, of the richest uses of reading and writing—exploration, celebration, learning, organization, remembering, recording, and discovering.

In relation to the purposes of literacy, we cannot continue to judge literacy merely by its communicative purposes and ignore the fact that all reading and writing is done as an attempt by readers and writers to realize personal goals within a social context. We should ask ourselves before creating literacy tests that ask people to read bus timetables whether these people ever need to take a bus, live in a community where buses are a way of travel, or care whether or not they ever take a bus. Each day I ride the Winnipeg Transit System. I observe people who may well be nominally functionally illiterate but who peer at bus schedules, check their watches, and adjust their behaviour accordingly—that is, literately. By the same token, I also know highly literate friends who, because they have no desire and no need ever to take a bus, would have no idea how to read a bus schedule and would tell you that they have no desire to learn. We could examine any literacy test or survey and make similar observations about every item. Until we understand that literacy must be placed in the context of people's competence to succeed in life, we will be placing false and unrealistic parameters around our population.

This leads me to a final point about social construction. Our national literacy policy has operated as if literacy is a personal, private skill. None of the research on and speculation about literacy that I know has supported that notion. Literacy must be conceptualized within the social contexts of literate behaviour, because that is where literacy is needed and used. With an expanding media, the terms of our literacy contract are changing; what counted socially as literacy a few decades ago no longer counts. Things that were hardly conceived twenty years ago now qualify as literate behaviour. Witness such things as keyboarding, responses to televised political campaigns, the literature of film, and the television "literacy". We must examine carefully our conceptualizations of literacy so that they adequately describe both the literate person and literate behaviour (Langer, 1987). We must become aware of the underlying notions that drive our literacy policy in an attempt to demythologize concepts of literacy and illiteracy (Morgan, 1990; Olson, this volume). We will be crippled if we try to enter the twenty-first century with nineteenth century conceptualizations of literacy and literate behaviour.

Acknowledgement

I would like to thank Pat Sadowy for reading drafts of this chapter and commenting on them.

References

Applebee, A., Langer, J., & Mullis, I. (1985). *The reading report card, progress toward excellence in our schools: Trends in reading over four national assessments, 1971-1984*. Princeton, NJ: Educational Testing Service.

Bogdan, D. (1986). Literacy response as dialectic: Modes and levels of engagement and detachment. *Cuadernos de Filologia Inglesa, 2*, 45-62.

Calamai, P. (1988). *Broken words*. Ottawa: Southam Newspaper Group.

Chomsky, N. (1957). *Syntactic structures.* The Hague: Mouton.

Dahl, S. (1981). Oral language and its relationship to success in reading. In V. Froese & S. B. Straw (Eds.), *Research in the language arts: Language and schooling.* Baltimore: University Park Press.

Davis, F. B. (1944). Fundamental factors of comprehension in reading. *Psychometrika, 9,* 185-197.

Durkin, D. (1986). *Teaching them to read.* (5th ed.). Boston: Allyn & Bacon.

Fish, S. (1980). *Is there a text in this class?* Cambridge: Harvard University Press.

Flower, L., Hayes, J. R., Carey, L., Schriver, K., & Stratman, J. (1986). Detection, diagnosis, and the strategies of revision. *College Composition and Communication, 37,* 16-55.

Frye, N. (1957). *Anatomy of criticism.* Princeton: Princeton University Press.

Gere, A. R. (1987). Teaching writing: The major theories. In A. R. Petrosky & D. Bartholomae (Eds.), *The teaching of writing* (85th yearbook of the National Society for the Study of Education, Part II). Chicago: University of Chicago Press.

Gilbert, P. (1987). Post reader-response: The deconstructive critique. In B. Corcoran & E. Evans (Eds.), *Readers, texts, teachers.* Upper Montclair, NJ: Boynton/Cook.

Goodman, K. S. (1970). Behind the eye: What happens in reading. In K. S. Goodman & O. S. Niles (Eds.), *Reading, process and program.* Urbana, IL: National Council of Teachers of English.

Goodman, K. S. (1985). Unity in reading. In H. Singer & R. B. Ruddell (Eds.), *Theoretical models and processes of reading.* (3rd ed.). Newark, DE: International Reading Association.

Gough, P. B. (1972). One second of reading. In J. F. Kavanagh & I. G. Mattingly (Eds.), *Language by ear and eye.* Cambridge, MA: MIT Press.

Guerin, W. L., Labor, E. G., Morgan, L., & Willingham, J. (1979). *A handbook of critical approaches to literature.* New York: Harper & Row.

Graves, D., & Hansen, J. (1984). The author's chair. In J. Jensen (Ed.), *Composing and comprehending.* Urbana, IL: National Conference on Research in English and ERIC Clearinghouse on Reading and Communication Skills.

Hansen, J. (1987). *When writers read.* Portsmouth, NH: Heinemann.

Harste, J. C., Woodward, V. A., & A. Burke, C. L. (1984). *Language stories and literacy lessons.* Portsmouth, NH: Heinemann.

Hirsch, E. D., Jr. (1987). Cultural literacy: What every American needs to know. Boston: Houghton-Mifflin.

Holub, R. C. (1984). *Reception theory: A critical introduction.* The Hague: Routledge, Chapman & Hall.

Hopkins, C. J. (1981). Evaluating children's oral language. In V. Froese & S. B. Straw (Eds.), *Research in the language arts: Language and* schooling. Baltimore: University Park Press.

Hunt, R. A. (1990). The parallel socialization of reading research and literary theory. In S. B. Straw & D. Bogdan (Eds.), *Beyond communication: Reading comprehension and criticism.* Portsmouth, NH: Boynton/Cook-Heinemann.

Hynds, S. (1990). Reading as a social event: Comprehension and response in the text, classroom, and world. In S. B. Straw & D. Bogdan (Eds.), *Beyond communication: Reading comprehension and criticism.* Portsmouth, NH: Boynton/Cook-Heinemann.

Just, M. A., & Carpenter, P. A. (1980). A theory of reading: From eye fixations to comprehension. *Psychological Review, 87,* 329-354.

LaBerge, D., & Samuels, S. J. (1974). Toward a theory of automatic information processing in reading. *Cognitive Psychology, 6,* 293-323.

Langer, J. (Ed.). (1987). *Language, literacy, and culture: Issues of society and schooling.* Norwood, NJ: Ablex.

Morgan, R. (1990). Beyond reader-response theory: The history and politics of reading. In D. Bogdan & S. B. Straw (Eds.), *Beyond communication: Reading comprehension and criticism.* Portsmouth, NH: Boynton/Cook-Heinemann.

Rosenblatt, L. M. (1978). *The reader, the text, the poem: The transactional theory of the literary work.* Carbondale, IL: Southern Illinois University Press.

Rumelhart, D. (1977). Toward an interactive model of reading. In S. Dornic (Ed.), *Attention and performance VI.* Hillsdale, NJ: Erlbaum.

Rumelhart, D. (1985). Toward an interactive model of reading. In H. Singer & R. B. Ruddell (Eds.), *Theoretical models and processes of reading* (3rd ed.). Newark, DE: International Reading Association.

Smith, F. (1984a). A metaphor for literacy: Creating worlds or shunting information? In D. R. Olson, N. T. Torrance, & A. Hildyard (Eds.), *Literacy, language, and learning: The nature and consequences of reading and writing.* Cambridge: Cambridge University Press.

Smith, F. (1984b). Reading like a writer. In J. Jensen (Ed.), *Composing and comprehending*. Urbana, IL: National Conference for Research on English and the ERIC Clearinghouse on Reading and Communication Skills.

Straw, S. B. (1990). Reading and response to literature. Transactionalizing instruction. In S. Hynds & D. L. Rubin (Eds.), *Perspectives on talk and learning*. Urbana, IL: National Council of Teachers of English.

Tierney, R. J., & Cunningham, J. W. (1984). Research on teaching reading comprehension. In P. D. Pearson (Ed.), *Handbook of reading research*. New York: Longman.

Tierney, R. J., & Pearson, P. D. (1984). Toward a composing model of reading. In J. Jensen (Ed.), *Composing and comprehending*. Urbana, IL: National Conference on Research in English and the ERIC Clearinghouse on Reading and Communication Skills.

Tompkins, J. P. (1980). An introduction to reader-response criticism. In J. P. Tompkins (Ed.), *Reader-response criticism: From formalism to post-structuralism*. Baltimore, MD: Johns Hopkins University Press.

Tuinman, J., Rowls, M., & Farr, R. (1976). Reading achievement in the United States: Then and now. *Journal of Reading, 19*, 455-463.

Vygotsky, L. S. (1978). *Mind in society* (1938). (Eds. & Trans. M. Cole, V. John-Steiner, S. Scribner, & E. Sonberman). Cambridge, MA: Harvard University Press.

Wimsatt, W. K., & Beardsley, M. C. (1954). The intentional fallacy. In W. K. Wimsatt (Ed.), *The verbal icon: Studies in the meaning of poetry*. Louisville, KY: University of Kentucky Press, 3-18.

Wittrock, M. C. (1984). Writing and the teaching of reading. In J. Jensen (Ed.), *Composing and comprehending*. Urbana, IL: National Conference on Research in English and the ERIC Clearinghouse on Reading and Communication Skills.

Part III
Social Perspectives

12

The Role of Native Language Literacy
in Third Language Learning

Merrill Swain, Sharon Lapkin, Norman Rowen and Doug Hart
Ontario Institute for Studies in Education

The main question that this chapter addresses is whether the learning of a third language is enhanced through literacy in one's first language. To some, it may seem self-evident that being literate in one's native language will positively affect the development of literacy skills in another language. However, educational practices in many parts of the world, including many parts of Canada, show no hint of accepting such a statement as self-evident. Indeed, examination of the beliefs of many parents, teachers, educational administrators, and policy-makers leads one to the contrary conclusion: that learning a second or third language is impeded by knowledge and use of the first language.

As evidence for this belief, consider the following: that many immigrant parents in Canada believe that by speaking or reading to their children in their own language, they will seriously slow down their children's acquisition of English; that initial education in a child's first language, be it Tagalog, Urdu, Arabic, Italian, etc., is seen as taking time away from the important task of learning a second language—that of the school and majority of society; that it is common practice for teachers to recommend to immigrant parents of children who are having trouble in school to use more English with their children (Bild, 1987). Such practices deny the possibility of positive transfer from the first language to another one. Similarly, many immigrants to Canada whose native language is neither English nor French believe that learning a third language should be deferred until the second (majority) language, in this case English, has been firmly established (Cummins, 1984; Cummins & Swain, 1986).

In this chapter, we consider first several research and evaluation studies that emanate from bilingual education programs for minority language children. Second, we describe a study we have completed recently that involved grade eight children who had been enroled in an English/French bilingual program since grade five. Some of the students in the program acquired a heritage language at home before they began school. We will use the term "heritage language" to refer to the first language a child learns if that language is other than English or French. For these students, English is their second language and French is their third language. For students who do not have a heritage language, English is their first language and French is their second language. Given that the focus of this chapter is on heritage language students, children whose first language is English are referred to as "no heritage language students".

Some of the students acquired literacy skills in their heritage language either at home or in Heritage Language Programs at school. All students in the program were literate in English before beginning the bilingual program. Our study examines their learning of French with respect to (a) literacy in and use of a heritage language compared to not having a heritage language, and (b) the type of heritage language spoken (Romance versus non-Romance). As it is possible that our observed effects on third language learning may be a consequence of socioeconomic variables related to heritage language proficiency rather than heritage language literacy per se, we examine these relationships in the third part of the chapter and conclude that literacy in the heritage language accounts for enhanced performance in third language learning. Fourth, we briefly explore the implications of our findings for educational programs for heritage language children.

Bilingual Education for Heritage Language Children

Some of the most compelling evidence for the positive impact that native language literacy has on second language learning comes from evaluations of bilingual education programs for heritage language children. In general, it has been found that children who are initially educated in their heritage language learn a second language better (and are academically more successful) than those who have no such foundation in their heritage language (Troike, 1981).

Different explanations for this phenomenon have been posited—some linguistic, others more social and attitudinal. In the latter category fall such explanations as "success breeds success". Children who are educated in a language they initially do not understand, and where many of their classmates are native speakers of the school language, often experience failure or fear. Provision of heritage language schooling provides the opportunity for children to understand their surroundings and to experience academic success, self-confidence, a stronger sense of personal worth, and positive feelings about school.

Linguistic explanations are more specific about the impact that first language literacy has on second language literacy learning. There is considerable evidence that, even when two languages use different writing systems, readers are able to apply the visual, linguistic, and cognitive strategies they use in first-language reading to reading in the second language (Ovando and Collier, 1985). "Readers apply what they figured out about the process in one language to reading in another language" (Hudelson 1987, p. 839).

In writing about the benefits of first language literacy, Hudelson (1987) notes two in particular:

> The first benefit of a strong native language literacy program is that it develops in children an understanding of what reading and writing are for, using the medium of a language that the children speak fluently and that they have used to make sense of their life experiences to this point in time ... the task will be more easily accomplished in a language that one speaks fluently, because the reader will be able to make more efficient use of the cueing systems of the language to predict the meaning of written forms (p. 830).

> The second benefit of using the children's native language is that native language literacy provided the children with resources to use as they moved into second language reading and writing. (p. 833)

Cummins (1981) provides a theoretical explanation of how first language literacy affects second language learning in his "linguistic interdependence hypothesis". He posits that the abilities that underlie the use and interpretation of "decontextualized" language (of which many literacy activities are prime examples) are crosslingual. Thus, for an individual who is acquiring a second language, learning in the first language to use language as a symbolic system—that is, as a means to gain and apply knowledge using language alone, and as a means to abstract, generalize, and classify—not limited to that first language.

Therefore, spending time learning in the language one knows best may benefit both languages equally with respect to developing those language-related skills basic to academic progress in our schools.

Let us consider the results obtained from an evaluation of an exemplary bilingual education program. We consider the program to be exemplary because it involved instruction in the heritage language, including literacy instruction, throughout the six years of the program. The program involved Navajo students in Rock Point in the United States. Navajo students in Rock Point used to be educated in English only, and their performance on standardized tests of English remained below the performance expected for their grade level through elementary schooling. In 1971, a bilingual program was set up in which reading in English was not introduced until grade two after children had learned to read in Navajo. From grade two to grade six, the program involved instruction in both languages. Students were administered standardized tests of English achievement and the results were compared to, among other groups, those of previous students at Rock Point who had not had bilingual education. Rosier and Farella (1976) who evaluated the program conclude that:

> Data presented suggest that the effects of continuous bilingual instruction may be cumulative: that while Navajo students who have recently (in 2nd grade) added reading in English to reading in Navajo may do no better on standardized achievement tests than Navajo students who began reading in English, they do achieve better test scores each year thereafter. Nor does the difference seem to remain the same. The students who learned to read in Navajo and who continue to learn through Navajo and English appear to obtain scores progressively higher in English than those who did not. In effect, their rate of growth helps them to achieve progressively closer to the 'national norms' in each grade third through sixth, instead of maintaining a 'continuously retarded' level of achievement. (pp. 387-388)

In a meta-analysis of 23 studies of bilingual education programs in the United States, Willig (1985) showed that heritage language students in bilingual programs (i.e., heritage language/English) scored significantly higher than heritage language students in unilingual English programs not only in reading English but in language, mathematics, and total achievement as well. For related findings, see also Troike (1978), Cummins (1981), Cummins, Swain, Nakajima, Handscombe, Green, and Tran (1984), Hakuta (1986), Genesee (1987), and Krashen and Biber (1988).

These results are corroborated by studies of immigrant students who arrive in their host country after having had initial schooling in their home country. Skutnabb-Kangas (1979, 1981) found that students who had taken most of their elementary schooling in Finland before moving to Sweden did better in Swedish after two years of study than Finnish students in Sweden who had been educated in Swedish from the first grade. Similarly, Troike (1986) reports an unpublished study by Gonzalez that found that Mexican children who had two years of schooling in Mexico before immigrating to the United States did better in English than those who had no schooling prior to immigration.

The evaluation of French immersion programs also provides data that corroborates the conclusion that first language literacy can positively affect second language learning. In these programs, a distinction is typically made between bilingual education programs for majority language children and for heritage language children (Swain, 1981), allowing for the fact that to produce bilingual individuals, different formats of bilingual education are appropriate. However, it should be noted in the context of the present discussion that the performance in French of early immersion students and late immersion students by the end of high school is quite similar, particularly in literacy-related tests (Swain and Lapkin, 1986; Wesche, Morrison, Pawley, and Ready, 1986), suggesting that rapid progress can be made in the acquisition of literacy skills in a second language once a firm foundation has been established in the first language.

The Metropolitan Toronto Study

The Context for the Study

Toronto is a multilingual city: over half the students who enter the English school system in Toronto do not have English as their native language. Many parents of these children feel that although they would like their children to learn both of Canada's official languages, priority must be placed on acquiring the language of the wider community in which they live. In such a context, it has been suggested that a program that begins instruction using English and introduces French as a language of instruction around grade four or five would be more suitable than an early total immersion program. One such bilingual program that begins at grade five exists in the Metropolitan Separate School Board in Toronto.

The Metropolitan Separate School Board instructs children initially using English, and in grade five the students enter a bilingual program where for half the day instruction is in English and for the other half instruction is in French. From grades one to four, the students in the bilingual program have exposure to French through short daily periods (20 to 40 minutes) of French as a second language ("core" French).

The main question our study sought to answer was how the French language proficiency of the Metropolitan Separate School Board students at grade eight compared to students in an early total French immersion program. To do this, data were collected in three other boards of education in the Metropolitan Toronto area that had early immersion programs (Hart, Lapkin & Swain, 1987a). For purposes of this chapter, we will focus on data obtained only from the Metropolitan Separate School Board students, because it is only in this board that the number of children whose native language is other than English or French and who were enroled in a bilingual program is sufficient to warrant analyses based on native language use and literacy practices.

Data were collected from 16 grade eight bilingual classes involving 380 students. Parental permission was obtained for 319 students (84%) to complete the student questionnaire and language tests of writing, reading, and listening skills in French. Tests involving speaking in French were administered to a random sample of eight students in each class plus any heritage language students who were not in the random sample of eight, for a total of 210 students.

Questions Addressed

As we have seen from the brief review of the literature on bilingual education, there is considerable evidence that indicates that the learning of second language literacy skills is enhanced through having developed such skills in the first language. To our knowledge, however, there are no studies that examine the impact of heritage language literacy knowledge and use on third language learning, particularly in the context where all those studied have learned to read in at least one other language—in this case English, their language of initial schooling. Furthermore, as the third language in question is French, it is of interest to ask whether there is differential impact on its acquisition depending on whether the heritage language is a Romance or non-Romance language.

Also, we begin to tease apart the impact of heritage language use that does not include literacy activities from heritage language use that includes them. In so doing, we are able to address the issue of the additional impact that heritage language literacy has above and beyond that provided by the oral use of a heritage language.

Finally, as literacy practices in the home tend to be associated with socioeconomic class, it is important to investigate the extent to which our findings may be confounded with socioeconomic variables. If there are third language learning differences associated with heritage-language literacy practices, it is possible that these differences relate as strongly to socioeconomic variables as they do to literacy per se. Therefore, we will examine the degree to which heritage language literacy practices are associated with key socioeconomic status variables such as parents' level of education and their occupations.

Measures Used

The instruments used to collect the French language and background data were developed for this particular study. Tests that measured both receptive (listening, reading) and productive (speaking, writing) skill areas were prepared and pilot-tested prior to their use in the main study. We sought to make the set of tests as communicative as possible while using formats that would allow specification of psychometric characteristics (Hart, Lapkin & Swain, 1987b). This involved using quasi-realistic materials and providing thematic links between tasks where possible.

The test set consisted of the Test de Compréhension Auditive for assessing listening comprehension; the Test de Mots à Trouver - a cloze test measuring reading comprehension; open writing and speaking tasks; and a sentence repetition task. The open writing task immediately follows the cloze test and is thematically linked to it. The open speaking task follows the sentence repetition exercise and both are thematically linked to different passages of the listening test. Additionally, students completed a questionnaire that asked for, among other things, information relating to the occupations and educational levels of their parents as well as for information about languages other than English and French used at home and their frequency and type of use.

Test de Mots à Trouver

The Test de Mots à Trouver is a cloze test based on a text concerning the Abominable Snowman, or Yeti, purportedly resident in the Himalayas. The original text was drawn from a French *Reader's Digest* article.

The scoring procedure yielded a maximum score of 25, using the "acceptable" method of scoring. The acceptable responses were based on those obtained from pilot data from immersion classes and from two Quebec Francophone classes and reviewed by at least two adult Francophones.

Open writing task

The context of the writing task incorporates the theme of the Test de Mots à Trouver: students are asked to state what they thought about reports of "strange creatures" and, specifically, to give their own opinion about whether the Yeti exists and their reasons for this view.

Several measures were obtained from the writing of the students. First, the number of words written were counted. Second, an error count was made of the non-homophonous grammatical errors (that is, errors that would sound incorrect if spoken). This second measure gives an indication of the students' control over the written manifestations of grammatical knowledge. Third, a global judgement of good writing was made that involved two dimensions: complexity of sentence structure and phrasing; and the incidence of spelling, grammatical, and syntactic errors. A rating of 0 indicated use of simple sentence structures and a high number of grammatical errors, whereas a rating of 3 indicated use of complex structures and relatively few grammatical errors.

Test de Compréhension Auditive

The Test de Compréhension Auditive requires students to answer multiple-choice questions based on passages they have just heard. The passages are recordings of French radio broadcasts including, for example, a news item, a weather forecast, and a segment of an interview. A mix of male and female voices are heard. There are 15 questions in total based on seven passages. Students listen to the passage twice and then hear the question twice. The multiple-choice answer options are presented to the students in written form as they are listening to the questions, thus providing them the possibility of increasing their comprehension through access to a written text of the questions.

Open speaking test

The context for the speaking task is the last passage of the Test de Compréhension Auditive, which is an interview with a Quebec student of Italian home background regarding parental strictness. In the speaking task, students are asked to comment on the strictness of their own and/or their friends' parents and to provide examples. The speaking task was administered individually to a random sample of students, always in a session following the administration of the Test de Compréhension Auditive.

The speech samples of the students were scored for fluency. A four point scale was used, with 0 reflecting poor attack skills ("debit"), uneven rhythm, inappropriate stress patterns, and use of frequent and prolonged pauses often in inappropriate places. The top rating of 3 reflects native-like rate of speech, rhythm, stress and intonation patterns, use of liaison, and avoidance of overly long pauses in appropriate places.

Sentence repetition task

In this task, students first read a text (slightly modified from the original) of a French language weather broadcast. The written text was then withdrawn and the weather bulletin was heard in its entirety. Next, each sentence was played separately and the student attempted to repeat it, although all sentences were too long to allow reproduction from short-term memory. Thus, as with the Test de Compréhension Auditive, this task included the possibility of making use of written text to support comprehension of the spoken passage.

Two scores were obtained from the sentence repetition data that are of particular interest here. First, a score of 1 was given if the meaning of the sentence was conveyed even if the exact wording of the original sentence was not given. Otherwise, the student obtained a score of 0. The scores were summed across sentences making 10 the maximum possible. This score was considered to indicate, along with the Test de Compréhension Auditive, the students' understanding of spoken French. Second, correct reproduction of specific syntactic features, discursive features, compulsory liaisons and syncopes (the dropping of the mute "e" in speech) were counted. Across all the sentences, 21 occasions of the particular features singled out for exact repetition occurred, thus making the total possible score 21. This measure was considered an indication of the students' spoken French proficiency.

Parental level of education

As indicated above, students were asked to complete a questionnaire. They were asked to indicate the highest level of education obtained by each of their parents. There were 8 levels: elementary, some high school, high school diploma, some community college or business/technical school, graduation from community college or business/technical school, some university, university degree, and graduate or professional degree.

Parental occupation status

As part of the same questionnaire, students were asked to indicate separately the kind of work done by each of their parents. Examples of homemaker, plumber, nurse, bank teller, and doctor were given. The occupational responses (excluding non-labour-force categories) were coded according to the Porter-Pineo Scale (Pineo, Porter, & McRoberts, 1977) as revised to fit 1980 census categorization. Both the occupational status and the educational attainment questions were sent home for completion by parents.

Heritage language use: literacy

Students were asked a number of questions in order to determine heritage language use patterns. To obtain categories that would indicate literacy knowledge in the heritage language, information from several questions was combined. The questions used asked students to list what languages, not counting English and French, they understand in written and spoken form; and to indicate the main ways in which these languages are used (for example, speaking to parents, writing to relatives, watching TV, reading letters or newspapers). Using this information, four categories were derived: (a) no heritage language; (b) heritage language, but unable to understand the written form of it (a heritage language non-literate); (c) can understand a heritage language in the written form and did not indicate any use of the written form (heritage language literate, but non-user); and (d) understands and uses a heritage language in the written model (heritage language literate, and user).

Heritage language use: frequency

Our frequency-of-use variable is based on information derived from asking students how often English and any other language is spoken in their home. Students circled one of five categories for each language: never, hardly ever, sometimes, about half the time, most of the time. For purposes of analysis in this study, we grouped the responses into two categories: (a) infrequent (never, hardly ever, and sometimes); and (b) frequent (about half the time and most of the time).

There were 38 students who listed a heritage language but who gave no information on their frequency of using it. Therefore, these students were excluded from this category.

Results

Impact of heritage language literacy

Table 1 shows mean scores on the French proficiency tests for the four categories of heritage language use (literacy). Overall, the results show that literacy knowledge in the heritage language regardless of whether learners are currently making use of those literacy skills, has a strong positive impact on the learning of a third language. Generally speaking, there is little difference between those who have no heritage language and those who do have one, but cannot read or write it. This is the case, even though all students have at least one language of literacy—English.

The first five measures shown on Table 1 deal with tests directly involving literacy skills. The next three measures represent results from tests involving primarily listening comprehension but, given the manner of test administration, they involve the use of literacy skills to provide additional information and context to the task at hand. The last measure is a measure purely of spoken French proficiency in which the task itself involved no reading or writing. With one exception (non-homophonous errors), the differences are significant at $p \leq 002$.

Table 12.1
Proficiency Measures by Heritage Language Literacy Groups

Measure	No Heritage Language			Heritage Language non-literate			Heritage Language literate, but non user			Heritage Language literate and user			sig.*
	X̄	sd	N	X̄	sd	N	X̄	sd	N	X̄	sd	N	
Reading													
Test de Mots à Trouver (max = 25)	9.82	5.07	119	9.89	5.83	46	13.15	4.62	47	12.87	5.15	99	.000
Writing													
Word Count	57.86	25.39	119	55.70	28.79	46	72.11	27.18	47	69.96	28.06	99	.000
Non-homophonous errors	2.47	1.61	118	2.28	1.91	46	1.77	1.49	47	2.21	1.89	99	.128
Global (% '0')	29.1		34	34.8		16	12.8		6	9.1		9	.002
Global (% '3')	5.1		6	8.7		4	17.0		8	15.2		15	
Listening Comprehension													
Test de Compréhension Auditive (max = 15)	7.92	2.93	119	7.63	2.67	46	9.62	3.28	47	8.83	3.14	99	.001
Global Understanding (max = 10)	3.35	2.70	49	3.93	2.56	40	5.67	2.92	36	5.66	2.70	85	.000
Speaking													
Total Features													
Repeated (max = 21)	4.82	4.54	49	3.65	2.68	40	5.39	4.44	36	7.21	4.30	85	.000
Fluency (0-3)	1.07	.87	44	.89	.69	38	1.39	.73	36	1.44	.76	82	.001

* Based on one-way analysis of variance for all measures except the global writing scores; for the latter, the significance level is for the chi-square value for the cross tabulations of the global written measure with Heritage Language groups.

The results for the cloze test, Test de Mots à Trouver, illustrate clearly the pattern of results noted above for most measures: there is virtually no difference between those students who have no heritage language and those who do but have no literacy skills in it. Similarly, there is little difference between those who are literate in their heritage language but claim not to be involved currently in literacy activities, and those who are literate and make use of those skills. This pattern is also seen with respect to the length of the opinion statements in French (word count), listening comprehension (Test de Compréhension Auditive and global understanding) and speaking (total features repeated and fluency). Subsequent analyses on these measures comparing the mean of student scores in the no heritage language and heritage language but non-literate groups to the mean of students scores in the heritage language literate but non-user and heritage language literate and user groups revealed a highly significant difference ($p \leq 002$) in all cases.

The fourth and fifth measures shown on Table 1 indicate that among those with no heritage language, 29.1% obtained a "0" (write using simple sentences with numerous grammatical errors) while only 5.1% obtained a "3" (write complex sentences with few grammatical errors). Similarly, among those who have a heritage language but are not literate in it, 34.8% obtained a "0" while only 8.7% obtained a "3". These figures contrast with those who are literate in a heritage language: a considerably smaller proportion obtain scores of "0" (12.8% for heritage language literates who are non-users and 9.1% for heritage language literates who are users) and a somewhat higher proportion obtain scores of "3" (17.0% for heritage language literates who are non-users and 15.2% for heritage language literates who are users, thus corroborating the pattern noted with the other measures of French proficiency.

The exception to the pattern noted is with non-homophonous errors. The figures in Table 1 represent error counts. Therefore the lower the figures, the better the results. The results shown in Table 1 are non-significant, indicating that whether or not students could engage in literacy activities in a native language made no difference to the number of grammatical or non-homophonous spelling errors they made while writing in French. As this measure would appear to represent the most surface level, technical features of written language tested—which are, in effect, language specific—it may be that prior literacy experience has little transferability.

To summarize, it appears that heritage language literacy has a generalized positive effect on third language learning; that is, its positive impact is not limited to literacy-related activities in the third language. What appears to be crucial is being able to read and write in the heritage language as opposed to making current use of such knowledge. Furthermore, our results suggest that the effect is related to literacy knowledge (whether currently used or not), rather than oral proficiency in the heritage language.

Relationship between heritage language frequency of use and literacy knowledge

One issue in interpreting the above findings is whether the results are due simply to a generally high level of proficiency in the native language or specifically to the impact of heritage language literacy. Cummins (1976) has argued that above a certain threshold, proficiency in the first language will benefit second language learning.

In order to tease apart general heritage language proficiency as a variable, and heritage language literacy as a variable, we examined test scores as a function of frequency of use and literate versus non-literate background. Doing so involved making the assumption that students who report frequent use (about half the time, most of the time) of a heritage language in the home are proficient in that language. Specifically, we looked to see whether, among those who reported their heritage language to be frequently used in the home, there was a tendency for those who are also literate in their heritage language to do better on test measures relative to those who are not. Results are shown in Table 2.

Table 2 shows that, with the exception of non-homophonous errors and fluency in speaking, differences between proficient heritage language students who are literate in their language and those who are not literate are statistically significant ($p \leq 05$). Thus, it appears that heritage language literacy enhances third language learning over and above general heritage language proficiency.

Table 12.2
Proficiency Measures by Heritage Language Literacy Groups for Students Proficient in their Heritage Language*

Measure	Heritage Language non-literate			Heritage Language literate			
	X̄	sd	N	X̄	sd	N	sig.
Reading							
Test de Mots à Trouver	10.39	6.75	18	13.14	5.00	96	.046
Writing							
Word Count	54.06	31.46	18	71.58	28.74	96	.021
Non-homophonous errors	1.61	1.46	18	2.07	1.78	96	.304
Listening Comprehension							
Test de Compréhension Auditive (max = 15)	7.39	2.66	18	9.11	3.25	96	.036
Global Understanding (max = 10)	3.72	2.32	18	5.78	2.78	85	.004
Speaking							
Total Features Repeated (max = 21)	3.94	3.24	18	7.08	4.45	85	.006
Fluency (0-3)	1.18	.73	17	1.44	.76	82	.193

* Frequency of Heritage Language use in the home is "about half the time" or "most of the time".

Relationship between heritage language literacy and SES variables

Literacy knowledge and use have been found frequently to be positively associated with socioeconomic variables. That is to say, the more literate a person's behaviour, the greater the probability that the person comes from a high SES home background. This means that, for the most part, in studies investigating the relationship between literacy and background variables, SES and literacy have been confounded. In such a case, it is impossible to know whether the relationship found is due to SES variables or to literacy per se.

For this reason, we considered it important to investigate the relationship between certain SES variables and literacy among our students. Our approach involved cross-tabulating our four-category literacy variable against a number of SES indicators: fathers' educational level, mothers' educational level, fathers' occupation, and mothers' occupation. As the pattern of results for mothers' and fathers' educational attainment and for mothers' and fathers' occupation are similar, only the results pertaining to fathers are given in the tables. Furthermore, only the extremes of the SES categories are shown, as little additional information is gleaned from the presentation of all the categories. The results are shown in Tables 3 and 4.

Table 12.3
Distribution of Fathers' Highest Educational Level (Polar Categories)within Heritage Language Literacy Groups

	elementary or some high school	university or graduate/ professional degree
no heritage language	13.4%	39.2%
heritage language non-literate	23.8%	21.4%
heritage language literate, non-user	33.4%	25.7%
heritage language literate, user	31.0%	28.7%

Table 12.4
Distribution of Fathers' Occupation (Polar Categories) within Heritage Language Literacy Groups

	semiskilled or unskilled workers	managers or professionals
no heritage language	13.5%	31.7%
heritage language non-literate	22.2%	15.6%
heritage language literate, non-user	34.1%	18.2%
heritage language literate, user	31.9%	19.1%

Table 3 shows the highest level of education attained by fathers cross-tabulated with language and literacy abilities of their children. Two categories of educational attainment are shown: fathers who have had only elementary school or some high school; and fathers who have completed a university, graduate, or professional degree. Table 4 shows fathers' occupation cross-tabulated against the language and literacy background of their children. Results are presented for two broad polar occupation categories: managers or professionals and semiskilled or unskilled workers.

Tables 3 and 4 present data indicating that the effects we have thus far ascribed to heritage language literacy are not, in fact, the masked effects of socioeconomic status. First, among students who have a heritage language, those literate in it are not disproportionately drawn from high SES families. There is a broad similarity in the distributions of fathers' education and fathers' occupation for heritage language literate and heritage language non-literate students. The proportion of university educated fathers is somewhat higher for heritage language literate students (25.7% and 28.7% versus 21.4%), but so too is the proportion of fathers without a high school diploma (33.4% and 31.0% versus 23.8%). In the case of fathers' occupation, the main difference between heritage language literate and non-literate students is the somewhat higher proportion of the former (34.1% and 31.9% versus 22.2%) whose fathers hold semiskilled or unskilled jobs. In summary, heritage language literate and non-literate students have broadly similar distributions regarding SES backgrounds. Thus, among students who have a heritage language, differences in third language proficiency associated with heritage language literacy cannot be ascribed to SES.

Tables 3 and 4 also indicate that SES is not a credible candidate for explaining differences in third language proficiency between students literate in a heritage language and those without heritage language. In comparison to students with no knowledge of a heritage language, a greater proportion of heritage language literate students have fathers who lack a high school diploma; a smaller proportion have fathers with a university degree. As Table 4 shows, a similar pattern appears regarding fathers' occupation. Fathers of heritage language literate students are more likely to hold semiskilled or unskilled jobs and less likely to hold managerial or professional jobs than fathers of students with no knowledge of a heritage language.

Thus, although it might be predicted that having parents with higher levels of formal education or more prestigious occupations and no heritage language would favour a student's performance on French language tests, these results suggest that this is not the case.

Impact of Romance versus non-Romance heritage language

A reasonable assumption about the influence of one language on the learning of another is that positive transfer will more likely occur between more closely related languages. We decided to explore this issue by examining the differential impact on the learning of French—a Romance language—of having a Romance versus non-Romance heritage language.

The students in the Romance heritage language group reported using one of the following heritage languages: Italian, Spanish or Portuguese. The students in the non-Romance heritage language group reported using one of the following heritage languages: German, Polish, Hebrew, Filipino/Tagalog, Chinese, Greek, or Korean.

The results are shown in Table 5. The first point to note is that in all cases there is a trend for Romance heritage language students to do better on the French proficiency measures than non-Romance heritage language students. However, the difference between these two groups is significant ($p \leq 05$) in only two cases: global understanding and fluency. Thus, although the results are in the expected direction, they are not strongly supportive of the hypothesis that positive transfer is more likely to occur when the first language is from the same language family as the language being learned.

The research reported in this chapter strongly supports the claim that literacy in one's native language enhances third language learning. It appears from this study that there is an effect of native language literacy per se independent of native language non-literacy skills, independent of the general level of heritage language proficiency, and independent of the linguistic and historical relationship between the two languages.

Four points are particularly worthy to note. First, it is clear that literacy in the heritage language adds something above and beyond literacy in the second language. This is to say, all the students in the study had learned to read in English, their initial language of schooling. Yet literacy in their heritage language appears to have contributed to a generalized higher level of proficiency in the third language. It is one of the weaknesses of the current study that we do not know when the heritage

Table 12.5
French Proficiency Measures by Heritage Language Background
(Romance versus Non-Romance)

Measures	Romance			Non-Romance			sig.
	X̄	sd	N	X̄	sd	N	
Reading							
Test de Mots à Trouver (max = 25)	13.50	4.61	86	12.40	5.45	55	.201
Writing							
Word Count	74.51	27.22	86	65.49	28.15	55	.060
Non-homophonous Errors	2.01	1.72	86	2.18	1.92	55	.584
Listening Comprehension							
Test de Compréhension Auditive (max = 15)	9.48	2.92	86	8.56	3.52	55	.097
Global Understanding (max = 10)	6.05	2.53	73	5.02	2.98	44	.048
Speaking							
Total Features Repeated (max = 421)	7.30	4.33	73	6.45	4.37	44	.309
Fluency (0-3)	1.57	.73	72	1.21	.72	42	.013

language students learned to undertake literacy activities in their heritage language: for some it is highly probable that they learned these skills in Heritage Language Programs offered at school to help them further develop their heritage language and learn about their heritage language culture. This means that their heritage language might not be their language of initial literacy. However, it might well be that heritage language literacy provides them a fuller understanding of "what reading and writing are for, using the medium of a language that (they) speak fluently" (Hudelson 1987, p. 830). Additionally, it may give them a feeling of success, pride, and self-confidence, which may breed further success.

Second, it appears from our results that knowledge of heritage language literacy is as important as using literacy skills. This finding supports the notion of linguistic interdependence. So, too, does our third point: that transfer appears least likely to occur with surface level and language-specific aspects of language. What is interdependent is knowledge and process.

Fourth, in the sample of students we considered in this research, SES does not appear to be confounded with heritage language literacy practices. This may be because heritage language literacy has been learned by some at school. Whatever the reason, it is unusual to be able to unconfound these two variables. We therefore place a great deal of importance on the finding that third language learning is enhanced through native language literacy independent of SES variables.

Our results contribute to the growing literature that indicates that bilingual education programs that promote native language literacy have an overall positive effect on the learning of other languages. They represent an extension of the findings that when the second language is required for academic success and participation in the target language society, the provision of a sound basis in a native language, including literate activities, is a wise investment.

References

Blid, E. (1987). *Minority language students in a French immersion program: Their French proficiency.* Unpublished master's thesis, University of Toronto, Toronto.

Cummings, J. (1976). The influence of bilingualism on cognitive growth: A synthesis of research findings and explanatory hypotheses. *Working Papers on Bilingualism, 9,* 2-43.

Cummings, J. (1981). The role of primary language development in promoting educational success for language minority students. In Office of Bilingual Bicultural Education, California State Department of Education (Ed.). Schooling and language minority students: A theoretical framework (pp. 3-49). Los Angeles: California State University, Evaluation, Dissemination and Assessment Center.

Cummins, J. (1984). Bilingualism and special education: Issues in assessment and pedagogy. Clevedon, Avon: Multilingual Matters.

Cummins, J. & Swain, M. (1986). *Bilingualism in education.* London: Longman.

Cummins, J., Swain, M., Nakajima, K., Handscombe, J., Green, D. Z., & Tran, C. (1984). Linguistic interdependence among Japanese and Viet-

namese immigrant students. In C. Rivera, (Ed.) *Communicative competence approaches to language proficiency assessment: Research and
application* (pp. 60-81). Clevedon, Avon: Multilingual Matters.

Genesee, F. (1987). *Learning through two languages: Studies of immersion
and bilingual education.* New York: Newbury House.

Hakuta, K. (1986). *The mirror of languages: The debate on bilingualism.*
New York: Basic Books.

Hart, D., Lapkin, S., & Swain, M. (1987a). *Early and middle French
immersion programs: Linguistic outcomes and social character.* Toronto:
Metropolitan Toronto School Board.

Hart, D., Lapkin, S., & Swain, M. (1987b). Communicative language tests:
Perks and perils. *Evaluation and Research in Education, 1*(2), 83-95.

Hudelson, S. (1987). The role of native language literacy in the education
of language minority children. *Language Arts, 64,* 826-841.

Krashen, S., & Biber, D. (1988). *On course: Bilingual education's success
in California.* Sacramento: California Association for Bilingual Education.

Ovando, C., & Collier, V. (1985). *Bilingual and ESL classrooms.* New York:
McGraw-Hill.

Pineo, P. C., Porter, J., & McRoberts, H. A. (1977). The 1971 census and
the socioeconomic classification of occupations. *Canadian Review of
Sociology and Anthropology, 14,* 91-102.

Rosier, P., & Farella, M. (1976). Bilingual education at Rock Point - some
early results. *TESOL Quarterly, 10,* 379-388.

Skutnabb-Kangas, T. (1979). *Language in the process of cultural assimila-
tion and structural incorporation of linguistic minorities.* Arlington, Va.:
National Clearinghouse for Bilingual Education.

Skutnabb-Kangas, T. (1981). *Bilingualism or not: The education of
minorities.* Clevedon, Avon: Multilingual Matters.

Swain, M. (1981). Bilingual education for majority and minority language
children. *Studia Linguistica, 35*(1-2), 15-32.

Swain, M., & Lapkin, S. (1986). Immersion French in secondary schools:
'The goods' and 'the bads'. *Contact, 5* (3), 2-9.

Troike, R. C. (1978). *Research evidence for the effectiveness of bilingual
education.* Arlington, VA: National Clearinghouse for Bilingual Education.

Troike, R. C. (1981). Synthesis of research on bilingual education. *Educational Leadership, 38,* 498-504.

Troike, R. C. (1986). *Improving conditions for success in bilingual educa-tion programs*. Report on Bilingual Education to the Committee on Education and Labor. Washington, D.C.

Wesche, M., Morrison, F., Pawley, C., & Ready, D. (1986). *Post-secondary follow-up of former French immersion students in the Ottawa area: A Pilot Study*. Ottawa: Department of the Secretary of State.

Willig, A. C. (1985). A meta-analysis of selected studies on the effectiveness of bilingual education. *Review of Educational Research, 55*, 269-317.

13

Concepts of Literacy and their Consequences for Children's Potential as Learners

Gen Ling Chang and Gordon Wells
Ontario Institute for Studies in Education

This chapter argues that it is in the activity of writing that the nature of literacy is most readily grasped and the potential of language for empowering thinking most fully experienced. Through the creation of a retrievable record of one's thinking that can be reflected upon and reshaped, one is able to develop structures of thought of a complexity and coherence that would otherwise be almost impossible. By the same token, reflection on the processes of writing permits one to gain a greater understanding of and control over the associated mental processes. Writing is thus a technology that can be intentionally used to extend the power of mind.

The implications of this conception of literacy were investigated in collaboration with two teachers by attempting to change the learning conditions in their classrooms. Discussion of the data addresses three issues: the connection between teachers' beliefs, provision of learning opportunities, and children's literacy development; collaboration as a mode of research; and writing-process theory as the basis for a model of inquiry.

Theoretical Background

For those of us whose intellectual development has taken place in a literate society, it seems self-evident that our intellectual achievements are dependent on the ability to read and write. And, at one level, that is certainly true. Without the knowledge that we have gained by reading, we should be much less well-informed; without the ability to write, we should be unable to take notes or summarize what we have learned, nor would our ideas achieve the wide circulation that publication makes possible. But such an assessment of the contribution of reading and writing both under-values and over-values their significance. On the one hand, much more is involved in using written language as a facilitator of thinking than is brought out by an emphasis on the archival function that written language serves in giving a permanent representation to information so that it can be widely disseminated. On the other hand, it would be arrogant to assume that, amongst those who, for whatever reason, do not learn to read and write, there are none who demonstrate the ability to think critically and constructively on a wide variety of issues, including issues demanding a high level of abstraction.

Nevertheless, it is this characteristic of the permanence (relatively speaking) of what has been written that is significant in making written language potentially such a powerful instrument for the development of thinking—for functioning as what Bruner (1972) calls a "cognitive amplifier". The existence of a text—a fixed verbal formulation—facilitates the recognition of the distinction between what was actually said and the various meanings or interpretations that can be derived from it (Olson, 1986). As a result, readers of texts are encouraged to ask about the facts contained in them, the adequacy of the evidence to support them, the relationship of these facts and evidence to their own experience, and so on. Such talk also leads quite naturally to the development of a metalanguage for talking about texts and about the thinking associated with their production and interpretation (Olson & Astington, in press). Written texts thus invite a discriminating, critical response, in the course of which the reader may extend and sharpen his or her understanding of the matter concerned whilst, at the same time, developing these language-related thinking skills more generally.

However, although reading texts written by others may provoke the reader to think or feel more profoundly and discriminatingly, reading itself leaves no record of its results to which future reference may be made. For that, it is necessary for the reader to become a writer, and attempt to formulate in his or her own text the understanding that has been gained. And then it is the malleability of written language that comes into focus as a facilitator of thinking and feeling. What has been written can be critically read, in the same way as can a text by another person, in order to see what it means; but it can also be rewritten, in order to develop ideas that were initially only incipient or to clarify those that were imprecise. Furthermore, the record that is left of these mental processes—that is, the written text—can be the basis for discussion with others, in the course of which another reader's response can be taken into account. In other words, by writing, rereading and rewriting, and by discussing the emerging text with others, one can work on one's own thinking in a conscious and deliberate manner (Bereiter & Scardamalia, in press).

From an educational perspective, then, what is important about reading and writing is not so much the specific information that is gained through engaging in these activities as it is the development of a way of thinking: the building up, metaphorically speaking, of a set of mental muscles that enable one effectively to tackle intellectual tasks that would otherwise be beyond one's power. However, this way of thinking is not dependent on reading and writing: to a considerable degree it can also be deployed in speech. When the appropriate conditions arise, literate people can "speak a written language"; and so too can those who are still in the process of learning to read and write.

To focus on literate thinking, then, is to draw attention to the centrality of literacy in education, but not literacy conceived simply in terms of the skills of coding/decoding print or those involved in the transmission of information through written texts. What is emphasized, rather, is the conception of literacy as thinking that deliberately makes use of language, whether spoken or written, as an instrument for its own development.

If this general line of argument is correct, there are very substantial implications for the way in which the teaching and learning of literacy should be approached in school, and indeed, there are similar implications for the curriculum as a whole. However, as our current observational research study shows, these ways of thinking are, as yet, largely unknown to teachers and so they have little impact on classroom practice. In the place of this broad and powerful conception of literacy as both means and model for creative and critical thinking, what we have elsewhere referred to as "epistemic literacy" (Wells, 1987), the conception underlying much actual classroom practice is both restricted and restricting. One of the aims of our current research project, therefore, is to bring about a closer relationship between theory and practice by working collaboratively with teachers to reflect on current practice with a view to improving children's opportunities for learning.

This chapter is based on work carried out with two teachers in one of the four participating schools in the Language and Learning Research Project—a three year ethnographic study of the classroom learning experiences of 72 children from four ethnolinguistic backgrounds— Chinese, English, Greek, and Portuguese—and across seven elementary grades, Senior Kindergarten to Grade Six.

The Two Classrooms Observed

Grade Five, located in Room 130, was a place in which all of the 26 children moved around freely and spoke to each other as much as to their teacher, whom we shall call Mr. Michael Dougherty. He believes firmly in books as a rich source of language input and, throughout the fall and spring terms, he devoted a substantial portion of each day to reading to and with the children. In language arts periods, children either worked individually or in small groups according to ability levels or commonality of interests; at other times children worked on teacher-directed tasks, for example on a series of problems in mathematics, or followed guided steps in science using the kits of materials provided. Yet it was not unusual for the Grade Five children to postpone or altogether forget about doing the work set, since Michael Dougherty was extremely lenient about checking the children's work. Indeed, his trusting attitude with respect to the monitoring of work to be done was often perceived by the children as a lack of clear expectations.

In Room 301, where the Grade Three class was located, Mrs. Margaret Thomson had developed a close relationship with her 22 children. Besides being expected to work individually at their desks, for example, on language and mathematics skill-related activities, the children also had opportunities to work in groups on theme-oriented activities. Often these group activities, which integrated language with curricular content, appeared to act as a bonus, because the children were encouraged to engage in them only after completing their daily seatwork. While the children worked alone or in groups, Margaret Thomson would frequently instruct individual children on a particular set of skills or grammatical point. She also regularly checked the children's work and kept a detailed record of the work completed by each child.

In both classrooms we observed that reading and writing were predominantly treated as skills and processes that required the allocation of specific times for their learning. In reading periods, it was not unusual to observe the children in both classes grouped according to reading-level, reading the group Reader and completing the accompanying exercises. Similarly, in writing periods, children wrote in folders or journals about their personal experiences or on story topics that were either selected by the writer or suggested by the teacher. When the topic was teacher-selected, there would usually be a period of oral preparation, in which elements to be included in the story would be discussed (Grade Three) or ways of generating possible content suggested (Grade Five). During the actual writing, there was little teacher intervention, although there was much discussion among peers. In neither class did we observe regular opportunities for children to share what they had written with their peers, nor were the teachers observed to devote a significant amount of time to the discussion of first drafts with their authors.

The major difference between the two classes was in the amount of teacher-directed practice of skills. In Grade Three, a substantial propor-tion of the reading period (25%) was devoted to phonics and grammar exercises; in addition, a separate period was devoted to work on spelling and handwriting. At no time was a child seen to engage in sustained reading of a book of his or her own choice. In Grade Five, by contrast, much less time was spent on individual skill-based seat-work (6%); instead, children spent approximately a fifth of their time engaged in silent reading of books of their own choice. In both classes, these periods allocated to the learning of reading and writing, although spent different-ly, accounted for 45% of curricular time. Some time was devoted to work in Science and Social Studies: approximately 10% to 20% according to our observations of the two classes. Most of this time was spent on whole-class discussion or on the completion of teacher-structured tasks (Grade Three) or on teacher-defined practical activities (Grade Five).

From such methods of classroom organization, we inferred that both teachers conceived of writing and reading primarily as language skills to be mastered as ends in themselves. Although they differed somewhat in the means they employed to achieve these results, neither teacher seemed to encourage active discussion of alternative interpretations of| the texts that the groups read together, nor did they seem to demonstrate to the children that writing could be a way of coming to know, and of communicating the understanding so acquired to others.

The Problem: Teachers' and
Researchers' Perspectives

By the middle of the school year, both teachers had become sufficiently accustomed to the presence of researchers in their classrooms for the
observations to be no longer perceived as threatening, and a relationship
of mutual trust was beginning to be established. Informal discussions
began to take place in recess time and at the end of the school day, in
which the teachers began to talk about their concerns. In both cases, the
poor quality of the children's writing was a topic that was frequently
raised. Since writing activities constituted a considerable proportion of
class time, the children's limited success as writers could not, in the
teacher's view, be the result of lack of opportunity. Instead, they tended
to attribute it to the children's limited command of English or to the
parents' inability to give support at home, either because of the long
hours that they worked, or because they were unaware of ways in which
they could help, despite their concern that their children should succeed
in school.

To have challenged these explanations directly would have been
inappropriate. In the first place, there was some truth in the observation
that the children's ability to write was affected by the fact that they were
simultaneously learning the language in which they were expected to
demonstrate their ability. (In the Grade Three class, 86%, and in the
Grade Five class, 92% of the children were from non-English-speaking
backgrounds.) In the second place we judged that a better approach
would be to try to bring about a change in the conditions for writing, by
engaging in teacher-researcher collaboration such that the children's
resultant behaviour and performance would lead the teachers to change
their opinions on the basis of empirical observations. In addition, we
hypothesized that the limited potential that the children manifested in
their writing was more apparent than real, and that it stemmed as much
from low expectations and the nature of the challenges set for them as
from any inherent limitations in the children themselves. Moreover, as
suggested above, an equally important constraint on the opportunities
for the children to display their full potential as writers, we believed, was
the teachers' underlying conception of literacy and its development.

Collaboration in Effecting Change

It is perhaps unusual to devote so much space to the description of the situation into which the researcher intends to intervene. However, we have felt it necessary to do so in order that the grounds for the intervention and the nature of the intervention itself should be understood. For, unlike those who work within what might be called the traditional paradigm of educational research and development, our intention was not to introduce an alternative curriculum package that we judged to be superior and then measure its effectiveness in some way. Of course, we had principles that we thought would underpin a more effective model of literacy in the curriculum, but we also recognized that any change in that direction would need to be organic—that is to say, it would have to be chosen by the teacher and would probably be achieved incrementally over a considerable period of time.

Our reasons for adopting this approach were twofold: first, we wished to support teachers' professionalism by inviting them to be co-agents with us in the determination of directions for change and in the means for achieving it; secondly, we saw the collaborative inquiry in which we were seeking to engage the teachers as itself an example of the sort of literate thinking we were hoping to promote. Through it, we hoped that they would experience a way of thinking and working that they could then share with their pupils. But first we had to discover what concerns the teachers had that might serve as starting points for our action-based inquiry.

Changing Writing Conditions in Grade Three

The opportunity first came with the Grade Three teacher. Having been introduced to the idea of cooperative learning at a professional development day, Margaret Thomson decided to devote part of each Wednesday morning to a series of pre-structured activities designed to develop the skills of cooperation. As this was a new way of working for her, she invited the researchers to participate and provide feedback on the experiment.

Over the six weeks of interchange, a working rapport developed between Thomson and Chang which facilitated the sharing of sensitive information, particularly about the connections between teacher beliefs, learning opportunities, and the children's participation. In her role as teacher, Thomson initially stressed preparation and planning as essential ingredients in the organization of group activities, being strongly influenced by her previous experience. However, in the light of Chang's observational insights, she began to question or re-think her own practices and to formulate possible connections and disjunctions across the range of learning conditions she provided, for example, between seatwork and activities-centre work, and between cooperative group learning and children learning cooperatively in groups. These discussions, which took place after a half-day observation or on the telephone a day or two later, often led to a sharing of ideas on alternative practices, with discussion of potential outcomes and effects.

As a result of these exchanges, teacher and researcher gradually became more critical of their own ideas and roles. Thomson also became more open to the use of observational data as a way of re-visiting phenomena to enable understanding to be more precise. Her growing epistemic stance toward research as a method for professional development moved from initial examination of transcripts of audio-data, through ethnographic analysis of observational data, to reading published papers on literacy in classroom contexts. Finally, in discussion with Wells, she agreed to allow video recordings to be made of teacher and researcher working with the children. This was an important development, for the role of reflective analysis of video-data in the process of changing the conditions for learning hardly needs to be emphasized. However, in retrospect, it was the evidence the video-data provided of children's structures and strategies in these varied conditions that was the most significant factor in empowering Thomson as agent of curriculum change with respect to literacy and group work.

The dinosaur story-writing event, which we now wish to discuss, was one example of change. It was an important occasion in that, for the first time, Thomson allowed the children to take the initiative in deciding on group membership and the allocation of roles; she also allowed the groups to interpret the task: to write a story about dinosaurs. After forty minutes of sustained group activity, their story read as follows:

> Baby DINOSAURS Schools were in VOCKANOS. Every 5 Years the Fire Drial would Go On as an ERUPTION. THEY WriHT About People. THE Paper was 10 mters long. And the Pencil is 5 mters long. There Close is poka Doted. And THERE Poget is about THE Fugter. THE Library is called Home read stone. And The books or made of saled Rock. THEY

live in haya rock. THERE Brians or as small as marbells. THERE LUnCH
is Brontobrgers. THERE TOYS ARE all With Batreries. THERE
HOUSES is MADE OF Pebulls. by Paulo, Maria, Carmina, Fei, and John.

Numerous studies of young children becoming literate from learning
to write (e.g. Ferreiro & Teberosky 1982; Goelman, Oberg, & Smith,
1984) have demonstrated the socio-cognitive processes of children using
writing for social interaction and for self-initiated expression, for instance very young children using squiggles to mark ownership and
labelling. However, current studies are more concerned with
demonstrating the reverse, i.e., children using interaction to develop the
requisite socio-cognitive-linguistic structures and procedures for writing
(e.g. Dyson, 1987; Heap, 1986; Langer, 1988). One strong claim made
about the value of providing interactive writing events (such as co-
authoring a story, teacher or peer conferencing, and letter or journal
writing) is that these learning conditions expose children to alternative
ways of composing, which in turn might facilitate their development of
a personal composing model. Furthermore, when children are in conditions of writing that call for justifications of conceptual or rhetorical
choices made, in the course of responding as authors, they could meaningfully begin to alter their less effective composing skills and perhaps
acquire new skills as well. In brief, interactive writing conditions enhance children's opportunities to become literate from learning to write.
This we see demonstrated in more than one way in our video-data of this
particular writing condition.

The on-line talk that accompanied the writing of this text, acts as a
window on the children's writing processes. The first point we notice is
that, like most writing tasks, the writing of this story represents a
challenge to the writer(s) to envision an audience. When Paulo, voted
scribe for the group, initiates joint composing with "How about—er—
You guys think too", the immediate responses of the co-writers concern
what would be interesting and fun for the reader. "It will be fun then"
says Carmina. And this consideration appears to guide most of the
suggestions made. In the case of this group of young writers, the
alternatives take the form of titles—one common child strategy for topic
identification and for marking the boundaries of their meaning construction. After approximately 25 turns, the writers finally agree on "Dinosaur
School". Their next task is to generate possible content.

(In the following transcripts, underlining indicates that utterances were spoken simultaneously; a period indicates approximately one second of pause; upper case denotes a word spoken with emphasis. Pseudonyms are used throughout.)

John: The dinosaur school is back in time

Paulo: No, the dinosaur school is underground

Maria: No, no

Paulo: How about in a cave?

Maria: No

Carm: No

Paulo: In a volcano? (Group laughs)

Carm: In a volcano

(The children all speak at once)

Maria: Baby dinosaurs go to school

Paulo: What

Maria: Baby dinosaurs can go to - into a volcano for school

Carm: Baby dinosaur

Paulo: Cor—

John: Then they put a bomb inside the volcano

Paulo: Then we try to put in tyrannosaurus rex? Get it? He wrecks everything

Evidently, these young writers first give their attention to finding a suitable starting idea rather than to deciding how the story should begin. Their child-driven strategy for accessing appropriate content is based, not on the consideration of what elements would constitute an effective beginning and the goals for one, but on generating ideas that their co-writers might like. In cases of expert writers co-authoring a text interactively, the response of either to what has been written is both audience-like and a judgement of whether negotiated intentions and goals have been met. However, the third-graders' process-talk is quite different from expert co-writers'. For example, in making their proposals for the topic-title, they act as if they have already established intentions and goals so no discussion is necessary. Taking this assumption as tacit underpins the children's approach to joint composing, quite unlike expert writers.

The five third-graders co-authoring the "Dinosaur School" demonstrate not only their abilities for social self-expression, but also their growing understanding of the influence of the audience on the composing process: the orientation to others within one's constructive efforts when thinking and writing (Heap, 1986). Indeed, it is the children's move beyond initial response to a word, phrase or sentence written, to engagement with ideas, that is remarkable in the following extract:

Paulo: Baby dinosaur schools are in—are in . volcanos

Maria: WERE in

John: WERE in

Maria: They are not right now, are dinosaurs living right now? 'were' (repeating as Paulo writes)

Paulo: But this is make believe

Maria: I didn't realize there's—there's really a dinosaur school

Another instance occurs when Maria reads aloud when Paulo is scribing and, noticing an inconsistency, she remarks:

Maria: Hm you put dinosaur
DinoSAURS (emphasizing the plural form)

Paulo: I can't do anything now

John: What did he do wrong?

Maria: Dinosaur he put . dinoSAURS (again emphasizing the plural) like thousands of them . more than one

Paulo: So—so that's what the school is

Maria: A school with one kid (laughs)

Carm: Dinosaur school . school of one kid

Here, we have evidence of the children's spontaneous willingness to explain, to question their own ideas in writing, and to play out hypothetical consequences of an alternative suggested in order to help the writer to understand what the text says and what it means, each time any of them was, so to speak, the writer. The role of writer moves fluidly from child to child, each taking control of the composition when it is his or her self-initiated turn.

A final example confirms this point. Maria's first suggestion for the second sentence is "Every five hundred years the fire drill will go on as an eruption". However, when this is objected to, she modifies her suggestion:

> **Maria**: Yeah five years . because they won't be alive in five hundred years
>
> **John**: Yes they would
>
> **Maria**: But they wouldn't be babies any more
>
> **Paulo**: Yeah
>
> **Carm**: They'll be five
>
> **John**: So they'll be in grade six
>
> **Maria**: They are in grade six They'll be in school . they'll be teenagers . not babies any more

From the interactive nature of the cycle of response to something written and feedback on an alternative suggested, we begin to witness the children's emerging ability to revise when provided with appropriate conditions to do so. We believe that numerous occasions of this kind of literacy condition will certainly nourish the recognition that writing in school does not have to be a completion of an assignment that is effortful and ill-understood. Instead, it can be a meaningful event for enabling various skills needed to compose a text that is to be understood by varied and unconvinced audiences.

Relating Science and Literacy in Grade Five

Several times during the year, Michael Dougherty had expressed his interest in teaching science in the junior grades. In the spring, he decided to devote a considerable amount of class time to the theme of energy, with the children working in self-selected groups on projects of their own choosing. A number of factors led to this decision, including an up-coming parents' evening at which he wished the children to have work to display, the talk about group-work in the staffroom, reading about another class in which similar theme-based work had been successful (Chang & Wells, 1988) and discussions on issues of literacy, learning, and language with the researchers. From the beginning, he was keen that the researchers' participation should extend beyond observation and video-taping, as he felt that to have other knowledgeable adults in the classroom would be of benefit, since there would be many groups simultaneously needing assistance.

He was correct in this judgement, and over the next month, Dougherty and Chang spent a considerable amount of time talking with various groups about their projects, helping them to clarify, plan, review, and revise their intentions as they worked toward their chosen outcomes. Wells' visits were less frequent, and were mainly devoted to video-taping, but on occasions he too worked with various groups.

Beside being facilitators of the small groups, Dougherty, Chang and Wells used the frequent discussions they had together to enable each other to work jointly toward Dougherty's intention of developing a community of speakers and audiences among his fifth-graders. But the more significant literacy objective to which the study of energy became integrated was that of empowering the children to take intentional control over their own thinking. To achieve this change was indeed a challenge, as Dougherty began to conceptualize the children's learning experiences and develop a new way of thinking about the connection between science, literacy, and language development. For these aims, Wells and Chang acted as catalysts and participant observers of the children working to know and learn, and the insights thus gained were the elements for establishing the collaborative relationship with Dougherty.

All ten groups of fifth-graders were introduced to the idea of using the library as a resource centre, especially during the topic-identification phase of their projects. Consequently, reading played a major role in almost every group's approach to their topic, as they sought out the information needed to formulate a feasible question for investigation. The role envisaged for writing was initially quite small but, through the group discussions, the children were alerted to the varied and important functions that writing could perform in carrying out their projects. However, for this chapter we will focus our analysis of the video-data on the structures and strategies that the children shared through talk as they moved from information externally located in people and books to understanding, in other words, on how these fifth-graders constructed knowledge under the learning conditions of group investigation.

Judith, Suyin, Vanda and Teresa were working on wind energy. Following a lengthy conference with Chang and Wells, Judith was asked by her teacher to share with the rest of the class the strategies her group had learned to use.

> **Judith**: We'll be doing about the history of the windmills, and like what they used the windmills for and we will . . . The sheet here of what we know about the windmills and what we need to find out. So we'll be doing that and we're doing a model and sheets so we won't have to do much job. Okay?
>
> **Dough**: Did you discover any special problems that you'll have to do—you will have to work on?
>
> **Judith**: What do you mean 'special'?
>
> **Dough**: Well, while you were making an outline of things that you know and things that you have to find out did you come across anything that—any part of it that's particularly difficult?
>
> **Vanda**: Now we have to find out how we're going to make it [the model]
>
> **Judith**: Yeah
>
> **Dough**: The actual construction?
>
> **Judith**: Yeah. It is to do—I don't know. We're not sure about size yet
>
> **Dough**: So you've got—so did you outline then the things you'll be needing?
>
> **Judith**: Yeah.

As can be seen in this extract, the teacher's monitoring of the children working in a group provided occasions for making small group talk a part of the learning process, and using public articulation as a learning tool. Whenever the fifth-graders had to explain, report, justify and illustrate their progress and the directions their investigations would be taking, not only did their knowledge on energy increase, but also the explicit and logical processes that underlay the articulation became more public. When both teacher and children were aware of this, and intentionally developed these processes, we observed the children reflecting and analyzing in terms of distinctions like "what we know" and "what we need to find out".

The location of inconsistencies or gaps, expressed as "special problems", is an example of the problem-solving framework that was being fostered, within which the children might conceptualize their inquiries. However, this mode of thinking about constraints encountered was still unfamiliar, as is evidenced by Judith's question: "What do you mean 'special'?" Nonetheless, this idea does not mean that the young researchers were without their own strategies for problem-solving. To the children, "the sheets" represented a documentation of their planning, monitoring and revising of their issues, work to be done and how it should be done. Examination of this tangible trace of the children's thoughts concerning their project indicates a systematicity in their construction of hypotheses, and in their categorization and reshaping of information taken from books according to their self-defined criteria.

So far, we have pointed to the literacy benefits that accrue when children are encouraged to make their group discussions and decisions public. Another literacy condition which was consistently fostered throughout this unit of science study was the request to share the group's findings and what each individual or the group as a whole had learned. This does not refer only to the presentation of final outcomes. It includes the sharing of results so far achieved, the examination of different aspects of the topic from a variety of perspectives and updating of their current understanding of the investigation.

For example, among our video-data are extracts from the various stages of learning that a group of four boys experienced in their joint construction of a model of a windmill. Having to address issues such as the relationships among various types of energy, and problems such as the measurement and synchronization of gears and parts of the model, Wen Kai, Jethro, Peter, and Kim Hock came to understand the significance of theoretical knowledge. Like all enthusiastic youngsters engaging in projects, the four fifth-graders initially thought that their common-sense thinking would be sufficient to carry out their chosen task. However, making a windmill to illustrate wind energy became a learning experience that tested out in observable phenomena the applicability of their lay knowledge. This had profound literate consequences for the boys. They began to recognize the difference between "common-sense knowledge" and "theoretical knowledge" when tested out in the tasks that they undertook.

For example, these young researchers were confronted with the task of meshing two cog-wheels to drive the gear shaft that turned the grinding stone in their windmill. First, they realized their investigation had moved from wind energy to mechanical energy, and, secondly, they discovered that their lay knowledge about how to cut two circular pieces of tin to form the cog-wheels was inadequate. Reference to theoretical knowledge such as the weight of the wheels in proportion to the weight of the shaft and grinding stone had to be considered for the wheels to function. Indeed, the thinking processes as well as the desire to make use of reference books that were generated in this context hardly need to be elaborated.

Conclusion

We began this chapter by arguing that it is in the activity of writing that the nature of literacy is most readily grasped and the potential of language for empowering thinking most fully experienced. For it is through engaging in the cyclical processes of composing and interpretation which any sustained piece of writing requires that writers come both to understand their subject and recognize the limits of their understanding. Through engaging in these same processes in a reflective manner, they can also learn to take intentional control of their own thinking. At the same time, it has to be recognized that goals such as these do not usually figure prominently in the teaching of literacy in the early school years. It is for these reasons that we have focused on writing in our examination of the attempts to change the conditions for literacy learning in the two classrooms.

However, as the evidence shows, to focus on writing need not be restricting. On the contrary, when writing is treated as a powerful means of thinking and communicating in the service of coming to know and understand substantive matters, the development of writing ability and the acquisition of domain knowledge will *both* be enhanced. For this to happen, writing needs to be perceived as a means for the development of literate thinking. We recognize, of course, that the data cited above fall far short of substantiating this claim. However, our aims were as much to investigate the change process itself and the means by which that change came about, as to demonstrate the results seen in terms of the children's performance. Nevertheless, we believe we have been able to demonstrate an uncovering of the children's potential.

An equally important aim has been to develop a framework for conceptualizing the relationship between literacy and the acquisition of domain knowledge for both research and educational purposes. Here too we have found a focus on writing helpful, particularly recent research on the writing process. In order to write, a topic has to be identified and specific goals set with respect to it; plans, both at the macro and micro level, have to be formed in the light of these goals and text composed and transcribed in order to achieve them; and goals, plans, and text have to be constantly subjected to monitoring and revision (Flower & Hayes, 1980). Finally, the whole process has to be under the writer's intentional control, that is to say, subject to metacognition (Bracewell, 1983).

At all levels, the process is dialectical. First, there is the dialectic between what one knows and the demands of the particular text that one is trying to create (Scardamalia & Bereiter, 1985). This, in turn, creates a second dialectic, between what one already knows and what one needs to find out. Finally, there is the dialectic between this particular text and the intertextual world of discourse in relation to which it will be interpreted. As all of these researchers have pointed out, writing is justifiably seen, therefore, as a particularly complex form of problem-solving, which has intellectual benefits that extend beyond the actual production of a particular text.

We wish to argue that this way of conceptualizing writing can be extended to provide a framework to aid in thinking about inquiry more generally, particularly as this is carried out in the classroom within a broad thematic unit of study (see Figure 1). Most types of inquiry have three major phases: (1) the collection of information relevant to the topic through reading, interviews, experimentation, etc. (Research and Inquiry); (2) the assembly, interpretation and organization of this information (Compose and Construct); (3) the communication of what has been discovered through publication, drama, models, oral presentation, etc. (Outcomes of the Inquiry). The three phases may be tackled sequentially or to a large degree simultaneously, but whatever the temporal relationship between them, each phase will involve, as in writing, the same four major processes of: Generating and Setting Goals; Planning; Doing; and

Revising. All four processes are subject to the control of an Executive
Monitor and involve various kinds of Problem Solving and Hypothesis
Construction and Testing.

Figure 13.1 Framework of Literate Conditions for Learning

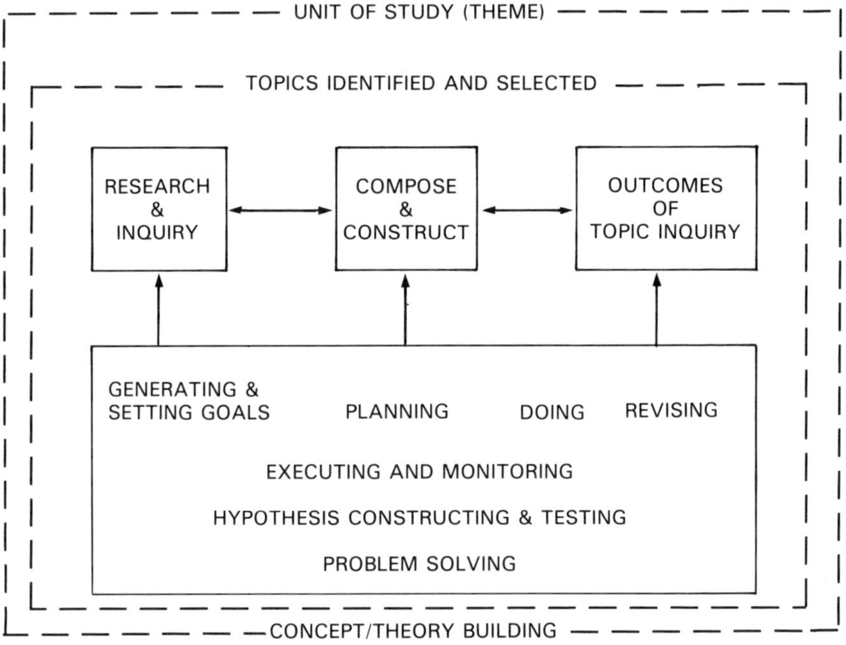

```
┌ — — — — — — — UNIT OF STUDY (THEME) — — — — — — — ┐
│  ┌ — — — — — TOPICS IDENTIFIED AND SELECTED — — — — — ┐  │
│  │                                                     │  │
│  │  ┌──────────┐      ┌──────────┐      ┌──────────┐   │  │
│  │  │ RESEARCH │      │ COMPOSE  │      │ OUTCOMES │   │  │
│  │  │    &     │◄────►│    &     │◄────►│    OF    │   │  │
│  │  │ INQUIRY  │      │ CONSTRUCT│      │  TOPIC   │   │  │
│  │  │          │      │          │      │ INQUIRY  │   │  │
│  │  └────▲─────┘      └────▲─────┘      └────▲─────┘   │  │
│  │  ┌────┴──────────────────┴────────────────┴─────┐  │  │
│  │  │ GENERATING &                                  │  │  │
│  │  │ SETTING GOALS    PLANNING    DOING   REVISING │  │  │
│  │  │                                               │  │  │
│  │  │          EXECUTING AND MONITORING             │  │  │
│  │  │       HYPOTHESIS CONSTRUCTING & TESTING       │  │  │
│  │  │               PROBLEM SOLVING                 │  │  │
│  │  └───────────────────────────────────────────────┘  │  │
│  └ — — — — — — — — — — — — — — — — — — — — — — — — — ┘  │
└ — — — — — — CONCEPT/THEORY BUILDING — — — — — — — — ┘
```

To justify this framework in detail, would take more space than is
available here. However, we believe that the analyses that we have
presented of the development of the third and fifth-graders' literate
thinking, and of the evolution of the teachers' own thinking, have
demonstrated the effects of moving toward the sort of learning opportunities that such a framework envisions. To be sure, its structure and
the language in which it is articulated emerged out of the ongoing
discussion and after-the-event reflection, rather than being prepared in
advance for delivery to the teachers. Yet it is precisely this hindsight
cognition that is our strongest evidence of the gains attained by teachers
and researchers, and also by the children, in the action of changing the
learning conditions to those that reflect a concept of literacy that empowers minds.

Acknowledgement

This research was jointly funded by the Ontario Ministry of Education under contract, by the Toronto Board of Education, and by the Ontario Institute for Studies in Education. We thank them for their support. However, the views expressed in this chapter are those of the authors and not necessarily those of the funding agencies.

We should like to express our gratitude to the teachers and children in the two classes for allowing us to work and learn with them.

References

Bereiter, C., & Scardamalia, M. (in press). Intentional learning as a goal of instruction. In L. B. Resnick (Ed.) *Cognition and instruction: Issues and agendas.* Hillsdale, NJ: Erlbaum.

Bracewell, R. J. (1983). Investigating the control of writing skills. In P. Mosenthal, L. Tamor, & S. A. Walmsley (Eds.) *Research on writing: Principles and methods.* New York: Longman.

Bruner, J. S. (1972). *The relevance of education.* Harmondsworth, Middlesex: Penguin.

Chang, G. L., & Wells, G. (1988). The literate potential of collaborative talk. In M. MacLure, T. Phillips, & A. Wilkinson (Eds.) *Oracy Matters.* Stony Stratford, England: Open University Press.

Dyson, A. H. (1987). *Unintentional Helping in the Primary Grades: Writing in the Children's World.* Technical Report No. 2. Center for the Study of Writing. Berkeley, CA.: University of California. Pittsburgh, PA.: Carnegie Mellon University.

Ferreiro, E., & Teberosky, A. (1982). *Literacy before schooling.* Exeter, NH: Heinemann.

Flower, L. S., & Hayes, J. R. (1980). The dynamics of composing: making plans and juggling constraints. In L. W. Gregg & E. R. Steinberg (Eds.) *Cognitive processes in writing.* Hillsdale, NJ: Erlbaum.

Goelman, H., Oberg, A., & Smith, F. (1984). *Awakening to literacy.* Exeter, NH: Heinemann.

Heap, J. L. (1986, March). Sociality and cognition in collaborative computer writing. Discussion Paper at the Conference on Literacy and Culture in Educational Settings. Michigan: University of Michigan.

Langer, J. (1988). A sociocognitive perspective on literacy. In J. A. Langer (Ed.) *Language, literacy and culture: Issues of society and* schooling. Norwood, NJ: Ablex.

Olson, D. R. (1986). The cognitive consequences of literacy. *Canadian Psychology, 27*: 109-121.

Olson, D. R., & Astington, J.W. (in press). Talking about text: how literacy contributes to thought. *Journal of Pragmatics.*

Scardamalia, M., & Bereiter, C. (1985). Development of dialectical processes in composition. In D. R. Olson, N. T. Torrance, & A. Hildyard (Eds.) *Literacy, language, and learning.* Cambridge: Cambridge University Press.

Wells, G. (1987). Apprenticeship in literacy. *Interchange, 18* (1/2): 109-123.

14

Socioaffective Factors in Literacy Development

William T. Fagan
University of Alberta

Researchers such as Bloome (1983) and Wilcox (1982) have pointed out that literacy development is more than the transmission of a body of academic skills. Literacy is a cultural value that develops through the interaction of individuals. Thus, teachers cannot be viewed as mere skill transmitters, separated from the goals and values that the use of the skills imply. Literacy development is an interactive process, one in which teachers' expectations alone do not necessarily control outcomes. Rather, such outcomes are often modified or even forsaken as teachers and students react to each other's behaviour (Bloome, 1983). Consequently, literacy development must be understood in a broader context than that of skill transmission and the treatment of cognitive or perceptual deficits (Johnson, 1985).

The purpose of this chapter is to demonstrate the validity of this thesis. In the following section the significance of the social context of literacy will be considered. Within this context, children are often differentiated and at times segregated according to the extent to which they meet school expectations. This topic is explored further in the next section, "Marching to a Different Drummer". The subsequent section provides a framework for understanding socioaffective relations and is followed by a description of research findings that seem explicable by this model. The implications of accepting that literacy development is as much influenced by socioaffective factors as by cognitive and academic ones are considered in the last section.

The Social Context of Literacy Development

Literacy as a sociocultural commodity must take its meaning from its use in sociocultural settings. Literacy development occurs not merely through the exchange of skills and ideas, but also through the reactions of individuals to the reactions of other individuals. Students never act as individuals even when they are working on a task on their own, because the task cannot be seen in isolation from what has gone before, what may come after, and even what is happening simultaneously.

When students are called upon to read orally, their relations with the teacher and other students may be as much a factor in how they perform as their actual skills in pronouncing words and constructing meaning. Students who feel that the teacher is "putting them on the spot" and that others may "snicker" at their performance are not only likely to do poorly, but also to develop negative associations with reading and to avoid it if possible in the future. On the contrary, those who feel positive about themselves and the reactions of others are more inclined to view the experience as an opportunity for approval and even admiration. Consequently, as Clark (1984) states, "The social context in which reading and writing are taught, learned, and used" can be either an enabling factor or a constraining one (p. 281).

McDermott (1977) believes that learning is best fostered in an atmosphere of mutual trust. He speaks of "trusting relations" manifested in "how the teacher and children can understand each other's behaviour as directed to the best interests of what they are trying to do together and how they can hold each accountable for any breach of the formulated consensus" (p. 199). In a study of 17,000 students, Goodlad (1984, p. 168) concluded similarly that "students' perceptions of their teachers' interest in them as persons were related to their satisfaction in the classroom".

Rarely does a teacher have an opportunity to study the interactions of a single student to the same extent as students have opportunities to study the teacher (Wolcott, 1974). The teacher's role in the social life of the classroom is conveyed in verbal messages. Kozol (1975) argues that teachers can never "present a neutral position in the eyes of children . . . . Teachers can never be non-political . . . The things a teacher does not dare say may well provide a deeper, more substantial and more lasting lesson than the content of the textbooks or the conscious message of the posters on the wall" (p. 101). The non-neutrality of teachers' behaviours has serious implications when it differentiates among students on the basis of meeting school expectations. The resultant segregations of students can be unfortunate, because the segregated students may have been "marching to a different drummer".

Marching to a Different Drummer

Teachers respond differently to visible minority groups (e.g., Brown, Palincsar & Purcell, 1986; Johnson & Winograd, 1983). However, visible minorities are not the only students who are victims of negative differential treatment in the classroom. According to McDermott (1974, 1977), a minority, pariah, or at-risk status is imposed, not naturally acquired. School is an environment that breeds minorities through the achievement standards that it sets. Differences in achievement make otherwise invisible minorities visible.

As a cultural institution, school is concerned with promoting a set of values that reflect the dominant community. It is the role of the teacher to initiate children into a particular set of identities (McDermott, 1974). Criteria for initiation are set by the school, and are often so subtle that even well-intentioned teachers employ them (McDermott, 1974). From the first contact with the child, the teacher draws conclusions about how "school-wise" the child is. As a consequence, a number of children who are not considered school-wise become immediately a visible minority—a status from which most never recover. Thus, the teacher's set of standards makes visible a particular group of students who continue to be singled out within the context of the school. In other words, they have achieved their minority status. According to Mc-Dermott (1974), the mixture of such children and well-intentioned teachers "can bring about the same disastrous school records achieved by either neurologically disabled children or socially disabled, prejudiced teachers" (p. 82). McDermott maintains that "we have been measuring achievements with a biased set of standards" (p. 94). Thus, the school, by the nature of its operation, sets up minorities for failure (Erickson, 1984). McDermott (1977) states, "Our school system is harsh on those who fall behind; it sorts children out, labels them and finally pushes them aside" (p. 209).

Many children become visible minorities because of a clash in cultural values—the culture of the home and the school. These children are not empty bottles to be filled with school knowledge. Instead, as McDermott (1974) states, they have already been initiated into a culture and have developed identities, statuses, and abilities. When they enter school they are simply behaving within their cultural norms. A problem occurs when different cultural statuses are seen as deficits rather than differences, and the school fails to take such differences into account. Thus, rather than accepting these differences and working within them, the school often sets up barriers that result in the collision of a dominant and a minority group. The children learn that they are not as accepted as others because they are different. The result of such negative messages, according to McDermott (1974) is that

> reading, writing, and arithmetic may take on very different meanings than they do for the child who is more successful in getting good feelings from the politics of the classroom. (p. 90)

Heath (1981) has described home environments from which children come to school "school-wise", and environments where the learning that takes place is not valued by the school. Middle-class mothers ask their children questions similar to those asked in school. These questions tend to be of a "known-answer" type. The question is asked so that the children can display their knowledge—knowledge already possessed by the questioner. A common form of this kind of questioning involves eliciting attributes of objects such as colour and shape. Interestingly, one of the subtests of the Illinois Test of Psycholinguistic Abilities involves this kind of questioning, and failure to respond correctly may result in a child being diagnosed as delayed in expressive language ability.

While the minority families of Heath's study provided just as rich an interaction, it was not of the sort valued or assessed by the school. A possible result of the home and cultural differences documented by Heath (1981) and by Au and Mason (1981) is that teachers immersed in the dominant culture and not aware of alternate forms of behaviour may, on first contact with students from other cultures, relegate them to language-delayed, inattentive, hyperactive, socially immature, or learning-disabled groups.

Another important source of collision between the school and minority groups lies in the meaning which the school in general, and literacy in particular, have for these groups. Teachers tend to believe that literacy is a good to which all children must aspire. As Spindler (1974) states, "educational systems are often charged with responsibility for bringing about change in the culture (actually the minority cultures). Schools become or are intended to become agents of modernization" (p. 303). However, not all students are convinced that schools can deliver what it offers. Many students know someone who engaged in the appropriate behaviours to acquire the rewards that schools promised, yet they did not attain the promised opportunity. Frustration rather than advancement resulted. To the students who know of such occurrences, the teacher's preaching of the merits of education and literacy tends to lessen the teacher's credibility. Those who don't aspire to this good, however, are often viewed with disdain by teachers. In fact, the term "illiterate" tends to have negative connotations.

Not only does literacy sometimes not lead to reward upon leaving school, but also it often has little meaning for students attending school. Literacy as taught in schools is often environmentally sterile. Children are drilled on phonics, answer questions requiring rote recall, and complete workbook exercises. Somehow, such activities are supposed to pay off for the diligent and the involved. But there is little relationship between the literacy activities of school and the literacy activities outside of school—reading for pleasure, taking phone messages, writing notes, reading forms, checking prices. Those children whose conception of literacy is based on these outside-of-school activities and who are not attuned to the school's notion of literacy may find themselves in a school-created minority group.

The above discussion focuses on subcultures as homogeneous entities. However, not all conflicts with the dominant culture of the school can be viewed as resulting merely from different home environments or subcultures. For instance, personality is a source of conflict for some children. In the following section, an attempt is made to provide a framework of the factors contributing to diverse interpersonal, socioaffective relations in the classroom.

A Framework for Understanding Socioaffective Relations

Human interaction is never static. Bateson (1958) suggests that such interaction is really a dynamic equilibrium in which changes in behaviour are constantly taking place. On the one hand, there are processes that tend to lead to greater differentiation in the behaviour of groups. On the other hand, there are processes acting to counteract differentiation.

Bateson calls this process of differentiation, "schismogenesis"—"a process of differentiation in the norms of individual behaviour resulting from cumulative interaction between individuals" (p. 175).

If differentiation is slight or negative, and forces tending to differentiation are continuously counterbalanced by ones counteracting differentiation, then harmony or a state of mutuality results. For example, a teacher may unintentionally slight a student (creating differentiation) but immediately realize what has happened and apologize. The apology increases the state of mutuality between the teacher and the student. When the differentiation is not redressed, it may take two forms, according to Bateson—complementary or symmetrical schismogenesis.

Complementary Schismogenesis

In complementary schismogenesis, one group or individual in a system of relationship accepts a passive or subservient role. Some children adopt this role out of fear. They fear their teachers and the teachers' punishment if they do not meet with their expectations. Consequently they do their work, do not create discipline problems, and are respectful, at least on the surface. This behaviour by the children reinforces the teachers' stance, which, in turn, will lead to more fear in the students. Thus, the roles of the teachers and students differentiate progressively. Shor and Freire (1987) think of such students as living in a culture of silence, in which "some silent students dutifully copy down notes and follow the teacher's voice . . . [while] others sit silently and daydream, unplugged from the repulsive conditions of the classroom" (p. 122). When socioaffective relations of this type have been established, students often band together in support of each other, not so much anti-teacher as pro-student (Wolcott, 1974). The whisper of a word to a peer who stumbles when reading orally, or the passing of a note with an answer are attempts to keep the peer from being detected, from being singled out. Such behaviour (as long as it is not known to the teacher) reinforces the complementarity of the situation.

However, Bateson cautions that there are always limits—the pendulum may be pushed too far. Some students are inclined to react with anger and resentment "provoked by the imposition of tedium and orthodoxy on them" (Shor & Freire, 1987, p. 122). However, they are unlikely to express this hostility openly, at least in the presence of the teacher. Others may regress to a state of helplessness and hopelessness—

a state which is often reinforced by their assignment to the lowest instructional group which, according to McDermott (1974), is a structure for organizing the statuses and identities of children in the class.

Many studies have documented the effects of low group assignments on differentiating students (e.g., Allington, 1983; Brophy, 1983; Brown, Palincsar & Purcell, 1986; Hiebert, 1983; Johnson & Winograd, 1983). Not only do teachers have a different attitude and emotional reaction toward children in the low group, they provide them reading instruction of a different nature. For good readers, teachers are more inclined to focus on comprehension instruction, interrupt less frequently, and provide more supportive and constructive feedback. For the low reading group, on the other hand, teachers spend more time drilling on phonics or isolated words, interrupting frequently usually to give a response (Brown, Palincsar and Purcell, 1986), and selectively calling on students to answer questions (McDermott, 1977). According to McDermott (1977), the low reading group spends only one-third as much time on reading tasks as the top group, even though they spend an equal amount of time in group work. Brown, Palincsar and Purcell (1986) state that "it would not be surprising if children in the low groups came to regard reading as a process of reading aloud to the teacher with acceptable pronunciation..." (pp. 115-117). However, what is even more disturbing is that these children are also likely to learn that they don't have a productive place in the school system and that an education is meaningless to their lives because they are unable to participate fully in the affairs of the school.

Another disturbing fact about the relegation of children to a low reading group is that their fate is likely sealed on admittance to the group. Cazden (1981) showed that when children who tested similarly in reading achievement were assigned to groups, those who were assigned to a low group performed more like poor readers, while those assigned to a higher group were more likely to perform like good readers. Considering such data, it is not surprising that Anderson, Hiebert, Scott, and Wilkinson (1984) concluded that "it is not so much ability that determines the future attainment of a young student but the reading group into which the child is initially placed" (p. 90).

Johnson and Winograd (1983) indicated that learned helplessness tends to result in deficits in three general areas: cognitive, motivational and affective. Children assigned to low ability groups often perform erratically and do poorly on tasks they had performed successfully earlier. They also tend not to use strategies effectively nor to monitor their performance on tasks. Affectively, they suffer from low-esteem, resignation, and apathy. They have a low expectation of success, do not perceive a relationship between their effort and achievement, and believe that factors leading to success are beyond their control.

Symmetrical Schismogenesis

When differentiation evolves within a symmetrical schismogenesis pattern it tends to be characterized by conflict and open hostility rather than by passivity. Shor and Freire (1987) refer to this conflict as cultural sabotage (p. 123). They maintain that "passivity is *not* a natural condition of childhood or adulthood" (p. 123), but believe that "students who sabotage the symbolic violence of the curriculum are defending their autonomy", although often in "self-destructive, and confused ways" (p. 123).

Students who are relegated to a minority status by the school often refuse to cooperate with the school's diagnosis of them as failures. Consequently, rather than "buckling under" and assisting with the school's self-fulfilling prophecy, they fight back and thus acquire a "more acceptable self-image than does agreement with the school's definition [of them]" (Erickson, 1984, p. 538).

When students resist, teachers sometimes attempt to control them through status degradation that often leads to "impersonal warfare, rather than trust and responsibility" and to many "children spend[ing] their time in relational battles rather than on learning tasks" (McDermott, 1977, p. 206). The outcome of resistance by students depends on how much peer support they can mobilize. If there is sufficient peer support, then teachers find themselves without the assistance of counteracting forces and the leadership status normally accorded the teacher is now accorded the students. In this situation, the teacher has lost control.

Relations among students also may be marked by complementary and symmetrical schismogenesis patterns—the same differentiation patterns that characterize teachers' and students' interpersonal relations. Richek, List and Lerner (1983) report a large body of evidence that "shows that poor achievers tend to be rejected by their classmates in school" (p. 30).

In fact, Asher, Renshaw and Hymel (1982) maintain that not only are positive peer relations important as support mechanisms in classrooms, but peer relations correlate with adjustment in later life.

Section Summary

Socioaffective differentiation characterized as patterns of schismogenesis may be represented diagrammatically as in Figure 1, a modification of a representation of stress reactions to reading depicted by Gentile and McMillan (1988).

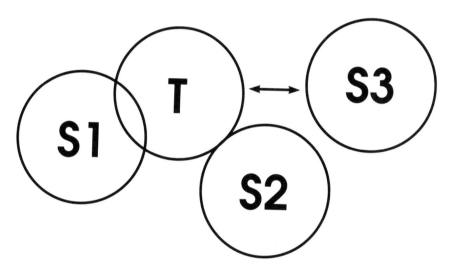

Figure 14.1 Interpersonal Relations: Teacher-Students

The intersecting circles suggest that the teacher and student 1 have mutually accepted goals for literacy and both cooperate in working to realize these goals. Consequently, there is harmony. The touching circles signify a pattern of complementary schismogenesis between the teacher and student 2. Students from three groups, as discussed in the section on complementary schismogenesis, typify this latter pattern: (a) those who passively accept the situation and tend to develop a learned helplessness syndrome; (b) those who seethe with anger and resentment, tend to be dismissed by the teacher, but give the appearance of "buying into the system" by not being trouble-makers; and (c) those who are part of the dominant student body through achievement. The latter group usually contains very bright students who either are able to achieve though doing little work, or who by their ingenuity can scheme their way through. Their high level of intelligence is often not recognized by the teacher.

The non-adjoining circles suggest symmetrical schismogenesis between the teacher and student 3. Two types of students may be characterized this way—those who fight and those who flee (Gentile & McMillan, 1988). One group resorts to flight by opting out of the school milieu (through, for example, truancy or as a result of work not completed). Students in this group are unlikely to achieve. The group that fights, engages in open conflict. Unless there are counteracting forces, students in this group, too, tend to be failures within the school system.

Figure 1 represents the possible interpersonal relationships between only the teacher and students. A description of classroom interpersonal relations and their consequences must also consider the interpersonal relations among students. Figure 2 suggests some indication of the complexity resulting from the potentially dominant roles played by the teacher, some students, and the many interactions between the teacher and students, and among the students.

Application of the Schismogenesis Model of Classroom Interaction

The research summarized below is part of a larger study, the purpose of which was to identify factors affecting literacy development. The goal of a strand of the research on socioaffective factors was to test particular tenets regarding socioaffective factors and interpersonal relations. Data on three of these tenets are given below and are arranged in chronological order beginning with a child's transition from home to school and concluding with the achievement of school status. The three tenets are: (a) some children enter school possessing values and statuses not congruent with those of the school (McDermott, 1974); (b) such children are likely to become visible minorities within the organization of the school (Au & Mason, 1981; Bateson, 1958; Heath, 1981; McDermott, 1974); and (c) the interpersonal relations between teachers and such children can be described as a complementary or symmetrical schismogenesis (Bateson, 1958; Erickson, 1984; Johnson & Winograd, 1983; McDermott, 1977; Shor & Freire, 1987).

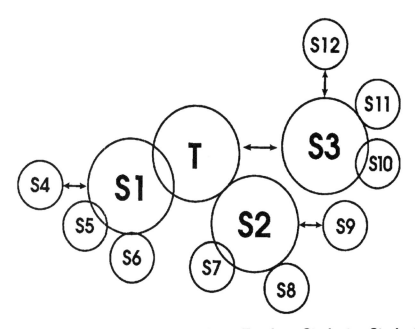

Figure 14-2: Interpersonal Relations: Teacher - Students - Students

Data were derived from two groups of low-literate adults and one group of achieving grade nine students. There were 26 individuals in each group. One group of adults consisted of prison inmates; the second group consisted of mainstream-society adults, whose economic status ranged from welfare recipients to successful business people. Through interviews, it was ascertained that all adults had negative experiences with school, while the achieving grade nine students related well to their school environment. The three tenets above were tested by comparing data on the adults to the grade nine student data.

Test of first tenet: The adults had entered school with values and status not congruent with those of the school. The adults came from different type home environments than did the grade nine students. A larger proportion of the parents of the adults worked at unskilled or semi-skilled jobs. The adults' homes seemed to exemplify different values for literacy than the grade nine students' homes. Almost all the grade nine students had been read to and had seen others reading and writing from their very early years. Seventy percent of them reported being read to on a daily basis. In contrast, only about one-half of the adults had been read to and had seen others reading and writing, and fewer than 15% reported being read to on a daily basis.

Almost one-half of the mainstream-society adults and 60% of the prisoners remembered disliking the idea of starting school. Only 9% of the grade nine students felt this way. On entering school, the adults did not find school accommodating. About 70% of the adults thought of school as a fairly structured environment where children had no input into decisions. One adult described school as a place where "the teacher had it all laid out or else", and another commented that she could never imagine how it would be possible to sit in a desk day after day, year after year, for 12 years and listen to teachers. Over one-half of the grade nine students believed they had considerable input into how school ran.

It seemed as if the adults had entered school already in conflict with the school's values and its expected status for children. McDermott, (1974) argues that schools must accept children as they are, rather than maintaining values which set them apart and make them visible as a minority. He believes that

> children are often more adaptable than their teachers. They are able and willing to develop new codes, indeed they do so every day on the playground. However, if the new code is used to degrade the children, as in the case for children in 'lower' ability groups, they will take flight and cut themselves off from whatever rewards the new code has to offer them. (p. 107)

McDermott concluded that children do not come to school disadvantaged; they leave disadvantaged (pp. 86-87).

Test of second tenet: The adults had been children who were not compatible with the school's expectations and became visible minorities within the school environment. During their school career, almost all of the prisoners had been assigned to a lower ability group or a remedial class for instructional purposes. This compares to 19 of the 26 mainstream adults and only one of the grade nine students. By contrast, 9 of the grade nine students had been assigned to higher ability groups. About one-half of the adults, already believing they were failures, accepted group placement as an opportunity for help. The other half, however, were inclined to believe they were put into groups for the teacher's convenience. A number of adults felt that group placement was the start of their problems from which they did not recover. They felt embarrassed and ashamed in front of their peers, felt segregated and the victims of differential treatment. One adult said, "It seemed like the teacher was more interested in fast learners and, while I wanted to learn, the teacher didn't pay attention to me. It seemed like I held up my arms for hours and then gave up."

Test of third tenet: The relationships of the adults (as children) with their teachers and other children could be characterized as a complementary or symmetrical schismogenesis. About one-half of the mainstream-society adults, but less than one-fifth of the prisoners could be described within a complementary schismogenesis framework. The behaviour of these adults as children is best summed up by one adult, "I was never a teacher botherer." The adults felt that teachers disliked them because they were not "good students", "because their work wasn't of high quality", or because they "came from the wrong side of the tracks". These adults were inclined to stay in school; some went to school for as long as 14 years even though their level of achievement was low and they experienced considerable failure. Perhaps, a factor in their remaining in school was that at some point in their school life, about one-half of them encountered a teacher who they felt really cared about them and this gave them hope.

One-half of the mainstream-society adults' and the majority of the prisoners' relationships with teachers and other children may be described best as symmetrical schismogenesis. They felt that they were discriminated against and did not get a fair chance. They were more likely to be punished for work left unfinished and felt that the teacher looked for an excuse to pick on them, while turning a blind eye to other students' behaviour. As one adult commented, "The vice-principal's kid could get away with anything." They were also more likely to be punished for tasks other than school work. Only 9 of the grade nine students felt such discrimination.

The prisoners especially were very much in conflict with the dominant culture of the school. A small number took flight by skipping school. Others had joined gangs. One subject said, "You don't get no rewards in school for not knowing how to read, but with your friends that doesn't count." The majority of the prisoners had resorted to "fight", and openly opposed school policy. Their infractions were more serious than those committed by the grade nine students, or even by the mainstream adults. Their behaviour was a good example of symmetrical schismogenesis being pushed to its limits of acceptability. Two prisoners as students had dealt drugs in school. Two of the prisoners committed their first crimes in junior high school by assaulting an assistant principal.

The prisoners as children were also more likely to have open conflict with their peers. Sometimes, the consequences of these conflicts were far-reaching, as they were for one prisoner who had beaten some kids who were ridiculing him. He was sent to the vice-principal's office for punishment, who declared that he would be expelled for two weeks. The prisoner said he left the office upset because he, and not the kids who had started the fracas, was punished. He was fearful of the consequences when his parents would find out, so he just wanted to get away. He went to the school parking lot and took one of the teacher's cars for a joy ride. This, of course, landed him in trouble with the law, and confirmed the vice-principal's belief that he was a "good-for-nothing".

The prisoners as students typified McDermott's (1977) portrait of students who spend more time in relational battles than on school tasks. It is little wonder that the majority saw school in general, and literacy in particular, as meaningless in their lives. For those who thought otherwise, they believed their chances for literacy attainment were low.

The experiences of the grade nine achieving students stand out in contrast. They were not singled out by school standards upon entrance to school, unless to be accorded a special status (high ability group placement). While the behaviours of some of them differed at times from the schools' standards, the difference was never too extreme. They achieved according to the schools' goals within an environment that was generally satisfying for them, that is, in harmony with their teachers and their peers.

Implications

Goodlad (1984, p. xvi) has stated that "if we are to improve school, we must understand it". According to Goodlad, school is more than academic; it also comprises social relations that, if negative, can be detrimental to learning. Amoroso (1984, p. 19) concluded that the "need for teachers to be caring and supportive is central to the concept of literacy as an act of becoming someone". The goals of the school cannot be separated from the backgrounds of the students who enter. This, of course, necessitates that teachers attempt to understand the statuses and identities of children as they come to school, and to modify the school agenda to accommodate various strengths and needs.

Teachers must be aware of school standards which are used (often subconsciously) to create visible minorities of high risk, potentially low-achieving children. This is not to say that schools should not attend to individual differences. School, in fact, is about individuality, but individuality based on both child and school criteria rather than school criteria solely. Guild and Garger (1985) state that

> if education is a people business, and if we know people are different, then education is a business about the diversity of people. It is about the different goals people have for education. It is about the different programs people want in schools. It is about the multitude of values and interests of all its constituents. (p. 5)

Providing a literacy program based on an understanding of individual differences means understanding the literacy environment and literacy needs of all students. School is not a place where literacy is taught, and then somehow students find a place for it in their lives. School, as part of students' lives, should provide literacy in meaningful contexts. Granted there are literacy skills that are more suitable for development in school; however, the way that these skills can be used in various meaningful literacy tasks should be clear to the students. Literacy materials in the classroom should not consist of just textbook materials, but rather a range of reading and writing tasks to enhance opportunities for students to make the most of the knowledge they have.

Given the diversity of individual differences, there is always the possibility of some students experiencing difficulty with academic tasks. However, Erickson (1984) reminds us "that we need to move beyond simple, single-factor explanations of school failure in literacy and reasoning" (p. 540). Children should never be locked into groups for all their school experiences. There may be times when students are grouped for special needs; in these cases the children should always understand why this is so.

There is also likely to be interpersonal conflict in school. Any institution, including the school must operate by a set of guidelines. As Shor and Freire (1987) say, a teacher must express authority, but not be authoritarian. Also, as Bateson (1958) indicates, schismogenesis does not have to be progressive. The teacher may halt the progression by varying the roles of the teacher and students (e.g., participating in activities in which the teacher becomes a peer, allowing student groups to set goals for a particular project), by changing tasks that are threatening, and by lightening a situation through humour.

Finally, as Bateson (1958) points out, there may be instances when schismogenesis leads to discomfort between teacher and students. Rather than blindly pursuing this course, Wolcott (1974) suggests that the teacher step back and take stock of the situation. He suggests that in such a situation the teacher consider himself or herself the enemy, and the student as a prisoner of war, whom the teacher is trying to persuade to defect to his or her side by showing the student what the school has to offer. Wolcott states that such a stance forces the teacher to come to grips with what the school really has to offer this student that is meaningful and desirous. It also directs the teacher's attention not to the student as a recalcitrant, but to the student's community with its history and its values. Such stocktaking on the part of educators would create a greater potential for the development of positive socioaffective factors in literacy development, and remind teachers that achieving literacy requires taking more factors into account than is traditionally the case in schools.

References

Allington, R. L. (1983). The reading instruction provided readers of differing reading abilities. *Elementary School Journal, 83*, 568-559.

Amoroso, H. C. (1984, April). *Adult conceptions and assumptions about literacy.* Paper presented at the American Education Research Association Meeting, San Francisco.

Anderson, R. C., Hiebert, E. H., Scott, J. A., & Wilkinson, I. A. (1984). *Becoming a nation of readers.* Washington, DC: The National Institute of Education.

Asher, S. R., Renshaw, P. D., & Hymel, S. (1982). Peer relations and the development of social skills. In S. G. Moore & C. R. Cooper (Eds.), *The young child: Reviews of Research* Vol 3, (pp. 137-158). Washington, D.C.: National Association for the Education of Young Children.

Au, K. H., & Mason, J. (1981). Social organization factors in learning to read: The balance of rights hypothesis. *Reading Research Quarterly, 7*, 115-152.

Bateson, G. (1958). *Naven (2nd ed.)*. Stanford, CA: Stanford University Press.

Bloome, D. (1983, April). *Definitions and functions of reading in two middle school classrooms: A sociolinguistic ethnography study*. Paper presented at the Annual Meeting of the American Education Research Association, Montreal.

Brophy, J. E. (1983). Research on the self-fulfilling prophecy and teacher expectations. *Journal of Educational Psychology, 75*, 631-661.

Brown, A. L., Palincsar, A. S., & Purcell, L. (1986). Poor readers: Teach, don't label. In U. Neisser (Ed.), *The school achievement of minority children* (pp. 105-143). Hillsdale, NJ: Erlbaum.

Cazden, C. B. (1981). Social context of learning to read. In J. T. Guthrie (Ed.), *Comprehension and teaching: Research reviews* (pp. 118-139). Newark, DE: International Reading Association.

Clark, C. M. (1984). Research into practice. Cautions and qualifications. In T. E. Raphael (Ed.), *The contexts of school based literacy* (pp. 281-294). New York: Random House.

Erickson, F. (1984). School literacy, reasoning and civility: An anthropologist's perspective. *Review of Educational Research, 54*, 525-546.

Gentile, L. M., & McMillan, M. M. (1988). Reexamining the role of emotional maladjustment. In S.M. Glazer, L. W. Searfoss, & L. M. Gentile (Eds.), *Reexamining reading diagnosis* (pp. 112-128). Newark, DE: International Reading Association.

Goodlad, J. (1984). *A place called school*. New York: McGraw-Hill.

Guild, P. B., & Garger, S. (195). *Marching to a different drummer*. Washington, D.C.: Association for Supervision and Curriculum Development.

Heath, S. B. (1981). Questioning at home and at school: A comparative study. In G. D. Spindler (Ed.), *Doing ethnography: Educational anthropology in action* (pp. 102-131). New York: Holt, Rinehart and Winston.

Hiebert, E. (1983). An examination of ability grouping for reading instruction. *Reading Research Quarterly, 18*, 231-255.

Johnson, P. H. (1985). Understanding reading disability: A case study approach. *Harvard Educational Review, 55*, 153-177.

Johnson, P. H., & Winograd, P. N. (1983, December). *Passive failure in reading*. Paper presented at the National Reading Conference, Austin, Texas.

Kozol, J. (1975). *The night is dark and I am far from home*. Boston: Houghton Mifflin.

McDermott, R. P. (1974). Achieving school failure: An anthropological approach to illiteracy and social stratification. In G. D. Spindler (Ed.), *Education and cultural process* (pp. 82-118). New York: Holt, Rinehart and Winston.

McDermott, R. P. (1977). Social relations as contexts for learning in school. *Harvard Educational Review, 47*, 198-215.

Richek, M. A., List, L. K., & Lerner, J. W. (1983). *Reading problems: Diagnosis and remediation*. Englewood Cliffs, NJ: Prentice-Hall.

Shor, I., & Freire, P. (1987). *A pedagogy for liberation*. Amherst, MA: Bergin and Garvey.

Spindler, G. D. (1974). The transmission of culture. In G. D. Spindler (Ed.), *Education and cultural process* (pp. 279-310). New York: Holt, Rinehart and Winston.

Wilcox, K. (1982). Ethnography as a methodology and its application to the study of schooling: A review. In G. Spindler (Ed.), *Doing the ethnography of schooling* (pp. 268-309). New York: Holt, Rinehart and Winston.

Wolcott, H. F . (1974). The teacher as enemy. In G. D. Spindler (Ed.), *Education and cultural process* (pp. 411-425). New York: Holt, Rinehart and Winston.

15

Ethnicity, English-language Usage, and Academic Attainment: Evidence from Australia

Rodney A. Clifton
University of Manitoba

Trevor Williams and Jeff Clancy
Australian Council for Educational Research

In many multi-ethnic countries, such as Australia, Canada, and the United States, the fate of minority ethnic groups within the educational system has become a central issue. According to one perspective, these countries are relatively meritocratic, so academic achievement results from what individuals bring to the school. That is, students from various ethnic groups interact and compete within the educational system according to universal criteria. This perspective assumes that these multi-ethnic countries are lands of opportunity. According to another perspective, the educational system discriminates against minority ethnic groups. Specifically, it is argued that individuals are assigned to classrooms, schools, and occupations on the basis of observable ethnic traits. As a result, minority ethnic groups believe that their improvement is blocked by institutional discrimination. Therefore, they often band together to counteract the discrimination and to improve their status. This perspective assumes that institutional discrimination against minority ethnic groups is rampant.

This chapter aims to assess differential ethnic achievement in terms of these two perspectives. More specifically, we attempt to assess the relative academic achievement of English, Greek, and Italian students in Australia in order to investigate the effects of English-language usage on Greek and Italian students' academic achievement and completion of secondary school.

The Theoretical Model

Blau and Duncan (1967) provide evidence that social and economic attainments are largely a function of performances within the educational system. They report a correlation of .538 between education and first jobs. Similarly, Broom, Jones, McDonnell, and Williams (1980) report a correlation of .507 between education and first job and a correlation of .363 between education and current income.

In the last two decades, researchers in a number of countries have elaborated the Blau and Duncan model of status attainment. Figure 1 presents the model that guides our analyses. This model follows the established conventions and assumes that individual status variables (ethnicity, socioeconomic status, number of siblings, and sex), selected academic performance variables (school attendance and year-level at age 14), and social context variables (family rurality, the type of school attended, and the state within which the student resided), are all exogenous variables. In turn, the English-language usage variables (parents' speaking English, students' speaking English, and family receiving English newspapers), and academic achievement (word knowledge, literacy, and numeracy) are intervening variables. Completion of all 12 years of secondary school is the final dependent variable of interest (Clifton, Williams, & Clancy, 1987).

As previously noted, the major independent variable is ethnicity. In Australia the research on ethnic group differences generally distinguishes between two groups of people—immigrants from non-English-speaking countries and immigrants from English-speaking countries—whose ancestors have resided in Australia for two generations or less. These two immigrant groups are often contrasted with Australians whose ancestors have resided in the country for more than two generations.

The distinction between immigrants and non-immigrants makes a certain amount of sense. Evidence from a number of countries suggests that recent immigrants enter menial, low-paying jobs where their chances for mobility are restricted (Olzak, 1983). In Australia, non-English-speaking immigrants are much more likely to have menial jobs than are English-speaking ones (Clifton, et. al., 1987). From this type of evidence, it has been argued that opportunities are more restricted for non-English-speaking immigrants than for English-speaking immigrants (Bullivant, 1981; Martin, 1978; Smolicz, 1979). These arguments are not entirely convincing because the analyses have often been based upon zero-order relationships without controlling for more obvious factors that may account, in part, for the discrepancies in occupational status between immigrants from English-speaking and non-English-speaking countries.

It has been suggested that there are three ways for restricted opportunities for non-English-speaking immigrants to occur. The first, and most commonly advocated, suggestion is that the channels for upward mobility have been blocked. That is, non-English-speaking immigrants have not been able to move up within the social structure because established English-speaking Australians have discriminated against them. Within this perspective, it has been argued that schools are one of the most discriminatory institutions within society (Bowles & Gintis, 1976; Smolicz, 1981). Discrimination can occur in schools because

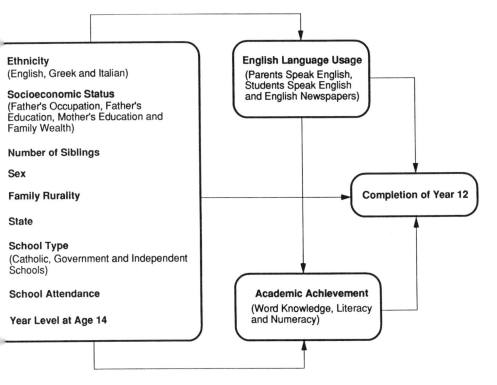

Figure 15.1 A Theoretical Model

non-English-speaking students interact with teachers and other students who are prejudiced against them (Clifton, 1981; Clifton & Bulcock, 1987).

Second, discrimination can also occur because the criteria used to assess students in schools are based upon fluency in the national language (Mehan, 1984). Therefore, it is important to distinguish between lack of fluency in the national language and ethnic prejudice as separate impediments to academic achievement and completing secondary school. Fluency in the national language is often seen as a legitimate criterion for assessing students, while ethnic prejudice is an illegitimate criterion.

Third, it has been argued that certain ethnic groups have distinctive cultural values that shape the development of abilities and aspirations of youth (Bullivant, 1978; Clifton, 1982; Mehan, 1984). Specifically, it has been argued that differences in ambition, persistence, and tolerance of deferred gratification can influence academic achievement, completion of secondary school, and qualifications for certain occupational status positions within society. From this perspective, ethnicity is often defined in the research literature by such markers as cultural, national and geographic origins, language, race, and religion. The boundaries defined by these markers provide the basis of "primordial" collective sentiments, ethnic solidarity, and identification by others (Stevens & Swicegood, 1987).

Thus, in our attempt to understand ethnic differences in academic achievement and attainment, we measured ethnicity on the basis of the country of birth and the native language of the students' parents. Specifically, we focused on students with both parents born in either England, Greece, or Italy. These students represent the three largest ethnic groups in Australia (Sturman, 1985).

Three measures of English-language usage form the first set of endogenous variables: the parents' use of English at home, the students' use of English with their parents, and the frequency with which their families receive English newspapers. These variables are included as intervening variables between ethnicity and academic achievement so that we can determine their effects upon academic achievement. Given the previous arguments, we expect that Greek and Italian students will use substantially less English at home than English students. Merrill Swain (personal communication, October, 1988) has noted that our measures of English-language usage may be a measure of fluency in either English or the students' native languages. Since we do not have measures of native-language fluency, we cannot determine if our measures serve as proxies for language fluency in general. If our measures are proxies for language fluency, then our arguments and interpretations would be more consistent with the arguments and interpretations proposed by Swain, Lapkin, Rowen, and Hart (this volume).

Three measures of academic achievement form the second set of endogenous variables: word knowledge, literacy, and numeracy. Since direct effects of ethnicity on these variables are net of a number of other variables that are also important determinants of academic achievement, then any effects found might result from differences in cultural values, differences in English-language proficiency, discrimination based upon ethnic prejudice, or some combination of these factors. More specifically, if any or all of the three impediments are present, we expect to find that generally the Greek and Italian students have lower academic achievement than the English students. Additionally, if the cultural values argument and/or the language proficiency argument is true, we expect to find that the direct effect of ethnicity is less for numeracy than for word knowledge and literacy because the numeracy test is less dependent upon English-language proficiency, as well as being less embedded in the context of the specific Australian culture (Clifton et al., 1987). If, on the other hand, the English-language proficiency argument is true, we expect to find that the lower academic achievement of Greek and Italian students, compared to English students, can be accounted for by the English-language usage variables. That is, the differences in achievement between English students and the Greek and Italian students will be mediated by the English-language usage variables, particularly by whether the students speak English with their parents and by whether their families receive English newspapers. Moreover, if the ethnic prejudice argument is true, we expect to find that the Greek and Italian students, in comparison with the English students, have similar and lower achievement on all three variables. Furthermore, if the ethnic prejudice argument is true, we also expect to find that the effects of ethnicity are not mediated by the English-language usage variables. One possible explanation for such results would be that these students have been exposed to teachers, counsellors, and other students who have discriminated against them. Nevertheless, because academic achievement is measured using standardized tests marked by independent evaluators, ethnic differences would not result directly from discriminatory evaluation procedures used by teachers.

Further, any direct effects of the three measures of academic achievement on completion of secondary school would indicate the degree to which academic proficiency leads to overall success in the institution. The indirect effects from ethnicity would indicate the degree to which English-language usage and academic achievement variables act as mediators. If the language proficiency argument alone is the explanation for ethnic differences, we expect to find that the effects of ethnicity will be completely mediated by English-language usage, particularly for the students speaking English with their parents and the families receiving English newspapers, and academic achievement, particularly word knowledge and literacy. If the cultural argument alone explains these differences, we also expect to find that the effects of ethnicity will be mediated by the English-language usage variables, because the Greek and Italian students will not use English at home and they will not receive English newspapers. This argument assumes that the Greek and Italian parents are bound to their cultures, and they realize that using English at home or receiving English newspapers separates them and their children from their cultural heritages (Stevens & Swicegood, 1987). Moreover, if this argument is true, we also expect to find that the effects of ethnicity will be only partially mediated by academic achievement because cultural values presumably affect all three measures of achievement as well as the completion of secondary school.

If the ethnic prejudice argument alone explains differences between the ethnic groups, we expect to find that the effects of ethnicity on completion of year 12 will not be mediated by the English-language usage and academic achievement variables. In this case, we expect that Greek and Italian students, irrespective of their use of English at home and their academic achievement, will have similar and lower completion rates than English students. Moreover, we also expect to find that the direct effect of ethnicity will be stronger on completion of year 12 than on academic achievement, because completion of secondary school is influenced by teachers who are presumably prejudiced against non-English-speaking students, while academic achievement is determined by standardized tests, which presumably are less affected by prejudiced teachers, counsellors, and other students (Clifton, 1981; Clifton & Bulcock, 1987).

Nevertheless, given the results of previous research, we expect that the academic achievement variables have direct and substantial effects upon completion of year 12 (Stryker, 1981). We expect, however, that the direct effects in this study will be less than the direct effects in most existing research where measures of academic achievement have been in terms of the grades awarded by teachers for classroom work. Teacher grades are an unknown mix of teachers' expectations for their students and academic achievement itself (Clifton, 1981). The standardized tests as used in this research are not contaminated to the same extent by teachers' expectations.

Methodology

Data

Data were obtained from a six-year longitudinal survey of youth in transition within and between education and the labour market (Williams, Clancy, Batten, & Girling-Butcher, 1980). The subjects made up a national probability sample of 6247 students who were included in a national assessment program focusing on achievement in basic literacy and numeracy skills. Assessment of these skills took place in 1975 when the students were 14 years of age, and between 1978 and 1984 members of the sample were surveyed each year to obtain data on their participation in education and the labour market. Data obtained in 1975 and over the years 1978 to 1980 are used in this study.

The original sample provided for state estimates and over-sampled in five of the six states and in both territories. To produce estimates representative of the national population of 14-year-olds who were students in 1975, the data were weighted to compensate for the over-sampling. Comparisons with published data suggest that this procedure was effective (Williams, Slater, & Clancy, 1984a).

Over the years from 1975 to 1980, 55% of the sample was retained (Williams, 1987). Proportionately more low-achieving students and students from low socioeconomic status backgrounds dropped out of the survey. This attrition has relatively little effect upon the mean values and standard deviations of the variables (Williams, 1987). Nevertheless, a further weighting adjustment was made to compensate for the effects of sample attrition between 1975 and 1980. In this adjustment, the sample was post-stratified on the basis of years of schooling completed, school system, and sex, and the data were weighted in order to preserve the covariance structure (Kalton, 1983). In short, non-respondents were replaced by respondents who were similar on all these variables. Comparisons of the means, standard deviations, and correlations for the weighted and unweighted data suggest that this procedure was effective (Williams, 1987).

Variables

Complete descriptions of the questionnaires and tests that were administered to the students are found in Bourke and Lewis (1976), and Williams et al. (1980). The following is a description of the variables used in the present study.

Ethnicity

In order to measure ethnicity, the students were classified on the basis of their parents' birthplace. Homogeneous ethnic groups were formed for students with both parents born in each of England, Greece, and Italy. These groups were the three largest ethnic groups in the population. Using this definition and the weighted data, 250 English students, 62 Greek students, and 130 Italian students were identified. Of the 442 students who were classified as belonging to the three ethnic groups, 56.7% were English, 14.0% were Greek, and 29.4% were Italian.

Socioeconomic status

Four student-reported measures were used as indicators of socioeconomic status. Father's occupation was reported as the father's occupational title and an accompanying description of his work. This information was used to assign prestige scores to each student, based on the Australian six-point occupational prestige scale developed by Broom, Duncan-Jones, Jones, and McDonnell (1977). Father's and mother's education were reported as the highest levels of education completed by each parent, and were coded into four-point scales that ranged from "primary school only" to "tertiary degree or diploma". Family wealth was measured by asking the students to report on family possessions at the time they were aged 14—for example, the number of bedrooms, bathrooms, and telephones in their homes (Broom et al., 1980). A weighted composite variable, with a range of 1.5 to 6.6, was created as an indicator of family wealth.

Number of siblings

The measure was obtained from the students when they were 14, and was coded into six categories ranging from "no siblings" to "five or more siblings".

Sex

The students reported their sex on the original literacy and numeracy questionnaire in 1975. Males were coded as "0" and females were coded as "1".

Family rurality

This variable is indicated by three measures taken from census data on the collector's district where the students resided when they were 14. The three indicators were: proportion of the work force in agriculture, forestry, and fishing; proportion of dwellings not connected to a sewage system; and proportion of families with three or more vehicles (Ross, 1983). These three indicators were weighted and summed. This measure ranged from -0.79 to 6.79 and had acceptable psychometric properties (Williams, Slater, & Clancy, 1984b).

State

The weighted proportions of students by state and territory were as follows: Australian Capital Territory, 1.3%; New South Wales, 25.3%; Northern Territory, 0.1%; Queensland, 6.5%; South Australia, 18.8%; Tasmania, 1.2%; Victoria, 34.0%; and Western Australia, 12.9%.

School type

The students reported the type of school they attended when they were 14 years of age: 14.8% attended Catholic schools; 81.7% attended Government schools, and 3.6% attended non-Catholic Independent schools.

School attendance

Teachers reported on their students' attendance in school on a four-point scale that ranged from "prolonged absence" (more than 20 days this year) to "regular attendance" (0-5 days absence this year).

Year-level at age 14

This refers to the year of school the students were in when they were 14 years of age: 34.6% were enroled in the eighth year; 58.9% were enroled in the ninth year; and 6.4% were enroled in the tenth year.

English-language usage

Three student-reported measures were used as indicators of the amount of English used in the home. The students were asked, "Do your parents use English to speak to each other at home?" The responses were coded into "Some English" and "Only English". The students were also asked, "Do you use English to speak to your parents?" The responses were coded into a four-point scale from "No English" to "Only English". Finally, the students were asked, "How often does your family get a newspaper in English?" The responses were coded into a four-point scale from "Never" to "Every day".

Academic achievement

Three achievement tests were used in the study. A word knowledge test, originally developed for the International Association for the Evaluation of Educational Achievement, was constructed from 40 word pairs arranged so that the students had to indicate synonyms or antonyms (Thorndike, 1973). A correction for guessing was used, and the scores ranged from -19 to 40. A literacy test measured reading skills (Bourke & Lewis, 1976), and had scores ranging from 0 to 33. A numeracy test included items on ability to read measuring instruments, to add, subtract, multiply, divide, to read graphs and tables, to do money and time calculations, to use decimals and fractions, and to interpret plans and maps (Bourke & Lewis, 1976). The total numeracy scores ranged from 0 to 33.

Completion of year 12

Completion of year 12 was determined from the follow-up questionnaires administered over the period 1978 to 1980. Respondents were asked to indicate the amount of education they had obtained. This variable was dichotomized into less than 12 years of schooling completed, representing 65.6% of the sample, and 12 years or more completed, representing 34.4% of the sample.

Results

Preliminary Relationships

A preliminary profile of the students forming the three ethnic groups is presented in Table 1. This table illustrates that the students differ on a number of factors. Not surprisingly, Greek and Italian students are less likely to use English to speak with their parents, and they are less likely to receive English-language newspapers than English students. Moreover, Greek and Italian students are more likely to have regular school attendance than English students. At age 14, a greater proportion of Greek students are in year 8, while a greater proportion of Italian students are in years 8 and 10. Similarly, a greater proportion of Greek and English students are enroled in Government schools, while a greater proportion of Italian students are enroled in Catholic schools. In terms of word knowledge and literacy, Greek and Italian students have lower mean scores than English students, and in both cases Italian students have lower mean scores than Greek students. On the numeracy test, English and Greek students perform the same while Italian students have a lower mean score than both. Finally, Greek students are more likely to complete year 12 than the students from the other two groups, while Italian students complete year 12 at a rate that is slightly higher than the rate for the English students. In essence, these results illustrate the importance of distinguishing between Greek and Italian students, rather than combining them as non-English-speaking immigrants as has often been done in previous research.

Multivariate Relationships

The correlation coefficients between all variables in the theoretical model are displayed in Table 2, along with the means and standard deviations for each variable. These coefficients are used in the multivariate analyses, and are computed on the basis of pair-wise deletion of missing data.

Table 15.1

Ethnicity, English Language Usage, and Selected Educational Variables

Ethnic Group	A. Students Speak English to Parents				B. Receive English Newspapers				C. School Attendance				D. Year Level		
	No English	Some English	Mostly English	Only English	Never	Some days	Most days	Every day	Prolonged absence	Frequent absence	Occasional absence	Regular attendance	Yr.8	Yr.9	Yr.10
English	1.1	0.0	3.2	95.7	0.7	9.6	9.6	80.1	9.3	14.8	30.3	45.7	26.7	67.8	5.4
Greek	27.3	59.3	11.0	2.5	5.3	33.9	31.9	28.9	0.0	4.8	26.9	68.4	35.1	61.2	3.6
Italian	14.2	55.8	23.6	6.4	9.1	25.5	25.6	39.8	1.2	7.4	23.8	67.6	49.6	40.8	9.6

	E. School Type			F. Word Knowledge		G. Literacy		H. Numeracy		I. Per Cent Completing Year 12	Weighted N_s
	Government	Catholic	Independent	X	SD	X	SD	X	SD		
English	87.8	6.9	5.4	15.7	8.7	28.4	3.4	27.5	4.4	29.6	250.3
Greek	91.6	5.1	3.3	10.5	7.8	27.0	4.7	27.6	5.4	58.2	61.7
Italian	65.3	34.5	0.2	8.8	9.4	25.5	4.5	23.4	7.2	32.3	129.8

Table 15.2
Correlation Coefficients, Means, and Standard Deviations for the Variables in the Theoretical Model

	1.	2.	3.	4.	5.	6.	7.	8.	9.	10.	11.	12.	13.	14.	15.	16.	17.	18.	19.	20.	21.	22.	23.	24.	25.	26.	27.	28.	29.	30.	31.	32.
1. English	—																															
2. Greek	-.460	—																														
3. Italian	-.738	-.260	—																													
4. Father's Occup'n	.275	-.131	-.203	—																												
5. Father's Ed'n	.639	-.228	-.528	.359	—																											
6. Mother's Ed'n	.646	-.256	-.518	.329	.781	—																										
7. Family Wealth	.197	-.159	-.090	.204	.205	.127	—																									
8. No. of Siblings	.147	-.105	-.080	-.086	.031	-.005	.127	—																								
9. Sex	-.024	-.146	.138	-.065	.039	-.008	-.060	.002	—																							
10. Family Rurality	.128	-.165	-.013	.171	-.016	-.032	.159	-.034	-.016	—																						
11. Australian N'l Territory	.029	-.008	-.026	.103	.069	.023	.070	-.048	-.033	-.020	—																					
12. New South Wales	.096	.054	-.145	.109	.056	.002	.013	.013	-.011	-.024	-.067	—																				
13. North'n Territory	-.002	-.012	.011	.007	.020	.024	.007	-.003	-.030	.004	-.003	-.017	—																			
14. Queensland	.028	-.034	-.004	-.046	.046	.058	.008	.053	-.012	.061	-.030	-.154	-.008	—																		
15. S. Australia	.080	-.023	-.069	-.005	.056	.088	-.090	.094	-.030	-.150	-.055	-.279	-.014	-.127	—																	
16. Tasmania	.088	-.038	-.067	.101	.073	.112	.075	.046	.006	.041	-.013	-.064	-.003	-.129	-.053	—																
17. Victoria	-.250	.077	.213	-.062	-.176	-.189	.017	.092	.040	-.032	-.082	-.417	-.021	-.190	-.344	-.079	—															
18. Western Australia	.078	-.111	.000	-.087	.026	.072	.122	-.033	.013	.199	-.044	-.224	-.011	-.102	-.185	-.042	-.276	—														
19. Catholic Schools	-.254	-.110	.360	-.027	-.207	-.207	.030	.030	.121	.012	.001	-.152	-.012	-.055	-.108	-.036	.239	.037	—													
20. Govt Schools	.179	.103	-.274	-.087	.067	.085	-.085	.015	-.100	-.051	-.011	.155	.014	.075	.118	-.034	-.230	-.056	-.878	—												
21. Indep't Schools	.111	-.006	-.116	.222	.192	.227	.192	-.088	-.023	.083	.020	-.033	-.006	-.011	-.041	.022	-.051	-.080	-.112	-.407	—											
22. School Attendance	-.266	.141	.181	.011	-.200	-.178	-.001	-.077	-.084	.048	.004	-.214	.022	.074	.116	.051	.230	.026	-.056	.133	-.022	—										
23. Year 8	-.190	.004	-.038	-.180	-.222	.113	.076	-.022	-.051	.068	.064	.306	-.021	-.052	-.273	.019	.073	-.169	-.080	.112	-.061	-.035	—									
24. Year 9	.206	.019	-.238	.057	.188	.220	.113	-.051	.015	-.103	-.047	-.220	-.003	-.065	.187	.073	.019	.029	-.112	-.073	.022	.004	-.873	—								
25. Year 10	-.045	-.045	.083	-.027	-.027	-.009	-.050	-.044	.012	.075	-.030	-.152	.047	-.031	.156	-.029	-.153	.270	-.112	.092	-.044	.076	-.190	-.313	—							
26. Parents Speak English	.666	-.378	-.436	.146	.421	.472	.107	.067	.073	.148	.020	.096	.017	-.055	.079	.061	.240	.135	-.172	.129	.061	-.200	-.188	.165	.033	—						
27. Students Speak English	.847	-.476	-.560	.259	.526	.537	.195	.132	.009	.177	.022	.035	-.002	.056	.126	.071	.283	.137	-.157	.108	.076	-.252	-.236	.233	-.011	.757	—					
28. English Newspaper	.422	-.230	-.284	.043	.233	.240	.106	-.043	.126	.024	.022	-.064	.013	-.028	.043	.074	.058	.103	-.025	.002	.043	-.109	-.133	.087	.085	.453	.479	—				
29. Word Knowledge	.336	-.106	-.285	.185	.185	.146	-.004	-.022	.038	.138	.071	.125	.010	-.060	.101	.058	-.240	.060	-.166	.053	.206	-.040	-.192	.126	.121	.307	.366	.198	—			
30. Literacy	.292	-.039	-.288	.219	.138	.141	-.024	-.080	-.027	.030	.044	.033	.003	.082	.030	.036	-.125	-.053	-.208	.131	.124	-.013	-.311	.242	.117	.234	.348	.280	.556	—		
31. Numeracy	.241	.090	-.331	.178	.097	.070	-.073	-.057	-.111	.016	.034	.067	.010	.094	.067	.024	-.154	.083	-.208	.131	.125	.030	-.258	.206	.087	.206	.304	.244	.606	.727	—	
32. Comp'n of Yr 12	-.115	.202	-.028	.205	-.013	-.054	-.036	-.183	-.085	.043	.092	.003	.012	.052	-.001	-.010	-.045	.083	-.176	.207	.156	.064	-.095	.055	.064	-.125	-.080	-.032	.348	.341	.390	—
Means	.567	.140	.294	3.157	2.233	2.073	3.198	2.253	.520	.799	.112	.431	.029	.245	.387	.187	.340	.129	.147	.817	.036	3.332	.346	.590	.064	1.731	3.146	3.358	12.923	27.366	26.310	.344
Standard Deviations	.491	.343	.451	1.501	1.011	.885	.830	1.180	.495	.401	.316	.495	.168	.430	.487	.390	.474	.335	.354	.387	.184	.874	.471	.487	.242	.440	1.057	.894	9.297	4.076	5.714	.471

The correlation coefficients are used to estimate the parameters of the model using ordinary least squares procedures (Duncan, 1975; Heise, 1975). Among the variables in the correlation matrix are four nominal variables—ethnicity, state, school type, and year—for which dummy variables have been created (Pedhazur, 1982). In order to estimate the effects for these variables, one of the dummy variables in each set is omitted to become the reference against which the remaining effect parameters are evaluated. For ethnicity, the English group is omitted from the equations because it represents the dominant immigrant group in Australia. Thus, the estimated effects of Greek and Italian are interpreted relative to English. Analogously, New South Wales (the most populous state), government schools (the type attended by the majority of students), and year 9 (the modal year for 14-year-old students) are omitted from the equations.

In Table 3 the standardized and unstandardized effect parameters are reported for the English-language usage variables. (In this table, and in Tables 4 and 5, the effects of the states and territories are not reported because of the difficulty of interpreting these effect parameters (Williams et. al, 1980). Thus, the results that are reported are analogous to analyses of covariance in which states and territories are covariates). As expected from both the theoretical argument and the results presented in Table 1, Greek and Italian students are less likely than English students to speak English with their parents and to receive English newspapers. Moreover, the Greek and Italian parents are less likely than the English parents to speak English with each other. In analyses that are not reported, ethnicity explains approximately 45% of the variance in the amount of English that the parents speak to each other, approximately 73% of the variance in the amount of English that the students speak with their parents, and approximately 18% of the variance in the frequency with which families receive English newspapers. As Table 3 illustrates, when the other variables are added to the analyses the amount of variance explained is increased only by approximately 4% for the amount of English the parents speak to each other, approximately 3% for the amount of English the students speak with their parents, and approximately 7% for the frequency with which the families receive English newspapers. In essence, these results illustrate that ethnicity is a very significant factor in explaining English-language usage of immigrant children in Australia.

Table 15.3
Standardized and Unstandardized Regression Coefficients and R^2s
for the English Language Usage Variables[a]

Independent Variables	Parents Speak English	Students Speak English	English Newspaper
Greek	-.473***	-.626***	-.377***
	(-.605)	(-1.927)	(-.981)
Italian	-.507***	-.714***	-.517***
	(-.494)	(-1.672)	(-1.024)
Father's Occupation	-.064	.038	-.068
	(-.019)	(.027)	(-.041)
Father's Education	-.066	-.020	-.049
	(-.029)	(-.020)	(-.044)
Mother's Education	.136*	-.031	-.063
	(.068)	(-.037)	(-.064)
Family Wealth	.003	.030	.058
	(.001)	(.039)	(.062)
Number of Siblings	-.019	-.002	-.133**
	(-.007)	(-.002)	(-.101)
Sex	.076*	.012	-.130**
	(.068)	(.025)	(-.235)
Family Rurality	.085*	.058*	-.059
	(.047)	(.076)	(-.066)
Catholic Schools	-.012	-.055*	.070
	(-.016)	(-.165)	(.178)
Independent Schools	-.015	-.014	-.005
	(-.037)	(-.082)	(-.025)
School Attendance	-.008	-.064**	-.007
	(-.004)	(-.077)	(-.008)
Year 8	-.079*	-.085**	-.013
	(-.074)	(-.190)	(-.026)
Year 10	.019	-.025	.091*
	(.034)	(-.108)	(.336)
R^2	.491	.756	.249

[a]Unstandardized coefficients in parenthesis.
* $p \leq .05$
** $p \leq .01$
*** $p \leq .001$

There are other important findings to note in Table 3. Specifically, rural families are more likely to speak English than urban families, but they are less likely to receive English newspapers. Another important finding is that students in Catholic schools are more likely to speak.

English at home than students in Government or Independent schools. School attendance has a negative effect upon the students' use of English at home. Moreover, students in year 8 are less likely to speak English at home, and their parents are less likely to speak English to each other, than students in years 9 or 10. Nevertheless, the families of students in year 10 are more likely to receive English newspapers.

In Table 4 the standardized and unstandardized effect parameters are reported for the academic achievement variables. In step 1 the reduced-form effect parameters are reported when the English-language usage variables are not included, and in step 2 the fully-recursive effect parameters are reported when the English-language usage variables are included as intervening variables.

This table reveals that the English-language usage variables mediate substantial proportions of the ethnic effects upon the academic achieve-ment variables. That is, for all three achievement variables, Greek and Italian students have significantly lower scores than English students before the English-language usage variables are included as intervening variables in the analyses. However, when these variables are included, the effects of being Greek and Italian are reduced, in most cases, to being non-significant. More specifically, the disadvantages of being Italian are substantially reduced for all three academic achievement variables when the English-language usage variables are added. Furthermore, when the English-language usage variables are added, the disadvantage of being Greek is reduced for word knowledge, while being Greek becomes an advantage for achievement in both literacy and numeracy. In fact, when the English-language usage variables are added, Greek students have an average score on the numeracy test that is 45.9% of a standard deviation (2.62 points) higher than the average score for the English students.

As expected, the English-language usage variables have independent effects upon the academic achievement variables. For all three achieve-ment variables, the most important language variable is the amount of English that .the students speak at home. Not surprisingly, receiving English newspapers also has significant effects upon both literacy and numeracy. It may not be surprising that whether or not the students'

Table 5.4
Standardized and Unstandardized Regression Coefficients and R^2s
for the Academic Achievement Variables[a]

Independent Variables	Word Knowledge		Literacy		Numeracy	
	Step 1	Step 2	Step 1	Step 2	Step 1	Step 2
Greek	-.232*** (-6.271)	-.069 (-1.875)	-.206*** (-2.442)	.020 (.234)	-.125* (-2.076)	.158* (2.622)
Italian	-.365*** (-7.526)	.179* (-3.682)	-.421*** (-3.803)	-.149*** (-1.345)	-.424*** (-5.366)	-.087 (-1.101)
Father's Occupation	.211*** (1.309)	.208*** (1.288)	.171*** (.464)	.164*** (.445)	.157*** (.597)	.149*** (.569)
Father's Education	-.047 (-.430)	-.038 (-.354)	-.128 (-.516)	-.119 (-.480)	-.080 (-.451)	-.068 (-.382)
Mother's Education	-.211** (-2.218)	-.208** (-2.185)	-.146* (-.672)	-.117 (-.538)	-.240*** (-1.553)	-.212** (-1.371)
Family Wealth	-.073*** (-.817)	-.081*** (-.910)	-.039 (-.193)	-.058 (-.283)	-.081 (-.560)	-.102* (-.702)
Number of Siblings	-.022 (-.172)	-.016 (-.130)	-.085* (-.295)	-.066 (-.229)	-.052 (-.253)	-.032 (-.153)
Sex	.082* (1.531)	.072 (1.352)	.002 (.017)	-.015 (-.127)	-.049 (-.570)	-.070 (-.813)
Family Rurality	-.059 (.682)	.045 (.523)	-.043 (-.219)	-.047 (-.240)	-.036 (-.255)	-.046 (-.325)
Catholic Schools	-.054 (-1.432)	-.067 (-1.782)	.082 (.958)	.054 (.621)	-.074 (-1.212)	-.107* (-1.747)
Independent Schools	.152*** (7.680)	.156*** (7.871)	.079 (1.757)	.084* (1.852)	.095* (2.936)	.100* (3.112)
School Attendance	.039 (.419)	.053 (.568)	.020 (.093)	.041 (.192)	.064 (.416)	.090* (.585)
Year 8	-.139** (-2.735)	-.117** (-2.313)	-.283*** (-2.445)	-.259*** (-2.238)	-.213*** (-2.582)	-.181*** (-2.197)
Year 10	.087* (3.350)	.089* (3.413)	.113** (1.907)	.109** (1.840)	.090* 2.129)	.087* (2.049)
Parents Speak English		.040 (.841)		-.071 (-.663)		-.046 (-.599)
Students Speak English		.211* (1.852)		.325*** (1.255)		.393*** (2.126)
English Newspaper		.031 (.325)		.147** (.671)		.154*** (.982)
R^2	.285	.302	.256	.300	.259	.321

[a]Unstandardized coefficients in parentheses.
*   p ≤ .05
**   p ≤ .01
***   p ≤ .001

parents speak "some English" or "only English" among themselves has relatively little effect upon the academic achievement of their children. In this respect, if the students speak English at home, word knowledge improves by 19.9% of a standard deviation (1.85 points), literacy improves by 30.9% of a standard deviation (1.26 points), and numeracy improves by 37.3% of a standard deviation (2.13 points). However, receiving English newspapers does not have such important effects upon the academic achievement variables. In this case, receiving English newspapers improves word knowledge by approximately one-third of a point, literacy by approximately two-thirds of a point, and numeracy by approximately one point.

It is also noted that other independent variables have relatively large effects upon the academic achievement variables. Specifically, the students' year level has a significant effect upon all three achievement variables net of the other independent variables. Not surprisingly, students with more regular school attendance have higher academic achievement, particularly for numeracy, than students with less regular attendance. Father's occupation is also important irrespective of ethnic background and all other variables in the model. That is, students from higher socioeconomic status families have higher achievement scores than students from lower socioeconomic status families. Additionally, students enroled in Independent schools do better on all three academic achievement variables than students enroled in Government schools. However, students enroled in Catholic schools have significantly lower achievement on numeracy than students enroled in both Independent and Government schools. Given previous research on Catholic schools, this result seems quite surprising (Clifton et al., 1987; Williams & Carpenter, 1988), and may exist because quite a large proportion of the immigrant students in Catholic schools are Italians, and they generally do less well on numeracy than English and Greek students (see Table 1).

In Table 5 the reduced form and fully recursive parameters for the variables that affect completion of year 12 are presented. As noted previously, these parameters are produced from ordinary least squares procedures. It may be argued that effect parameters produced from logit procedures would provide a better statistical model. That is, logit analysis has the advantage of meeting the formal statistical assumptions of a dichotomous dependent variable (Maddala, 1983). However, there are two reasons for not using logit analyses. First, logit analysis requires that there are no missing cases in the data set, and we have missing cases in our data set. Second, we cannot calculate indirect effects with logit procedures in a way that is directly comparable with the indirect effects calculated with ordinary least squares procedures. Nevertheless, the results in Table 5 are very similar to the results provided by logit analysis (Knoke & Burke, 1980).

This table illustrates that ethnicity plays an important role in determining completion of secondary school. Other things being equal, Greek students, and to a lesser degree Italian students, are more likely to complete twelve years of schooling than English students. Specifically, 28.9% more Greek students and 13.5% more Italian students complete year 12 than English students. Note that the English-language usage variables suppress the relationship between ethnicity and completion of year 12. This is particularly evident for the Italian students, though also true for the Greek students. That is, when these variables are added (step 2), the positive effects of being Greek and Italian are increased. Moreover, the academic achievement variables also suppress the relationship between ethnicity and completion of year 12 for the Italian students (step 3). This implies that for both Greek and Italian students, in comparison with English students, their lower usage of English at home inhibits their completion of year 12, while for Italian students their lower academic achievement also inhibits their completion of year 12.

It is not surprising that academically successful students are more likely to complete year 12 than less academically successful students. When academic achievement is added to the model, the explained variance is increased from 20.7 to 34.8%. The effect of word knowledge is .223, the effect of literacy is .087, and the effect of numeracy is .226. In total, these results suggest that successful academic achievement provides a strong positive impulse for completing secondary school.

Table 15.5
Standardized and Unstandardized Regression Coefficients and R^2s for Completion of Year 12[a]

	Completion of Year 12		
Independent Variables	Step 1	Step 2	Step 3
Greek	.200***	.233**	.211**
	(.274)	(.319)	(.289)
Italian	.012	.057	.129
	(.013)	(.059)	(.135)
Father's Occupation	.199***	.191***	.097*
	(.063)	(.060)	(.030)
Father's Education	.040	.037	.072
	(.019)	(.017)	(.033)
Mother's Education	-.121	-.102	.003
	(-.064)	(-.054)	(.002)
Family Wealth	-.042	-.047	.000
	(-.024)	(-.027)	(.000)
Number of Siblings	-.120**	-.117**	-.101*
	(-.048)	(-.047)	(-.040)
Sex	-.050	-.048	-.047
	(-.048)	(-.046)	(-.045)
Family Rurality	.023	.027	.032
	(.014)	(.016)	(.019)
Catholic Schools	.142**	.133**	.167***
	(.191)	(.178)	(.224)
Independent Schools	.185***	.185***	.120**
	(.473)	(.473)	(.308)
School Attendance	.077	.084	.048
	(.042)	(.045)	(.026)
Year 8	-.100*	-.098*	-.009
	(-.100)	(-.098)	(-.009)
Year 10	.021	.022	-.027
	(.040)	(.043)	(-.052)
Parents Speak English		-.101	-.093
		(-.108)	(-.100)
Students Speak English		.108	-.056
		(.048)	(-.025)
English Newspaper		.034	-.020
		(.018)	(-.011)
Word Knowledge			.223***
			(.011)
Literacy			.087
			(.010)
Numeracy			.226***
			(.019)
R^2	.203	.207	.348

[a]Unstandardized coefficients in parentheses.
* $p \leq .05$ ** $p \leq .01$ *** $p \leq .001$

Finally, it is noteworthy that the English-language usage variables do not have much effect upon the completion of secondary school. In fact, when the English-language usage variables are added to the model (step 2) the amount of variance explained in completion of year 12 is increased from 20.3 to only 20.7%. Moreover, the effects of the English-language usage variables are not significant in any of the analyses. Nevertheless, when the academic achievement variables are added to the analyses, the effect of the students speaking English at home decreases from .108 to -.056. This implies that the positive effect of speaking English at home is mediated by the academic achievement variables. That is, speaking English at home has a positive effect upon academic achievement (Table 3), and academic achievement, particularly word knowledge and numeracy, have positive effects upon completing year 12. In other words, virtually all of the effects of the English-language usage variables upon completing secondary school are mediated through the academic achievement variables.

Conclusion

Two perspectives have generally been advanced to explain the fate of minority ethnic groups in the educational systems of many multi-ethnic countries. On the one hand, it is argued that these countries are relatively meritocratic, and that academic achievement is the result of resources that individuals bring to school. On the other hand, it has been argued that there is institutional discrimination that blocks the academic achievement of minority ethnic groups within the educational system.

In turn, there are three arguments used to support the thesis that institutional discrimination blocks the academic achievement of minority ethnic groups. First, it is argued that students from minority ethnic groups are discriminated against by counsellors and teachers, and this accounts for their relative lack of success in the educational system. Second, it is argued that some ethnic groups are able to achieve in spite of discrimination, because their cultures place a premium on ambition, persistence, deferred gratification, and social mobility. Third, it is argued that students from certain ethnic groups lack sufficient knowledge of the national language that is required for success in the educational system.

The major objective of this research was to investigate differential ethnic achievement and attainment of English, Greek, and Italian immigrant students in Australia in terms of these three arguments. The findings reveal that ethnicity is a very significant factor in explaining English-language usage of these immigrant children. Moreover, it was also found that the English-language usage variables mediate a substantial proportion of the effects of ethnicity upon the academic achievement variables. That is, for all three achievement variables, Greek and Italian students have significantly lower scores than English students before the English-language usage variables are used as intervening variables. But, when these variables are included, the effects of being Greek and Italian are reduced, in most cases, to being non-significant. In the case of the Greek students, however, their disadvantage turns out to be an advantage for achievement in both literacy and numeracy. Finally, ethnicity plays an important role in determining completion of secondary school. Other things being equal, Greek students, and to a lesser degree Italian students, are more likely to complete secondary school than English students. Within this context, the English-language usage variables and the academic achievement variables suppress the relationship between ethnicity and completion of secondary school. That is, when these variables are added to the analyses, the positive effects of being Greek and Italian are increased.

Given these findings, it seems reasonable to conclude that ethnic differences in the academic attainment process in Australia is a function of competition within an essentially meritocratic educational system. In this respect, perhaps the school is an institution that provides no more than opportunities to learn. Thus, there is *de facto* institutional discrimination, but it is directed toward students who are handicapped or advantaged by their cultural values and their proficiency in English. To put it simply, teachers do not force students to learn; rather they provide the opportunities for them to learn. The resources and motivational factors necessary for students to capitalize upon the opportunities provided by the school are derived from the individual student, his or her past success and failure, particularly within school, and his or her cultural background, particularly within the family.

In this respect, there is little doubt that English language proficiency is a major requirement for success in Australian schools. The fact that some Greek and Italian parents use their native languages in speaking with their children limits the students' proficiency in English. In addition, the fact that the parents of the Greek and Italian students have relatively low levels of education and are from lower socioeconomic status positions, in comparison with the parents of the English students, further limits their children's English language proficiency. Thus, the Italian students, and to a lesser extent the Greek students, are not only less proficient in word knowledge and literacy, they are also more likely to be a year behind their English peers.

Overall, these results do not seem to support the argument that channels for upward mobility of non-English-speaking immigrant students are blocked in the educational system in Australia. Rather, the results seem to suggest that Greek and Italian students are limited by their lack of proficiency in English but they are supported by their cultural values. That is, Greek and Italian students seem to have been socialized within ethnic cultures that provide support for their completion of secondary school, though they limit their academic achievement by using their native languages at home (Blau & Duncan, 1967).

Although the achievement of socioeconomic status is not a simple product of education, completion of secondary school is the single most important predictor of income and occupational status (Broom et al., 1977; Broom et al., 1980; Williams et al., 1980). Even if certain minority ethnic groups encounter discrimination, they do seem to understand the economic values associated with completing secondary education. In this respect, the sacrifices that certain immigrant parents are willing to endure in order to support the education of their children is a persistent folk image in many multi-ethnic countries. Considerable sociological research supports this folk image, and informs us that cultural values are the primary reason why some ethnic groups have been successful in both the educational system and the socioeconomic system. The irony may be that the cultural values that support academic attainment seem to be dependent upon ethnic languages which in turn limit academic achievement.

Acknowledgements

The longitudinal study providing data for these analyses was supported by the Australian Government through the Department of Education, the School Commission, and the Tertiary Education Commission. The first author was supported by a leave fellowship from the Social Sciences and Humanities Research Council of Canada.

References

Blau, P. M., & Duncan, O. D. (1967). *The American occupational structure.* New York: John Wiley.

Bourke, S. F., & Lewis, R. (1976). *Australian studies in school performance II: Literacy and* numeracy in Australian schools: Item report. Canberra, A. C. T.: Australian Government Publishing Service.

Bowles, S., & Gintis, H. (1976). Schooling in capitalist America. New York: Basic Books.

Broom, L., Duncan-Jones, P., Jones, F. L., & McDonnell, P. (1977). *Investigating social mobility.* Canberra, A. C. T.: Australian National University Press.

Broom, L., Jones, F. L., McDonnell, P., & Williams, T. (1980). *The inheritance of inequality.* London: Routledge and Kegan Paul.

Bullivant, B. M. (1978). *The way of tradition: Life in an orthodox Jewish school.* Hawthorn, Vic.: Australian Council for Educational Research.

Bullivant, B. M. (1981). *The pluralist dilemma in education: Six case studies.* Sydney, N.S.W.: George Allen and Unwin.

Clifton, R. A. (1981). Ethnicity, teachers' expectations, and the academic achievement process in Canada. *Sociology of Education, 54,* 291-301.

Clifton, R. A. (1982). Ethnic differences in the academic achievement process in Canada. *Social Science Research, 11,* 67-87.

Clifton, R. A., & Bulcock, J. W. (1987). Ethnicity, teachers' expectations, and students' performances in Ontario schools. *Canadian Journal of Education, 12,* 294-315.

Clifton, R. A., Williams, T., & Clancy, J. (1987). Ethnic differences in the academic attainment process in Australia. *Ethnic and Racial Studies, 10,* 224-244.

Duncan, O. D. (1975). *Introduction to structural equation models.* New York: Academic Press.

Heise, D. R. (1975). *Causal analysis.* New York: Wiley.

Kalton, G. (1983). *Compensating for missing survey data.* Ann Arbor, MI: University of Michigan, Survey Research Center.

Knoke, D., & Burke, P. J. (1980). *Log-linear models.* Beverly Hills, CA: Sage.

Maddala, G. S. (1983). *Limited-dependent and qualitative variables in econometrics.* Cambridge: Cambridge University Press.

Martin, J. J. (1978). *The migrant presence: Australian responses, 1947-1977.* Sydney, N.S.W.: George Allen and Unwin.

Mehan, H. (1984). Language and schooling. *Sociology of Education, 57,* 174-183.

Olzak, S. (1983). Contemporary ethnic mobilization. *Annual Review of Sociology, 9,* 355-374.

Pedhazur, E. J. (1982). *Multiple regression in behavioral research.* New York: Holt, Rinehart and Winston.

Ross, K. N. (1983). *Social area indicators of educational needs.* Hawthorn, Vic.: Australian Council for Educational Research.

Smolicz, J. J. (1979). *Culture and education in a plural society.* Canberra, A. C. T.: Curriculum Development Centre.

Smolicz, J. J. (1981). Cultural pluralism and educational policy: In search of stable multiculturalism. *Australian Journal of Education, 25,* 121-145.

Stevens, G., & Swicegood, G. (1987). The linguistic content of ethnic endogamy. *American Sociological Review, 52,* 73-82.

Stryker, R. (1981). Religion-ethnic effects on attainment in the early career. *American Sociological Review, 46,* 212-231.

Sturman, A. (1985). *Immigrant Australians and education: A review of research.* Hawthorn, Vic.: Australian Council for Educational Research.

Thorndike, R. L. (1973). *Reading comprehension education in fifteen countries: An empirical study.* Stockholm, Sweden: Almqvist & Wiksell.

Williams, T. (1987). *Participation in education.* Hawthorn, Vic.: Australian Council for Educational Research.

Williams, T., & Carpenter, P. (1988, April). *Private* schooling and public achievement in Australia. Paper presented at the meeting of the American Educational Research Association, New Orleans, LA.

Williams, T., Clancy, J., Batten, M., & Girling-Butcher, S. (1980). *School, work, and career: Seventeen-year-olds in Australia.* Hawthorn, Vic.: Australian Council for Educational Research.

Williams, T., Slater, J., & Clancy, J. (1984a). *Surveying youth in transition.* Hawthorn, Vic.: Australian Council for Educational Research.

Williams, T., Slater, J., & Clancy, J. (1984b). *Measuring rurality.* Hawthorn, Vic.: Australian Council for Educational Research.

Subject Index

A
Alphabet, 26
Argument
  competence in, 77, 134
  literacy and, 79, 81
  logic of, 80
Artifact as text, 53, 63, 66
Asante religion, 31

B
Background knowledge, 7, 77, 130, 132, 135, 141,
  157, 161, 163, 171-172, 175-176
Basal readers, 8, 149, 151-155, 164
Bilingual education, 186, 188-190, 204-206
  Navajo students in, 188

C
Canada
  global village, 127
  small-town, 7, 127-128
Citizens
  informed, 66, 131
  literate, 64, 66, 131-132
  scientifically savvy, 131
Classrooms
  interaction in, 239
  social life of, 230
Closed system, 41, 45, 50
Co-authoring, 217-219
Collaborative inquiry, 215
Competence, 2, 4, 11, 16-19, 21, 38, 40, 51, 73, 77,
  116, 134, 178, 205
Composition, teaching of, 92
Compulsory school attendance, 110
Computer, 5, 114, 119-124
  programmability of, 7
Context of meaning, 5, 70
Correspondence problem, 37, 42, 47
Counter-elite, 62-63, 129
Critical consciousness, 7, 129
Critical pedagogy, 88, 90
Critical reading, 20, 53
Critical thinking, 68, 84, 92, 101-102, 127, 130,
  132-134, 136, 138, 141, 143, 210-211
Cultural capital, 89-90
Cultural tradition, 23, 25-26, , 91, 102
Curriculum theory, 24

D
Daily life, effective functioning in, 16, 18, 20, 22,
  37, 40-44, 46-48, 50
Decisionistic society, 64
Deductive reasoning, 112
Deferred gratification, 250, 267
Deskilling, 62
Discrimination in schooling, 247, 267-268
Documents, understanding, 17, 18, 27, 51, 127, 129
Dominant culture, 86-89, 91, 232-233

E
Empowerment, 2, 7, 54, 57, 105, 129-130, 132,
  134, 138, 141
Engineering theory, 59-61
Epistemology, 24, 134, 167
Ethnic differences, explanations of, 251-252
Ethnicity, 247, 248, 250-252, 260, 265, 267-268,
  270
Explanation, reasoning to best, 72, 79

F
Frame predetermination, 45
Functioning
  text-aided, 4, 40, 47, 50-51
  text-based, 4, 23, 30, 39-40, 50-51
  text-omitted, 4, 40

G
Goals, personal and collective, 38-39
Grapholect, 97

H
Heritage language children, 186-187, 189
Homeless mind, 113
Hypothesis formation, 71-73

I
Inductive discovery, 112
Inference, warranted, 75
Intellectual independence, 132, 134, 138
Interaction period, 170

K
Knowledge
  common-sense, 223
  embodied, 3, 23, 30
  incremental, 32
  justified-true-belief theory of, 25
  tacit, 61, 103
  technological, 54, 57, 59, 131, 133, 141
  textual, 24, 32

L
Learning, literate conditions for, 225
Literacy
  academic attainment and, 247, 267-270
  as cultural politics, 5, 86, 98-99, 101, 104
  as cultural value, 10, 229
  children's definition of, 233
  computer, 69-70, 83
  cultural, 2, 5, 69-71, 77, 79-83, 104, 130, 132, 180
  definition of, 2, 8, 28, 38, 54, 69, 96, 132, 165-
  169, 171, 178, 209, 211, 214, 233
  epistemic, 211
  functional, 3-4, 8, 16-20, 37-41, 49-51, 165-166
  goal of, 100, 129, 134
  heritage language, 186, 191, 194-195, 198-199,
  201-204
  historical perspectives on, 6, 107, 122
  lay, 3, 18, 26-27, 36
  mathematical, 6-7, 109-110, 122-123, 125
  models of, 85, 101, 173, 215

Author Index

Emig, J., 54, 56, 67
Erickson, F., 236, 238, 243, 245
Evans, E., 179
Evans, J., 121, 124

F

Fagan, W. T., 10-11, 229
Farella, M., 188, 205
Farr, R., 166, 181
Feibleman, J. K., 61, 67
Ferreiro, E., 217, 227
Feurzeig, W., 120, 123
Fey, J. T., 112, 124
Fish, S., 179
Fisher, A., 84
Fitzclarence, L., 87, 103
Fleming, R. W., 4-5, 53, 63, 67, 129
Flower, L. S., 174, 179, 225, 227
Forester, A., 157, 163
Foucault, M., 27, 35
Freire, P., 234, 236, 238, 243, 246
Froese, V., 179-180
Frye, N., 170, 179

G

Gadamer, H. G., 33, 35
Gallivan, P., 104
Garfinkel, H., 38, 40, 52
Garger, S., 243, 245
Gates, A. I., 150, 164
Gauld, C., 131, 142
Genesee, F., 188, 205
Gentile, L. M., 237-238, 245
Gere, A. R., 168, 179
Gilbert, P., 167, 179
Gintis, H., 86-88, 103, 249, 269
Girling-Butcher, S., 253, 271
Giroux, H. A., 87-91, 103-104
Glazer, S. M., 245
Globe and Mail The, 22
Goelman, H., 217, 228
Goffman, E., 45, 52
Goldman, S. L., 56, 67
Goodlad, J., 230, 242, 245
Goodman, K. S., 154, 156, 164, 170, 179
Goodman, Y. M., 156-158, 164
Goody, J., 29-31, 35-36, 50, 52
Gosling, D., 131, 142
Gough, P. B., 169, 179
Govier, T., 82-83
Graff, G., 101, 104
Graff, H., 20, 22
Grant, R., 120, 123
Graves, D., 176, 179
Gray, W. S., 152, 164
Green, D. Z., 188, 204
Green, W., 86, 104
Gregg, L. W., 227
Grundy, S., 56, 67
Guerin, W. L., 167-168, 179
Guild, P. B., 243, 245
Guthrie, J. T., 245

H

Habermas, J., 34, 36, 54, 64, 67
Hakuta, K., 188, 205
Handscombe, J., 188, 204
Hansen, J., 176, 179
Harste, J. C., 172, 179
Hart, D., 9, 11, 185, 190-191, 205, 251
Haugeland, J., 72, 83
Haussler, M. M., 158, 164
Havelock, E., 24-25, 36
Hayes, J. R., 174, 179, 225, 227
Hayter, E. W., 63, 67
Heap, J. L., 4, 18, 37, 39, 50, 52, 217, 219, 228
Heath, S. B., 232, 238, 245
Heise, D. R., 260, 270
Hersh, R., 117, 123
Hiebert, E. H., 155, 163 235, 244-245
Hildyard, A., 180, 228
Hirsch, E. D. Jr., 96-97, 102, 104, 166,   180
Hoggart, R., 90-91, 104
Holdaway, D., 154, 157, 164
Holton, G., 131, 139, 142
Holub, R. C., 171, 180
Hope, J. A., 113-114, 124
Hopkins, C. J., 174, 180
Hoyles, C., 121, 124
Huck, C. S., 154, 164
Hudelson, S., 187, 203, 205
Hughes, T. P., 58, 60, 67-68
Hull, D. L., 131, 142
Hunt, R. A., 170, 173, 180
Hurd, P., 132-133, 142
Hymel, S., 237, 244
Hynds, S., 173, 180-181

I

Illich, I., 24, 26-28, 36
Inglis, F., 90-91, 99, 104

J

Jaggar, A., 163
Jensen, J., 179, 181
Jewett, J., 112, 124
John-Steiner, V., 181
Johnson, P. H., 229, 231, 235, 238, 245
Johnson, R. H., 81, 83
Jones, F. L., 248, 254, 270
Jungeblut, A., 37, 42-43, 47, 52
Just, M. A., 169, 180

K

Kahneman, D., 65, 67
Kalton, G., 254, 270
Katz, M., 20, 22
Kavanagh, J. F., 179
Kerber, J. E., 164
Kieran, C., 6-7, 109
Kierkegaard, S. A., 35
Kirsch, I. S., 37, 42-43, 47, 52
Kline, S. J., 54-56, 67
Knoke, D., 265, 270